ACCLAIM FOR *SOPHIE SCHOLL AND THE WHITE ROSE*

"The animated narrative reads like a suspense novel."
The New York Times

"This is a story that commands our attention."
Newsweek International

"Inspiring – and could not be more timely."   Studs Terkel

"Superbly written."   *Library Journal*

"Unusually powerful and compelling . . . Among the indispensable literature of modern political culture."   Hans-Wolf von Wietersheim, *Das Parlament* (Official publication, German Bundestag)

"Heart-wrenching and inspiring . . . a story few readers will forget."
San Francisco Chronicle

"Could change your life forever."   *Dayton Daily News*

"Dumbach and Newborn have told their compelling story beautifully."
Washington Jewish Week

"This is an impressive, highly readable and beautifully researched account of two brave German youths and their comrades who rejected Hitler's demonic vision and fought to open their countrymen's eyes to the horrors that lay ahead—at the cost of their lives . . . This book drives home the high cost of courage in world gone mad, and the brilliant light these brave young people shone into the dark night of Nazi Germany."
Susan Rubinowitz, Political Reporter, New York

"A must for anyone, especially young people, to read."
Evelyn Rubin, author of *Ghetto Shanghai*

"A dramatic story of courage during the darkest period of the 20th century . . . And it's a story with new chapters unfolding. This book is a fundamental resource and a memorable read."
Toby Axelrod, author and reporter, Berlin & New York

"This book, chapter by chapter, builds into an incontestable argument for the power and possibilities of action over passive acceptance and apathy."
Jewish Chronicle

TESTIMONIALS ABOUT THE WHITE ROSE BY NOTABLE CONTEMPORARIES

"Good, splendid young people! You shall not have died in vain; you shall not be forgotten. The Nazis have raised monuments to indecent rowdies and common killers in Germany—but the German revolution, the real revolution, will tear them down and in their place will memorialize these people, who, at the time when Germany and Europe were still enveloped in the dark of night, knew and publicly declared: 'A new faith in freedom and honor is dawning.'"

Thomas Mann, Nobel Laureate (Broadcasting from exile to
Germany on the radio series "German Listeners",
June 27, 1943)

"If [the White Rose manifesto] is genuine, and there is no reason to doubt that it is, we can see in it the beginning of the end of the nightmare period in Germany itself . . . These young Munich students—few or many—representative or otherwise—rose gloriously . . . protesting in the name of principles which Hitler thought he had killed forever. In years to come we, too, may honor Sergeant [sic] Hans Scholl, Sophie Scholl, Christophe Probst, Alexander Schmorell, Kurt Huber and William Graf, slain in Munich for a cause that is also ours."

The New York Times ('Young German Martyrs', Lead Editorial
Eulogizing the White Rose, August 2, 1943)

"I will never forget the excitement when a leaflet was pressed into my hand by somebody in the editorial room of the *Allgemeine Zeitung.* The leaflets were being circulated by White Rose followers in Hamburg. Something inflammatory, heartening—yes, magical!— emanated from these typewritten and hectographed [mimeographed] lines.

"We copied them off and passed them on. A wave of enthusiasm swept over us—we who risked so damned little in comparison."

Ursula von Kardoff (reporter at Nuremberg War Crimes
Tribunal, 1945)

"I never saw these two young people. In my rural isolation I got only bits and pieces of the whole story of what they were doing, but the significance . . . was such that I could hardly believe it. The Scholls are the first in Germany to have had the courage to witness for the truth. The movement they have left at their death will go on . . . They died in all radiance of their courage and readiness for sacrifice, and thereby attained the pinnacle in lives well lived . . . We will all of us, someday, have to make a pilgrimage to their graves and stand before them, ashamed."

Friedrich Reck-Malleczewen, 1943, memoirist; author of
Diary of a Man in Despair

"When we heard about what was happening in Munich, we embraced each other and applauded. There were, after all, still human beings in Germany."

Former Concentration Camp Inmate

"I realized that she (Sophie Scholl) was the same age as me, and I realized that she was executed the same year I started working for Hitler. At that moment, I really sensed it was no excuse to be young and that it might have been possible to find out what was going on."

Traudl Junge, *Blind Spot: Hitler's Secretary*

"DESPITE EVERYTHING, THEIR SPIRIT LIVES ON!"
"SCHOLL LIVES!"

Anonymous graffiti appearing on walls
(Munich, February and March, 1943)

MODERN-DAY TESTIMONIALS ABOUT THE WHITE ROSE

"THE MOST IMPORTANT WOMAN OF THE TWENTIETH CENTURY"

Brigitte Magazine's readers (circ. 4,000,000) voted Sophie Scholl the most important woman of the last century, over Madeline Albright and Madonna.

"OUR BEST—THE GREATEST GERMANS"

ZDF, a German TV station, in 2005 invited its viewers to nominate the greatest Germans ever. Hans and Sophie Scholl of the White Rose were voted into fourth place, above Bach, Goethe, Albert Einstein, Willy Brandt, Gutenburg, and Bismarck. Among young people, they were voted first.

"'Rip off the cloak of indifference . . . choose before it is too late.' A half-century has passed since the White Rose called out these words before their arrest and death . . . Each new generation, including our own, realizes that those words are really addressed to us. Again and again, we feel their deep echo . . . Each person is responsible for what he does and for what he allows to happen. In the darkest moment of 20th century history, the White Rose demonstrated this truth."

Richard von Wiezsäcker, former President of Germany, in a special introduction to the German edition of this book

We will not be silent. We are your bad conscience.

Sophie Scholl
and the
White Rose

Annette Dumbach
Jud Newborn

The White Rose will not leave you in peace!

ONEWORLD

OXFORD

A Oneworld Book

First published in USA as *Shattering the German Night* in 1986
This revised, expanded international edition first published by
Oneworld Publications in 2006
Reprinted 2006 (three times)
This new edition published by Oneworld Publications in 2007
Reprinted 2009, 2010

ISBN-13: 978-1-85168-536-3

Typeset by Jayvee, Trivandrum, India
Cover design by Henry Steadman
Printed and bound by Thomson-Shore Inc, USA

Oneworld Publications
UK: 185 Banbury Road, Oxford, OX2 7AR, England
USA: 38 Greene Street, 4th Floor, New York, NY 10013, USA
www.oneworld-publications.com

The publishers are very grateful to George Wittenstein for permission to reproduce the photographs on p. iv, & Plates 2–5, & 8–13. Copyright © George Jürgen Wittenstein, 1942. The photograph on Plate 16 Copyright © Jud Newborn, 1983. The publishers would also like to thank Dr Wolfgang Huber for permission to reproduce the photograph of Professor Huber, and would like to express their sincere gratitude to Ursula Kaufmann, at the White Rose Stiftung, whose cheerful help in locating images has been invaluable. The publishers have made every resonable effort to identify and contact the owners of the copyright to the photographs included in this book, and to attribute copyright accordingly. Any errors are accidental and will be corrected in future printings upon advice to the publisher.

The authors are grateful to Bund Verlag for permission to use their own translation of a poem by Eugen Nerdinger appearing in "*Halts Maul—sonst kommst nach Dachau!*" edited by Sabine Asgodom. The authors are grateful to Harper & Row for permission to reprint the following material: Excerpts from *The Short Life of Sophie Scholl* by Hermann Vinke, translated by Hedwig Pachter. Copyright © 1980 by Otto Maier Verlag Ravensburg. English translation copyright © 1984 by Harper & Row, Publishers, Inc. Special permission granted by Harper & Row to the authors to use their own translation. Excerpts from the book *Hans Scholl and Sophie Scholl: Letters and Notes*, edited by Inge Jens. Copyright © 1984 by Fischer Verlag. English-language translation published by Harper & Row, Publishers, Inc., December 1986. Special permission granted by Harper & Row to the authors to use their own translation.

Photograph on title page shows Hans Scholl and Sophie Scholl, & Christoph Probst, July 1942.

CONTENTS

Not in the flight of thought
But in the act alone is there freedom.

DIETRICH BONHOEFFER
From "Stations on the Way to Freedom," written in prison,
July 1944
Executed by hanging in Flossenbürg Concentration Camp,
April 1945

Dedication

Even before Adolf Hitler took power, and during the twelve brutal years of National Socialist rule, there existed what is known as "the other Germany." Its voice was not the prevailing one—at times it was weakened and nearly choked off—but those individuals who sang with vibrant clarity while the world around them was shouting shared an energy, grace, and courage unsurpassed anywhere.

Statistics are inaccurate guides to reality, but sometimes we have very little else. One million Germans are said to have passed through the concentration camps and prisons; according to conservative estimates, at least 40,000 Germans were killed in the Nazi terror, 15,000 of them civilians executed for political crimes.

To the German men and women who resisted, this book is dedicated.

LIST OF ILLUSTRATIONS

AUTHORS' ACKNOWLEDGMENTS

THE HISTORICAL RECORD of the White Rose resistance has always demanded some degree of informed interpretation. It could not be otherwise: the White Rose operated under conditions of secrecy. But more significantly, there is nothing predictable about the fact of their resistance; in many ways they transcended their time, place, and social class. The process whereby they coalesced, moving together from "inner emigration" into active resistance, was a delicate one, even enigmatic; therein lies the challenge to the writer and historian.

Years of living in Germany helped both of us in our attempt to understand the personalities and events described here—but nothing could replace the careful historical research upon which this book is based. We interviewed surviving friends and family members of the White Rose, worked with primary written sources in the archives, including Gestapo interrogation records, studied the secondary literature, and attended official events commemorating their resistance. At times it has been necessary to sort through sometimes conflicting testimony and evaluate varying secondary interpretations, as well as to make our own decisions about emphasis and literary style; we have done our best to create what we feel is a responsible and credible account.

We would like to extend our gratitude to all those who were gracious enough to be interviewed, opening up a painful chapter in their lives—and not one without controversy—so that we might better understand the actions and motivations of those who resisted in a time when to do so required enormous courage. The insights of Dr. Birgit Weiss-Huber were especially important in making the

White Rose members come alive before our eyes. We also thank Anneliese Knoop-Graf for providing us with photocopies of the original White Rose leaflets.

We would like to thank the Bayerische Staatsbibliothek, and particularly Dr. Helmuth Auerbach of Munich's Institut für Zeitgeschichte, for facilitating the use of special archival materials on the White Rose, and for taking time to discuss with us a subject that has long been of special interest to him. The Institut für Zeitgeschichte granted permission to the authors to use quoted material from the memoirs and firsthand testimony housed in the institute's White Rose Collection, and most recently Frau Kaufmann and the Weisse-Rose-Stiftung for their cooperation in obtaining important materials.

We would like to thank Inge Aicher-Scholl and Harper & Row, for permission to quote from the letters and diaries of Hans and Sophie Scholl; Anneliese Knoop-Graf and Dr. Klaus Vielhaber, for permission to quote from the diaries and letters of Willi Graf; Dr. Michael Probst, for permission to quote from the letters of Christoph Probst; Dr. Erich Schmorell, for permission to quote from the letters and diaries of Alex Schmorell; and Mrs. Clara Huber and Dr. Birgit Weiss-Huber, for permission to quote from Professor Kurt Huber's farewell letter.

The accomplishments of many authors who have written previously on the White Rose, and on the Third Reich in general, were important to us, including the works of Hamilton T. Burden, Klaus Drobisch, Hubert Hanisch, Richard Hanser, Inge Jens, Günther Kirchberger, Anneliese Knoop-Graf, H. W. Koch, Mario Krebs, Melita Maschmann, Christian Petry, Inge Scholl, Michael Verhoeven, Hermann Vinke, and Klaus Vielhaber.

We also wish to thank Ingrid Schick and Arthur Thornhill, Jr., for their faith in the significance of this project, and Robert Berkvist and Ken Emerson of the *New York Times* for extending themselves. We are also grateful to Studs Terkel for his generosity in providing the foreword.

There are many friends, relatives, colleagues, and teachers to thank for their help, inspiration, and support, including Sheila Abrams, Ariela Baranov, Rabbi Moshe Birnbaum, Lenore Brooks, Nelson Chipchin, Horst Conrad, Dan and Nan, Arthur Flug, Rose Gatens, Lillian Gorfinkle, Nick Grillo, Eckard Holler, Ken Kleinberg,

Hans Kohn, Robert Morgenthau, Eva Newborn, Ira Newborn, and Kym Newborn, especially; Susan Peirez, Walter Renn, Susan Rubinowitz, Barbara Saidel, and Liz Smith.

Charlotte Sky, Vic Skolnick, and Dylan Skolnick of Long Island's Cinema Arts Centre have supported this undertaking with generosity and conviction, recognizing in their own mission a kinship to the spirit of the White Rose. Ruth Silverman shares in that spirit as well; her personal devotion and expertise is a gift freely given and with grace. As for Karen Frankel, her support cannot be quantified. She uses her wisdom daily to save the world, again and again, one person at a time.

And our deepest gratitude goes to those closest to us. Annette Dumbach wishes to thank Julius and Tatiana Chipchin Epstein who made the sounds, smells and voices of Russia and the claims of politics and history part of their daughter's birthright, and most of all, her husband, Otto Dumbach who shared his memories of growing up in a terrible time. Jud Newborn wishes to thank Solomon and Rita Newborn, for the gift of their faith and love, and for showing their son, with wisdom and compassion, how Jewish values are lived.

PREFACE

A visitor in postwar Germany may have had some disorienting and ambiguous reactions during his early days in the country. Perhaps most striking was the absence of discussion about the war and destruction, in spite of the jagged remains of bombed-out buildings that stood in just about every city and town.

The country lived in a shocked and sullen ambivalence about its recent past. This was perhaps not so surprising, considering that the rest of the world was also struggling to come to terms with the deeds of the war. However, when we first heard, and tried to learn more about the White Rose, the Munich group whose members sacrificed their lives to protest against the tyranny of the Nazi regime, our questions were met with silence. Instead of a willingness to talk about these courageous young students—one of the few examples we had yet come across of people trying to resist the Reich—our questions were met with silence and a bristling resentment at our raising them at all. Some said angrily that the White Rose members were traitors to their country in a time of war. Others said the students were spoiled adolescents who showed no concern for their unknowing families and friends who ended up paying for their suicidal acts. Another widespread opinion was that they were university-bred romantics who enjoyed the daring and danger of playing games with the Gestapo.

It was the same kind of silence one encountered if the concentration camps and death camps were mentioned. The hostility was strong and the message was clear: these subjects were taboo and not to be brought up in company. Even though the White Rose and the

German Resistance in general, however small in numbers, were not directly related to what later became known as The Holocaust, the tension and silence surrounding them both were almost palpable.

And the taboo surrounding these two topics remained until an unexpected bombshell hit via television in the late 1970s, in the form of the US series "The Holocaust". At least fifty percent of the adult German population viewed at least one episode of the show, and special telephone lines were set up to deal with the thousands upon thousands of calls the network received from viewers expressing anguish, grief, rage, shock, horror, disbelief—the gamut of human emotion. Critics pointed out that the series was a Hollywood version of what happened, not a German one, and many felt that their own suffering—day-and-night bombings, the terrifying treks from the East, the death of their own men at the front, the loss of their homes, cities, belongings—was being disregarded by the outside world.

The wound had been opened. Soon afterwards, two well-known Munich film-makers introduced the White Rose to the screen. Michael Verhoeven's "The White Rose" and Percy Adlon's "The Last Five Days" won numerous awards and made a deep impression on the German public. It was a searing experience for an audience to watch Hans, Sophie and Christoph go to their death by guillotine. As the picture ended, photographs of the real protagonists flashed on the screen reminding the viewer that these events were true and had actually happened.

At the same time these films came out, survivors and witnesses from both the Resistance and the Holocaust began to appear and were ready to speak, to pass the truth on to coming generations. They visited classrooms all over the country, and spoke to young people not as baleful Cassandras, but as grandparents or friends, without judgment or shame. Their act of witnessing, and their willingness to come forward, has helped make their words part of the school curricula in many parts of the country.

The fall of the Wall in 1989 was probably the most exciting break with the past for all Germans. In this atmosphere of disclosure, Steven Spielberg's film "Schindler's List" broke box office records. It presented the death-camp in all its unbearable horror, but it also showed a man named Schindler, who in spite of his foibles and contradictions, proved to be a decent and courageous human being—and a German. Classes came in droves to see the film, theatres were filled to the last seat, discussions were held all over—in schools, churches, in community gatherings and private interchanges.

Around this time, new transcripts of Gestapo interrogations, including some involving Hans Scholl, were discovered, which cast new light on the interrogation methods used by the Nazis, and revealed in more detail the personalities of the people questioned. Our book was translated into German and has since joined a growing collection of works now available on the German Resistance and the White Rose. A number of these concentrate on Sophie Scholl; her simplicity, innocence and courage have caught the hearts of many. Her bust now stands in Valhalla, the Hall of Great Germans, one of the very few women selected for this honor. Another has been placed near the carving of the White Rose in the atrium of the University of Munich, where she and Hans were arrested.

The members of the White Rose have captured the imagination of Germans throughout the country. In a popular television program called "Our Best: The Greatest Germans," the White Rose came in fourth, before such greats as Goethe, Bach, and Beethoven. They came in first place if you considered only the votes of the young viewers. The White Rose Foundation, supported by families and friends as well as by the University of Munich and open to the general public, offers an exhibition of photographs and written materials about all the members. Streets and schools in German cities and towns now bear the names of the members of the White Rose. A literary award has been established, the Geschwister-Scholl-Prize, which offers a yearly prize to a book that demonstrates original, independent thinking; that promotes moral and intellectual courage; and that raises public consciousness of important current issues.

Richard von Weizsäcker, one of the most esteemed former Presidents of Germany, spoke at the University of Munich while receiving the Geschwister-Scholl Prize. He began his talk by quoting a few lines from one of the White Rose leaflets: " 'Rip off the cloak of indifference you have placed on your hearts. Decide—before it is too late!' " He then addressed the audience in his own words. "More than half a century has passed since the White Rose made this call in their next-to-last leaflet, shortly before their arrest and death. But every era, including ours, sees itself as the addressee of these words. Again and afresh we feel deep inside an echo of the sign of the White Rose."

It is in this context that we wish to present our book on the White Rose. We feel their message of youth, moral courage and unflinching conviction in the face of adversity is one that needs to be heard and celebrated throughout the world.

The story of the White Rose is far from over. We fervently hope it never will be.

FOREWORD

By Studs Terkel

Jud Newborn and Annette Dumbach have captured a very important aspect of the Nazi era. In this marvelous work, they explore something extraordinary that was happening among a remarkable group of young German students—particularly a brother and sister, Hans and Sophie Scholl.

Whenever I see a white rose, I think immediately of those two, and of their heroism amidst the horror. They let us know that even in Nazi Germany there were some among the young, however few in number, who represented the best that there was in the world.

The authors have done a truly wonderful job in conveying the significance of the White Rose. This is a book worth reading anytime, anywhere.

The gallantry. The humanity.

SOPHIE SCHOLL AND THE WHITE ROSE

PROLOGUE

February 25, 1943

IT WAS GROWING DARK in Berlin; a raw night was setting in. A slim young man in a slightly shabby field-gray uniform was pacing up and down beside the Kaiser Wilhelm Memorial Church, a solemn and massive structure that loomed above the fashionable section of western Berlin.

The soldier walked back and forth as if he were waiting for someone. It was 1800 hours—6:00 PM. People were still leaving work at that time, and some were going into the shops that had not yet closed for the evening.

The young man in uniform, Falk Harnack, had been raised in Berlin but had spent years away, studying in Munich, and now was on military duty, stationed at a town near what used to be the Czech border. He had a sensitive, finely chiseled face, light hair, and pale eyes—an artist's face. In fact he was an artist, a dramatist, and had been a director at the National Theater at Weimar—before the war.

The city's appearance undoubtedly depressed him. Germany had been at war for about three and a half years now, and each week of combat on faraway fronts made cruder and deeper lines in Berlin's weary countenance. Each time Harnack came to the capital, fewer of the elegant shops on Tauentzienstrasse and Kurfürstendamm were still in business; the lights were dimmer on each visit.

Falk Harnack probably had no right to be in Berlin that day: he may not have had a pass, or permission to leave his unit at Chemnitz. But like many others, he could have calculated on slipping through the variety of spot checks and military controls on the trains. There were so many men in uniform in the Third Reich, it was impossible to check them all.

Harnack was supposed to meet Hans Scholl at the Kaiser Wilhelm Church at six. As the minutes passed, he might have surveyed the passing scene, perhaps lit a cigarette and tried to relax. On the streets around the traffic island where the church was located were men in uniforms much like his own, only theirs were dusty or smeared. Some of the soldiers had bandaged arms and legs, some walked on crutches or with canes. Berlin was a major transit-point for troops returning from the Russian front; even the walking wounded would take advantage of a few hours' layover to take in the sights of the capital city. There were army uniforms everywhere: no one even seemed to notice them amid the scattering of men in the smart blue of the air force— Göring's elite, the gentlemen fliers—and the Party men, in well-pressed brown with their red armbands, emanating health and importance.

It was time for Harnack to move on. Hans Scholl, the student from Munich he was expecting, had not arrived. However, a second rendezvous had been set up for seven o'clock if the first didn't work out. Harnack might have reflected about where to go to spend the three-quarters of an hour or so that remained, and perhaps even considered entering the church—not that he was much of a believer. But the very presence of the church, its bleak power, might have triggered raw memories that would be impossible for any man in his situation to repress totally.

On Christmas Eve, two months before, the Harnack family had joined together to sing a hymn, "I Pray to the Power of Love." Arvid Harnack, Falk's elder brother, had requested that the family sing it, after his death. Arvid had been executed by the Gestapo at Plötzensee, a fortresslike prison on the outskirts of Berlin, a few days before Christmas.

Perhaps Harnack chose instead to stroll down the blacked-out streets rather than enter the church. He would blend in easily and inconspicuously with the pale and expressionless passersby on Ku-damm. But his thoughts and reflections could not be ordinary ones. His brother, a prominent official in the Economics Ministry, had been arrested, tortured, and executed as a member of the skeletal German resistance, and now, only ten days ago, his American sister-in-law, Arvid's wife Mildred, had been executed in the same way. Mildred Fish Harnack, an American woman who had met Arvid at the University of Wisconsin at Madison years before, had given up her homeland and family to share the challenge and perils of living in an alien land that grew colder and more implacable with every passing year: she too was gone.

In all likelihood, the young man didn't allow himself to dwell on such thoughts. He was in Berlin to meet Hans Scholl and introduce him and his friends in Munich—the group that signed its clandestine leaflets "The White Rose"—to the "center" of the German resistance; at least that was the way Hans Scholl had put it when they met in Munich a few weeks before.

Scholl was a South German type, not at all Prussian in mentality or appearance; he was a tall, dark fellow, with brown eyes and enormous intensity. He was in his mid-twenties, just five years younger than Falk, although undoubtedly Harnack felt decades older in experience and outlook. When he had first met Hans Scholl and his friend Alex Schmorell and they talked about organizing resistance, the two South Germans had struck him as enraged innocents, a volatile combination. They had seemed almost unaware of the dangers they were exposing themselves to. But Mildred and Arvid had known the dangers, had had no illusions about the kind of enemy they were dealing with; had that knowledge helped them?

Mildred's hair had turned completely white in those months in the Gestapo cell, her face had become smaller but even more vibrant and alert. She had been given a six-to-ten-year prison sentence at the secret trial, while the men in the network were sentenced to death: her sentence was almost an act of mercy. But it was countermanded by Adolf Hitler himself and Mildred had to die, like Arvid and the others, strangled on a rope attached to a meat hook. The prison pastor reported that as they took her away her last words were "And I loved Germany so much. . . ."

Hans Scholl and Alex Schmorell. Harnack mixed up those names—Scholl and Schmorell—although the two youths were strikingly different. Alex was tall, lean, had tawny brown hair; there was an ironic gleam in his gray eyes and he had a light, casual way that made people around him want to smile. One sensed in him that rare breed in the Third Reich, a man who held on to life with easy reins, not taking it too seriously, ready to break out onto new paths. He needed the spice of adventure or risk to make the daily humorless routine bearable. Alex was half-Russian and his friends called him Shurik, one of the Russian nicknames for Alexander. He was odd man out, the fair, feckless Slav in a gray Wehrmacht uniform. He wanted to be a sculptor even though he was a medical student—a kindred spirit to Falk, the artist in the gray phalanx. Falk and Alex had hit it off right away: if times were different, they might have become friends; actually, they almost looked like brothers.

Harnack had first encountered Hans and Alex at his military base at Chemnitz when they journeyed there illegally to meet him. It must have seemed like years ago, but in fact it had only happened some four months before.

Why had he agreed to meet them at all? His sculptress friend Lilo in Munich had asked him to, maybe that was the main reason, but perhaps he was also just a bit curious as to who they were: students in Munich—which was not exactly a bastion of resistance.

Harnack himself had been a student at the University of Munich; he had watched the brownshirts take over the university and the city in 1933. He and his friends had fought back—but that was ten years before, early in the reign of terror. He, Günther Groll, and the others had also put out leaflets calling on the people to resist Hitler; they had tried to sabotage Nazi buildings in Munich, had had fistfights with brown-shirted students. They had not believed, could never have believed in those days, that Hitler would remain in power, that the country would watch in passive silence as the men and women who spoke up or fought back were destroyed, swatted to death, as if a crazed giant were annoyed by small and insignificant gnats.

Harnack and his friends called for a university strike in 1938; it was a total failure. Soon after that he had left Munich for his theater activities at Weimar, having earned a doctorate in theater sciences.

Hans and Alex had visited him on a Saturday morning last November. They met outside his barracks and went to the Sächsischer Hof, an inn in nearby Chemnitz, the same place where Arvid and Mildred had spent the night when they visited him.

The three of them talked all day and through the night, in the small tavern downstairs and, later, up in their room. There had been no need to play conspiratorial games; trust was—and had to be—absolute. They handed Harnack copies of the White Rose leaflets written, duplicated, and mailed out in Munich since the summer of

1942; there were four of them, typed single-spaced and badly, on cheap duplicating paper; four leaflets of condensed rage.

They waited impatiently for his reaction. He was blunt in his response; he told them that the leaflets were academic, intellectual, and much too flowery to have an impact on the masses. One could see immediately that they were created by intellectuals living in a world of literature and philosophy who didn't speak the language of the working people.

They agreed with him. They were determined to learn, to develop the skills of the underground; they realized leaflets were not enough, just a place to start, and they wanted to link up with the network of German resistance. They had been isolated in Munich, a handful of students, and a few of them had briefly been posted to the Russian front; that experience redoubled their determination. The war had to be stopped and Hitler destroyed: it was the only way to save Germany and restore it to its rightful place in the community of peoples.

Harnack warned them that the resistance was not based on well-meaning intellectuals and their outrage, but on coldly rational premises. It had to be a wide anti-Fascist front in every city in Nazi Germany, from Communists on the left, through the Social Democrats and liberals, to the conservative and military opposition on the right. People who had loathed each other in the Weimar days had to forget the past and work together for one goal: kill Hitler, overthrow the government, and negotiate peace with the Allies.

Alex and Hans seemed excited; it was likely they had not anticipated hearing such ambitious plans. The three talked on for hours, even exploring what the world would look like once they succeeded with their plans. Hans wanted to give up medicine after the war and go into politics. It is often the case that conspirators have a great need to be visionaries.

Harnack's plans for Hans Scholl in Berlin are not completely clear, but one appointment had been fixed: he would take Scholl to the Bonhoeffer residence immediately.

Harnack had already paid a visit to Dietrich and Klaus Bonhoeffer at their flat that afternoon at four. He had come to know the distinguished pastor and his brother better after his brief and final visit to Gestapo headquarters before his brother Arvid's execution: Arvid had instructed him to maintain contact with the resistance. Dietrich Bonhoeffer, whether one was a committed Protestant or not, was a man who inspired enormous admiration. His very appearance, his warm face behind round, scholarly spectacles, invited trust and almost a sense of relief that such a man could exist in this time and place. Bonhoeffer had studied theology with Harnack's uncle at the University of Berlin, and was one of the founding and leading members of the Confessing church, a segment of the Lutheran church of Germany that refused to accommodate itself to Hitler, Jewish persecution, foreign conquest, and murder.

Bonhoeffer *was* resistance. His execution in 1945 in the Flossenbürg concentration camp days before Allied liberation had a kind of somber inevitability—the destiny of a man who stood for everything decent and creative his nation had produced and now rejected. An inmate in prison with him in the last years of the war reported later that "when he walked into a room you could no longer be a coward." He believed in direct engagement with and for one's fellow man; he believed that piety alone was not Christianity, but a hollow excuse to ease the conscience. Bonhoeffer, in February 1943, had links with the officers, government officials, and aristocrats who, in 1944, would be involved in the plot to take Hitler's life, as well as with leftists like Arvid Harnack and his circle. Bonhoeffer was committed to a united resistance, and its ideological and sectarian roots were secondary, if not irrelevant.

During Harnack's visit that afternoon, Bonhoeffer had undoubtedly expressed his heartfelt condolences at the loss of Arvid and Mildred; what probably remained unspoken was the fact that both Bonhoeffer and the Harnack couple had refused the chance to escape. On separate occasions they had all visited the United States in the late thirties. All three had been offered refuge; friends begged them not to return to Germany. They had turned down the offers. Bonhoeffer wrote to Reinhold Niebuhr at the Union Theological Seminary in New York that he could not stay in America, that he had to share the trials of the German people in order to have the right to take part in the reconstruction of a moral and just German society after the war.

Harnack returned to the meeting point at seven. Scholl was not there. The minutes were crawling by. It had been only three weeks ago, in early February, that Harnack had gone to Munich and seen Scholl. He met the group during a period of two days at Scholl's rented room on Franz-Joseph-Strasse in Schwabing, the bohemian section of town not far from the university. Hans Scholl lived in typical student digs: French-impressionist prints tacked on the walls, piles of books and manuscripts. It was a provisional chaos, the sort perhaps permitted only students— if anyone—in the tidy and organized society of the Third Reich.

Alex informed Harnack that the leaflets *had* made an impact in Munich. Students had staged an improvised protest when the gauleiter (district party leader) of Bavaria had given an offensive and boorish speech at a university commemoration in January. The leaflets surely had helped give them the courage. Schmorell and Scholl and their friend Willi Graf had now gone even further: they were painting anti-Nazi graffiti on the walls of the university and other major public buildings at night—and carrying loaded guns to protect themselves. The Nazis were using forced female laborers from the East to scrub away the words "Down with Hitler" and "Freedom," but the traces were still visible.

Harnack felt the overcharged tension in the room; these people seemed to have been without sleep for days. He was uncomfortable about various objects in the room that indicated carelessness: hand-written essays that might have been drafts for new leaflets, and lists of names and addresses.

The next day, Hans insisted that Harnack go with him to the university and persuade Professor Kurt Huber, the one academician who sympathized with them and had even gone so far as to help them create leaflets, to join them for a group meeting at Hans's room that afternoon. They waylaid him after his seminar. He was reluctant to come, and obviously felt wary about Harnack and his leftist politics. But Hans was persistent and Huber came.

With the exception of Christoph Probst, the core of the group was there, all in heavy coats and mufflers; the building had run out of heating fuel.

Sophie Scholl, Hans's sister, was dark, serious, and quiet. She listened intently but made no contribution to the discussion. Willi Graf, with thinning blond hair and deep blue eyes, was intent and silent, probably the least accessible personality in the group. Professor Huber was haggard and upset; Harnack had attended his lectures years earlier and was very aware of Huber's deeply conservative political and social attitudes.

The discussion quickly turned into conflict, Harnack saying little, although it seems clear that he was the focal point of the dissension. Schmorell argued with Huber, but the bitter encounter was between

Huber and Hans Scholl, the student he had encouraged, supported, and inspired. The moment of ideological rupture had arrived: now it was not just a question of resistance. Huber refused to work with Communists on any level. He believed that the Nazis were a domestic version of Bolshevism, and it was for this reason that he detested them.

Harnack finally left; the atmosphere was filled with tension. But the date of meeting in Berlin had been agreed upon—today, Thursday, February 25, 1943: the group was determined to go on.

It was now almost 7:20 PM . . . the second meeting-time had passed some time ago.

Hans Scholl was not coming.

Harnack didn't know why, but he must have known that something had gone wrong. He could not have known how wrong. The news had not yet reached the general populace in Berlin.

Three days earlier, Monday, February 22, 1943, Hans Scholl, his sister Sophie, and their friend Christoph Probst had been tried for treason by the People's Court in Munich. At five o'clock in the afternoon of the same day, they were beheaded.

Falk Harnack could also not know that of all those present at that last meeting in Munich, he would be the only one left alive by the end of the year.

ONE

The first week of May 1942

A S THE TRAIN pulled out of the Ulm railway station, Sophie Scholl sat back in her seat. It was an unusually warm day for early May and the trip promised to be a pleasant one. She was alone in the compartment as the train began to move in the direction of Munich, some 150 kilometers to the southeast. On the rack above her head was a suitcase; next to her on the seat was a small bag containing a bottle of wine and a cake.

There was nothing exceptional about the young woman's appearance; she was slender, with shoulder-length brown hair and brown eyes. She was dressed simply, in a chocolate brown pleated skirt and a pink pullover; perhaps the fresh daisy she wore behind her ear was unusual, and it did make her look younger than her twenty-one years. She was neat and respectable-looking, wore no makeup, setting no great store on physical appearances.

The train began to pick up speed, clattering through the outskirts of the city. From her window the young woman would be able to see the sweep of Ulm's tall cathedral spire, soaring hundreds of feet above the old city center to the northeast; beneath it, on the square surrounding the cathedral, was the home of her parents.

Although her face may not have shown it, the departure from her home had aroused strong feelings in her. In a few days she would celebrate her twenty-first birthday, and the trip to Munich was a pivotal one. She was going to study at the university there, a goal she had worked and waited for since she was eighteen and had finished her *Abitur*, the high-school graduation exam.

The train roared over the Danube, whose surface glistened in the sun; the river vanished. Already the outskirts of the city were opening up to fields drenched in the golden yellow of dandelions. No matter how excited she was, she would make a mental note of these flashing images to record later in her diary.

The world of nature meant a great deal to her: the sight of a stream or the rolling contours of the land gave her a sense of peace and provided a pathway to some inner haven of calm; her diaries, letters, and old school essays were filled with descriptions of nature.

> Just as I can't see a clear brook without at least stopping to dangle my feet in it, I can't see a meadow in May and simply pass by. There is nothing more seductive than such fragrant earth, the blossoms of clover swaying above it like a light foam, and the petal-bedecked branches of the fruit trees reaching upward, as if they wanted to rescue themselves from this tranquil sea. No, I have to turn from my path and immerse myself in this richness....
>
> When I turn my head, my cheek grazes the rough trunk of the apple tree next to me. How protectively it spreads its good branches over me. Without ceasing the sap rises from its roots, nurturing even the smallest of leaves. Do I hear, perhaps, a secret heartbeat? I press my face against its dark, warm bark and think to myself: homeland, and am so indescribably happy in this instant.

Sophie Scholl's lyrical thoughts may not have been the musings of an average German girl in the spring of 1942, in the midst of total war, but they were not extraordinary either. Since the late nineteenth century, young people in Germany had been turning to nature to escape the constricting society they found around them. The *Wandervogel* (birds of passage) were groups of youths, especially students, mostly male, who hiked through the mountains and across the hills, camped along lakes and rivers, sang folk songs and recited poetry into the night. They had become a German tradition and a way of life. To commune with living things, to move with the sun and the water and the creatures of the earth, was a way to find freedom, a way to protest the rules and restrictions of bourgeois society, a way to reject the ugly smear of factories and mill towns that were eroding the meadows and the forests, a way to affirm youth and purity.

Literature and philosophy as well as song and poetry had grown out of this tradition, and until the onset of war in the early years of the 1940s, an unceasing stream of young people spent their summer and winter holidays scaling the mountains and trudging together through the valleys of their country, some even going abroad for a tramp through Finland, Yugoslavia, or Italy. Perhaps in no other country in the world was nature—not just its existence, but the idea of grappling with it as a group, trying to become a part of it, taking on its severe challenges and searching for its deeper truths—more profoundly a part of life than it was among the educated youth of Germany in this century.

Their yearning for freedom did not, however, translate into political activity or movements for social change. Their deep admiration for "exotic" folk cultures all over the world did not necessarily imply an acceptance of ethnic minorities at home. And their otherworldliness ultimately left them ill prepared to cope with those who later would abuse their hopes and appropriate the forms of their protest.

After 1933 and the establishment of the Third Reich, aspects of this youth movement were incorporated into National Socialist ideology and into Hitler Youth programs and excursions. Protesting this, some young people formed clandestine youth groups, which they tried to maintain in defiance of the Party and at no small cost to themselves.

By the spring of 1942, however, there were few young people at home with concerns like these. Most of them were in the military—a considerable number of them fighting in Russia—or in compulsory activities related to the war effort. After training as a kindergarten teacher, Sophie Scholl had been stationed for six months at a work camp that was run like an army barracks; from there she was sent into the fields, helping out farmers whose labor supply was running short after total mobilization. Then she had to work yet another half-year in the kindergarten attached to a munitions factory in Blumberg.

But all this was behind her; now, the landscape danced by in a golden shimmer. In a few hours she would celebrate her birthday with her older brother Hans, who would be waiting for her when the train arrived in Munich.

Sophie Scholl was an unusually reflective young woman. Her diaries and her letters to her unofficial fiancé, Fritz Hartnagel, an officer on the front lines in Russia, showed a deep concern with the realities of war and a fierce unwillingness, no matter how difficult things might be for her, to feel self-pity, or indeed any form of egotism, when men and women were suffering and dying in a savage and meaningless war. Even her own profound pleasure at finally achieving the long-sought goal of entering the university—not an easy matter in a nation where the quota on female students had been limited to 10 per cent of the student body—was probably mixed with feelings of guilt, as well as concern for Fritz and all her other friends at the front. These ambivalent feelings about experiencing pleasure, about having the right to enjoy oneself when others were in agony, had become characteristic of the entire Scholl family.

Life in the Third Reich had been a complex and ambivalent experience for the five Scholl children. Sophie, the fourth child and youngest daughter, had always known emotional and relative economic security; her parents were a harmonious and loving couple. Her father, Robert Scholl, had been mayor in several small towns in Swabia, an area of southwest Germany known for its rural charms, thrifty people, and spirit of independence, before settling in Ulm, where he opened his own office as a tax and business consultant. He was a big, rather heavyset man, with strong opinions and an unwillingness, if not an inability, to keep those opinions to himself. His views were never fashionable ones: he had worked as a medic in the First World War because of pacifist convictions, and during the war had met Magdalena, a Protestant nursing sister, who was to become his wife.

Mrs. Scholl was a gentle and soft-spoken woman who made her husband, home, and children the center and purpose of her life. In traditional style, she was the serene foil to her dynamic and strong-willed husband. She tried to soothe troubled waters and maintain the peace; Robert Scholl was not a man who adopted the prejudices or values of the rural and small-town folk among whom he happened to live. Even when he was *Bürgermeister* in the twenties, he did not find it necessary to visit the local pubs and have desultory chats with farmers and shopkeepers over a glass of wine or beer. When the political climate became increasingly conservative toward the end of the decade, he lost his mayoral post for advocating too liberal a position. Later, in Ulm, he would maintain some contact with Jewish friends and business associates despite the pressures around him, as well as with young artists who, like him, despised the new regime.

The Germans have a word for individuals with Robert Scholl's kind of personality—*Einzelgänger*, a man who goes his own way, alone. He brought up his children in the same manner; it was a hard but full and rich life. The price he ultimately paid was the heaviest that can be exacted from a father.

Sophie must have felt a twinge of uncertainty at the idea of separation from her family in Ulm, which over the years had become more and more an island of safety in a society gone mad. It had been different at first. In the days when her brother Hans was an active Hitler Youth leader—all the children had been members of the movement—the most disturbing aspect of their lives had been the conflicts this had aroused with their father. But those days were long over. All of the Scholl children had grown disillusioned with National Socialism, and after a few tension-filled years, the family was reconciled. Where before the children seemed to have sided with youth against their own parents, now their political and social attitudes were in tune again with their natural affections. Along with a loose network of like-minded friends, their family stood posed against a regime that was making increasing inroads into the peace and autonomy of their lives.

The train on the stretch between Ulm and Augsburg moved slowly east through Bavaria. Looking out her compartment window, Sophie would still see a countryside much like Swabia with its patterns of brown and green neatly cultivated fields. As the train approached small towns and the outskirts of Augsburg itself, the land along the tracks would be lined with small, orderly gardens. These were plots rented out to industrious employees of the German railroad, the Reichsbahn; they were carefully fenced with white pickets, and in the center of the plot a small toolshed often stood, designed to resemble a one-family house, complete with flower boxes beneath the windows. Owning one's own piece of land was part of the German image of earthly perfection; and even if it was not truly one's own, it made for pleasurable weekends in nature and gave people a sense of being rooted in the landscape, like the flowers and vegetables they tended.

In the spring of 1942, these gardens had gained in importance: they had become part of the home-front effort to produce enough to feed the population and the faraway military forces, in a time of increasing food shortages and rationing. The German people had just endured a difficult winter, worsened by a campaign against the Soviet Union that was heralded as another blitzkrieg victory but instead had bogged down. Hitler had been angered by the sinking public morale that winter: "If the German *Volk* is not prepared to assert itself for its own survival," he had said, "fine, then let it vanish." By spring, however, there came a change; the winter had been gotten through and the mood of the population was tentative but hopeful; there were no significant signs of opposition. People were particularly enthusiastic about the successful U-boat campaign against Allied shipping, and Hitler had promised in March that the "Bolshevik hordes," which had not been defeated that past winter, would be annihilated in the coming summer months. Even the new Allied technique of saturation bombing seemed to strengthen the resolve of the German home front, although it also spread a terrible fear of the unexpected. Only three weeks before Sophie passed through Augsburg, that city of renaissance facades had been hit in a major air raid—and in broad daylight—to the shock of its inhabitants.

The winter of 1941/42 had been a difficult time for Sophie Scholl. More than two years earlier, she had passed her *Abitur* and received her diploma, despite the warnings of her high-school principal, who had been informed about her lack of enthusiasm for National Socialism. But then a series of delays had occurred, preventing her from joining Hans at the university. First came a period of training as a kindergarten teacher, which she had tried to use as a stopgap to avoid compulsory farm work with the National Labor Service. But that failed and she had to suffer six months of heavy labor and indoctrination under the thumb of fanatical Nazi women leaders. After that she had thought she was free to study. But the conscription order came from yet another government agency, the War Assistance Program, demanding an additional six months from her as an attendant in a kindergarten attached to a munitions factory in Blumberg, near the Swiss border. She had to resign herself; there was no way out.

The mothers whose children she looked after worked in a brick factory that produced metal parts for the military. Blumberg itself was a small and unattractive industrial town. It was hard for Sophie to find any saving graces here, even though she did become fond of the children. But her chores were menial and exhausting, and as she labored, she was aware always that her work helped indirectly to perpetuate a war she deplored, conducted by a regime she had gradually come to consider criminal.

There were no like minds in Blumberg, no one to talk with; it was a dark period. "Many people think of our times as being the last before the end of the world," she wrote later in her diary.

The evidence of horror all around us makes this seem possible. But isn't that an idea of only minor importance? Doesn't every human being, no matter which era he lives in, always have to reckon with being accountable to God at any moment? Can I know whether I'll be alive tomorrow morning? A bomb could destroy all of us tonight. And then my guilt would not be one bit less than if I perished together with the earth and the stars.

During the course of her work at Blumberg, Fritz Hartnagel was called back temporarily from Russia to train new soldiers for the North African front. On several weekends Sophie was able to escape the kindergarten and join Fritz in nearby Freiburg. They had met at a dance in Ulm when Sophie was sixteen years old and Fritz was twenty; his courtly manners and gentle personality had made an immediate impression on her. But she soon became aware of troubling political differences between them. Fritz had been raised in a milieu that was conservative, although not National Socialist, and had gone on to become a career soldier. For him, loyalty to the Wehrmacht had been an honorable tradition long before the rise of Adolf Hitler; Fritz seemed to think that he could keep the two aspects of Germany separate.

Sophie wrote honestly to Fritz of her feelings about their relationship as it developed, but she did so in the probing and contradictory way of a headstrong and sensitive teenager. "It is true, isn't it," she wrote him in one letter, "that sometimes in the evening you think of me? You dream occasionally of our vacations together. But don't just think of me as I am; think of me also as I would like to become. Only then, if you still can care for me, will we truly understand one another."

As a soldier, Fritz needed to know Sophie was waiting for him at home. But later, as the war progressed and her horror of it increased, Sophie felt it urgent that Fritz understand her political passion, which was not just a female whim but a fundamental part life. "I've always been aware subconsciously of the career to which you are committed," she wrote. "I can't imagine how two people with such differing perspectives . . . could live together." Nonetheless, she continued to write him; he began gradually to change his attitude, and her deep feelings for him persisted. "When I was able to get home," she wrote Fritz in February 1941, shortly after he had been in Ulm on leave, it first hit me that you had left and I couldn't do anything about it. Every day before that an evening with you was waiting for me after school, now no more, strange feeling. I had grown too accustomed to your warmth. That is also a danger. At home I looked at the notebooks that you had bought and I got the stupidest surge of hope that I'd find something of you, something especially meant for me. I would so much like to have something of you that I could always keep by me, that nobody else would notice.

Past Augsburg, the flatter Bavarian fields leading to Munich were now visible from Sophie's train window and in twenty minutes her train would be pulling into Munich Central Station, with its arching ceilings and great clock. Its bustling ramps would be filled with young people arriving and others waiting to greet them, many of the young men in soldiers' uniforms. Somewhere on the platform, Hans would be standing, waiting for her.

During the last months at Blumberg, Sophie got the news that someone had denounced her father; she was deeply shocked. The informer—his own secretary—was a woman whom the Scholl family had thought was well disposed toward them. One day she overheard her employer say in a moment of anger that Hitler was a "scourge of humanity." Apparently she had felt it her duty, as a loyal German citizen, to report his comment to the Gestapo; they arrived at the Scholl home shortly thereafter, and hauled off Robert Scholl to be questioned. But almost immediately he was released, his trial put off indefinitely. The reason given was that his private consulting firm was in the midst of a crucial, long-range project for Ulm's municipal Finance Department, a project that was not to be interrupted.

From that day on, Robert Scholl and his family lived with the fear of his impending trial. And they could never be sure that one day the Gestapo might not show up again; once Robert Scholl was in Gestapo hands, anything would be possible.

Sophie found some solace from these troubles in a small chapel at Blumberg, where she could practice on the organ. During these stolen moments, her thoughts would turn to profound questions, intertwined with her anguish over the conditions she experienced around her. The last months, and all of the years since she had rejected National Socialism, had been difficult ones for her, but they had been important ones as well. "Isn't it a riddle," she wrote to a friend back home,

. . . and awe-inspiring, that everything is so beautiful? Despite the horror. Lately I've noticed something grand and mysterious peering through my sheer joy in all that is beautiful, a sense of its creator. . . . Only man can be truly ugly, because he has the free will to estrange himself from this song of praise.

It often seems that he'll manage to drown out this hymn with his cannon thunder, curses and blasphemy. But during this past spring it has dawned upon me that he won't be able to do this. And so I want to try and throw myself on the side of the victor.

But the dark days at Blumberg were over now, and Sophie was on her way to Munich, to her brother, to a free, cosmopolitan life. All of the delays were behind her; she had no regrets. The experiences of the past few years had toughened her, made her self-reliant, nourished her search for a life of the spirit. Her father's favorite line from Goethe had taken on personal meaning: *Allen Gewalten zum Trotz sich erhalten*— "Despite all the powers closing in, hold yourself up."

By now the train was moving slowly through the flat industrial outskirts of Munich. Before long she would see Hans on the platform at the station, a tall and handsome man, undoubtedly scowling intently into each window of the train as it passed him. She would descend with her suitcase and birthday bag and make her way to meet him.

His intense features would soften, his face lighting up in a broad smile of welcome; he was accompanied, as so often, by an attractive young woman, Traute Lafrenz.

As she and her brother embraced, Sophie's self-restraint and patience would have been rewarded at last. She had arrived, she was with Hans, it was spring, her new life had begun.

TWO

B Y THE TIME Sophie arrived in Munich in May 1942, Hans Scholl had already made the crucial and secret decision that would determine their fate. The young man on the train platform had already crossed an invisible and perilous boundary line, although precisely when that occurred remains unclear. Sometime in the spring of 1942, however, Hans and his friend Alexander Schmorell, had decided to *act*, to move from the realm of "spiritual resistance," or "inner emigration," and commit themselves to overt opposition to the Nazi regime.

The moment of crossing that line—the line separating private (if outwardly conforming) rejection of National Socialism from active resistance—is a hard moment to seize, not only in the case of the White Rose but in countless recorded instances of workers, housewives, and other "ordinary" Germans who resisted the Third Reich. It is as if there was no single discrete, conscious moment of decision when someone said, "Yes, I will act," but rather an accumulating force of rage, of incredulity, of desperation that came together inexorably, gathering its strength over months and years until it crested— and drowned personal fear and doubt. One gets the impression, from the accounts of these men and women all over Germany who did cross the line, that thoughts about "courage" or "protest," or even asserting one's rights as a human being, played an insignificant role in the process. It would seem, too, that introspection or self-analysis may be luxuries pertaining to a world at peace and to countries that have managed to keep their governments on a leash.

In any event, when Sophie arrived in Munich that day, she knew nothing about the decision made by Hans and his friend Alex, and Hans had no intention of involving her in conspiracy and danger.

He and Traute Lafrenz brought Sophie to his rented room in Schwabing, the section of Munich with a bohemian history, although not much was left of its early spirit after the nine years of Nazi persecution of writers and artists.

Before the First World War, this quarter—and Munich itself—had been one of the brilliant artistic centers of Europe, at least since the turn of the century. The fin de siècle school of painting and decor—Jugendstil, or art nouveau—had sprung up there, followed later by the Blue Rider expressionist movement; Kandinsky, Klee, and Franz Marc all found creative nourishment in the ambience of Munich and Schwabing. Thomas Mann—who actually was scorned by the Schwabing set as a consummate bourgeois—made Munich his residence, as did such writers as his novelist brother Heinrich, the poet Rainer Maria Rilke, and a major, almost cultlike figure, poet Stefan George, who was devoutly admired by the youth movements. Munich in its short-lived bloom attracted a wild variety of dreamers and utopian planners; Lenin lived there briefly during his long exile, and the hungry and embittered artist manqué Adolf Hitler arrived there before the First World War and fell in love with the city.

Munich's contradictions abound, which is a reason for its charm. It has a long history of monarchy, of separatism, and of provincial reactionary values; but it supported Napoleon in his wars with much of the rest of Germany and Russia. It is an elegant city, spacious, with Renaissance-like vistas, palaces, baroque churches, splashing fountains, and enormous public parks. It is a city of peasants who seem to have just arrived from the hinterlands, and aristocrats wearing expensive loden. A deeply Catholic city, it is also easygoing and Italianate, and it has an air of light and freedom—especially when the föhn blows and the blue-white Alps loom up in the south—that few, if any, other German cities possess.

Munich was also, briefly, the center of a workers-and-peasants republic, modeled on the Soviets of the Russian Revolution in the last months of the First World War. People recalling that time explain it as the final and heady moment of the reign of Schwabing. But a few months later, the Bavarian republic was savagely annihilated by the Freikorps and other right-wing groups from all over Germany.

Schwabing was never again to recapture its notoriety and exquisite pleasure in the notion of anarchy, sexual liberation, and artistic experimentation. In the twenties artists and writers abandoned it, moving on to Berlin, a harder and colder city that was in social and political ferment. In Munich the wave of reaction congealed; it was becoming a fortress for a variety of chauvinists and radical nationalists, and it was home country for the growing movement called National Socialism.

Even though much of this history may not even have been known by Sophie Scholl in the ninth year of the Third Reich, and even though the streets of Munich had grown dingy and shabby with the passing years of war, there still was a frisson of pleasure in young people, especially South Germans, when they arrived in the city and in Schwabing. Schwabing was a neighborhood still swarming with students who frequented small winehouses and cafés. It certainly offered liberating opportunities compared to the city of Ulm where Sophie had grown up.

Hans's friends came to greet Sophie and celebrate her coming birthday; the bottle of wine and the cake her mother had baked were a great success. In this time of growing shortages and expanded rationing of almost all foodstuffs and clothing, the birthday fare was a rare treat.

That day Sophie met Alex Schmorell, mild, pipe-smoking, deep-voiced, who spoke German with a Bavarian intonation oddly mixed with Russian overtones; she had heard much about him from Hans on his weekend visits home. Hans and Alex—or Shurik, as she quickly began to call him—were stationed as army medics at the Bergmann School in Freimann, an outlying area of the city. They were "furloughed" to continue their study of medicine at the university, and apart from required roll calls, ideological harangues, and marches a few times a week at the base, they were able to take quarters in town, study, and work a few hours a day at nearby military hospitals looking after the wounded. Hans's other friends, Christoph Probst and Willi Graf, who also came that day, were in much the same situation, studying medicine and attending other lectures at the university, while being attached to units of medics.

The rather free and casual style of life of these young men during wartime—attending concerts, taking fencing lessons, and joining Bach choral societies—is surprising. Nothing like it happened in the United States during the Second World War, and one would expect even less to find that such freedom and informality existed in Nazi Germany.

The informal and mobile life-style may help explain the form of resistance these young men had already chosen. They were planning to write, duplicate, and distribute leaflets in Munich, informing a selected audience of students, professional people, and intellectuals about the evils occurring in their midst, and warning that Hitler's war would inevitably be lost.

To be able to do that, one needed physical resources and time. The seed money came from Alex, whose father provided him with a generous allowance; and with that money and with whatever each of the others could afford, they procured a duplicating machine, a typewriter, stencils, and stationery. Through Hans and his large array of contacts, they were fortunate enough to find a place to store the clandestine equipment right in Schwabing, near Hans's room.

At Sophie's party, no mention was made about leaflets or their development; at that point perhaps none had been printed or even written, but it is likely that the procurement process had begun—and it was no easy matter, regardless of the young men's relative privileges.

They broke open the bottle of wine, ate the cake, and settled in for a long and balmy evening together. The mood was light, the talk not particularly serious. Hans read poetry aloud and the guests tried to guess who the author was. There were "political" overtones in the conversation—political at that time meaning anti-Nazi—as there often were among like-minded people who quietly despised the regime.

But even casual banter or a sarcastic remark or a joke about the war or Adolf Hitler constituted "malicious, anti-German activities," if not treason, and they all knew it. Such gatherings implied total confidence in one another. Years of practice had sensitized their antennae: Hans often said he could tell immediately when he met a stranger if he was "PZ"—the initials for the German words meaning "politically reliable"—and there was no question that Willi Graf, Christoph Probst, Alex Schmorell, Traute Lafrenz, and his sister Sophie were trustworthy; there would be no betrayals.

This group of young people meeting that day to celebrate Sophie's rise to adulthood and maturity, constituted—with Professor Kurt Huber, who was not present—the nucleus of "The White Rose." But the scene is still not clear: their coming together and acting together were only the final links in a process of personal evolution that had begun years before for all of them.

THREE

SOPHIE SCHOLL was less than twelve years old at the time of the Nazi takeover; her brother Hans, a little over fourteen. Against their father's advice, Hans joined the Hitlerjugend—the Hitler Youth—and Sophie followed, along with their sisters Inge and Elisabeth, and the youngest child, Werner. Boys and girls between the ages of ten and fourteen enrolled in the Jungvolk (Young Folk) and Jungmädel (Young Maidens); thereafter, boys were transferred to the Hitler Youth proper until age eighteen, while girls became members of the Bund der deutschen Mädchen (League of German Girls), or BDM. In 1933 membership was still voluntary—but of course Jews were excluded. Other youth organizations of the Weimar era continued to exist, but these were under increasing pressure, not only from the state's voracious official youth movement but, eventually, from the Gestapo itself, to dissolve their groups and join the Hitler Youth.

For the first few years of Nazi rule, all of the Scholl children were infected by the excitement that permeated their schools and community—the wearing of uniforms, the marching in torchlit processions through the streets of Ulm, the camping out in the country—and felt themselves a part in the rebuilding of their deeply divided and demoralized nation.

Inge Scholl, trying later to convey the gradual steps that had transformed her brother and sister into so-called *Volksfeinde* (enemies of the people), remembered the fervor of those early days: "We heard so much talk about the Fatherland and comradeship, the '*Volk* Community' and love of one's home—this impressed us, and we listened with rapture. . . . We were told that we should live for something greater than ourselves; we were taken seriously, in a strange sort of way."

For the Scholl children, three or four years would pass before disillusionment set in; but the seeds of doubt and opposition had been there from the start, planted by Robert Scholl. The same could not be said for all young people. One Berlin youngster who went on to become a ferociously ambitious Hitler Youth leader recalled her feelings and experiences the night Adolf Hitler took power:

> At one point somebody suddenly leaped from the ranks of the marchers and struck a man who had been standing only a few paces away from us. Perhaps he had made a hostile remark. I saw him fall to the ground with blood streaming down his face and I heard him cry out. . . . The image of him haunted me for days.
>
> The horror it inspired in me was almost imperceptibly spiced with an intoxicating joy. "For the flag we are ready to die," the torchbearers had sung. It was not a matter of clothing or food or school essays, but of life and death. . . . I was overcome with a burning desire to belong to these people.

In the early thirties, even the Scholl children felt something of this thrill. Youth was to be the cutting edge in the struggle ahead for a new Germany; indoctrination was the means to hone that edge. "Our youth must be tough as leather, hard as Krupp steel, fleet as greyhounds," Hitler had told the children at Nuremberg rallies as they stood immobile under the broiling sun, their arms rigidly outstretched in salute. Long before he came to power, he had already described his aims for youth. "My system of education is a harsh one," he said. "Weakness must be stamped out. The world will shrink in terror from the youngsters who grow up in my fortresses. A violent, masterful, dauntless and cruel younger generation—that is my goal. There must be nothing weak and soft about them. Their eyes must glow once more with the freedom and splendor of the beast of prey."

On April 3, 1933, two months after the Nazi takeover, the Hitler Youth used Storm Trooper tactics with an expertise born of years of street righting. They occupied the Berlin headquarters of the Committee of German Youth Associations, booting out the manager and staff and ransacking the offices. The Hitler Youth thereby gained control of files containing information ranging from the ages and religious backgrounds to the political affiliations of six million

German youths. Most disastrous was the seizing of the files on the Communist and Social Democratic youth organizations, which ultimately put serious opponents of the new regime in Gestapo hands.

Like the Scholls, most German children joined the Hitler Youth with excitement. It had numbered a hundred thousand members at the end of 1932; it rose to almost four million by 1935.

Unlike many other parents, who welcomed—or tried to believe they welcomed—Hitler and the Nazis, Robert Scholl loathed the National Socialists with every fiber of his being. He was not a political man in an ideological sense, and he was not a member of a formal political party; but he was liberal and open-minded. He was chagrined at the corruption, violence, and confusion that had characterized society in the Weimar Republic. But what came after, in 1933, was far worse.

The Scholl children, especially Hans—who seemed to resemble his father in many ways—at first did not accept Robert Scholl's views on National Socialism and the New Order. Controversy shook their home for years. The pattern was to repeat itself in uncounted German homes, where parents who were somehow immune to the fever of nationalistic furies and who privately opposed the new regime, watched in horror as their children slipped away from them. In many cases parents could no longer speak openly in their own living rooms, for fear that their children would report them to their teachers or youth-group leaders. Zealousness replaced reason, denunciation replaced loyalty and affection; a chilled silence invaded the home. As often happens, the generations moved away from each other, and a frozen space crystallized between father and son; but in this instance, ironically, it was youth that stood for state power and authority, while it was the older generation—or at least a fraction of it—that mutely clung to other values.

But Robert Scholl did not remain mute. He expressed his opinions, often loudly and incautiously. "The Nazis are wolves, wild beasts; they misuse the German people terribly," he told his hotheaded eldest son. Sophie, who loved and admired both her father and her older brother, would witness these scenes in silence.

The Hitler Youth demanded that its members throw themselves into the national struggle, even if this only meant staying out of school to march about town with jaws set and eyes ablaze. Hans's strong personality and good looks quickly made him stand out from the crowd; he seemed destined for leadership. Not long after his entry into the Hitler Youth movement, he was named a *Fähnleinführer* (squad leader) of a Jungvolk unit of about 150 boys.

It is difficult to imagine Hans straying too far from the humanism with which he grew up in the Scholl household—all the more so when one remembers at what cost he returned to these values later. Nonetheless, to attain such a position of leadership in the Hitler Youth as Hans did meant having the right ideological attitude and an eagerness to express it in action.

Hitler Youth had their chance to do so when, dressed in full uniform, they entered the classrooms of those teachers not yet properly "coordinated" with the movement. A squad leader in a position like Hans's commanded more than a hundred smartly outfitted boys, while a schoolteacher did not have more than perhaps forty pupils in a class. The Hitler Youth leadership provided new guidelines for teachers, reminding them that although Hitler Youth were pupils, their authority was not to be impaired in the eyes of their classmates. "Should a remark against the Hitler Youth be uttered in the heat of the moment," teachers were cautioned, "the trust between pupils and teaching staff will be damaged and not easily restored. But the more effort a teacher makes to enter into the spirit and code of the Hitler Youth, the greater will be his success."

In reality, the Hitler Youth tried to coerce teachers to develop the "correct" spirit. One section leader used the best beer-hall tactics of the Storm Troopers to physically disperse a meeting of a local teachers' association; another group broke the windows in the apartment of a Latin teacher reputed to have given out unpopular grades. "Youth is, in a higher sense, always right," the Hitler Youth leadership told teachers who stood aloof from the spirit of the new age. Soon, however, even the leadership had to concede that stringent regulations were necessary to control unruly boys and permit political "coordination" to develop more smoothly.

The year 1936 was a signal one for the Hitler Youth. Ever since 1933, each year had been devoted to one goal or another, be it physical training or leadership; 1936 was designated "The Year of the German Jungvolk." The entire age-group of boys and girls born in 1926 and now eligible for membership in the Jungvolk would be the object of a major recruitment campaign, the goal being to have them "volunteer" en masse. On April 20, Hitler's forty-seventh birthday, the lines of bare-kneed ten-year-olds would be presented to him as a gift; by the end of the year, membership in the Hitler Youth would become compulsory for all.

Hans's duties as squad leader meant the physical training and ideological indoctrination of his charges, passing on to them what he himself had received. This usually included "comradeship evenings" in the clubhouse—evenings spent listening, for example, to the nationally broadcast radio program of the Hitler Youth; its words blared out of the *Volksempfänger*—the official Nazi radio sets that Hitler had made available to the public as cheaply as possible, but which could only be tuned to ideologically pure (and that meant domestic) radio stations.

A Nazi propaganda film of the time, *Youth of Iron and Steel*, showed Hitler Youth marching resolutely through a craggy alpine landscape, their voices raised to chant a song that compared them to the steel being produced out of raw German iron ore for tanks and armaments. In like fashion, boy leaders across the country guided their squads over hills and through fields, drilling them in the official Hitler Youth Anthem:

> *Forward! Forward!*
> *resound the fanfares brightly.*
> *Forward! Forward!*
> *Youth knows no danger! ...*
>
> *We're marching for Hitler through night without dread,*
> *with the flag of youth, for freedom and bread.*
> *Our flags lead us on,*
> *our flag is the new age ...*
> *Yes, the flag means more to us than death!*
>
> *Youth! Youth!*
> *We are the future soldiers! ...*
> *Yes, we'll drop anyone with our fists*
> *who tries to stand against us.*
> *Führer, we belong to you,*
> *we your comrades.*

But Hitler Youth boys often demanded a song popular all over Germany, written by a former member of the Catholic Youth.

> *The rotten bones of the world*
> *are trembling before the coming war.*
> *We've broken the back of the terror,*
> *for us this was a great victory!*

We'll go on marching forever,
even if everything falls to pieces.
For today, Germany belongs to us—
and tomorrow the whole world.

Songs like these were a mainstay of the Nazi movement. Each formation had its own songbooks; even the SS. For the Hitler Youth these songs were especially important, and accompanied every activity. Their subjects were those of national pathos; sometimes they seemed childlike and naive, but often, in the same breath, arrogant, brutal, even crude: "Wave flag, wave from your tower—whoever spits on you is a worm, and like a worm he'll be squashed, with no chance to pray!"

A young Berliner who, unlike the Scholls, remained true to the Nazi movement, recalled marching through the streets of the city singing an unofficial but popular song: "When Jewish blood spurts from the knife, then things will go all the better" (Wenn das Judenblut vom Messer spritzt . . .). Of her BDM troop leader she wrote: "She would often make us march in three ranks along the Kurfürstendamm and cover part of the distance on the double. When doing this we had to stamp our feet as loudly as possible. 'This is where the rich Jews live,' she would say. 'They need a bit of waking up from their afternoon naps.'"

Anti-Semitism had no place in Hans's family, and in any event his horizons were less parochial than those of the usual Hitler Youth. Hans displayed this breadth of character even then, accompanying himself on the guitar as he sat with his boys around the campfire, singing not only the standard songs of the movement, but lilting Norwegian tunes and the poignant strains of Russian folk songs he had collected on his own. His youth-movement superiors chastised him for this; such songs were forbidden. Hans laughed over the restriction until he found himself threatened with punishment—an early confrontation that raised within him doubts about the organization to which he was devoting so much of his being. It was an organization that had no room, he would find, for the things that ultimately were the most important to him.

As a leader among boys, Hans Scholl had an opportunity in 1936 not only to participate fully in the year's important events, but to assume the tools of totalitarian power and make them his own. For many leaders of the Hitler Youth, the SS was only a step away; the temptation to join the cream of the racial and party elite was one few young men could resist.

The Nuremberg Party Rally of 1936 began on September 8, and Hans was chosen to bear the banner of his Ulm Hitler Youth section in the festivities. The distinction did not come as a surprise to many; Inge Scholl remembered how the girls in Ulm would say to her, "Your Hans, he looks so handsome—he's the right one to carry his company's banner at the rallies." But although Hans set out enthusiastically for Nuremberg on the gaily bedecked special train, when he returned to Ulm, his sisters and brother would note that a change had taken place in him.

Nuremberg had been selected as the site of the Party rallies for good reasons. The home of the great Renaissance painter Albrecht Dürer, Nuremberg had enjoyed a long history as an important center of commerce and German culture since the Middle Ages, and later came to be thought of as a quintessentially German city. In the modern period, Nuremberg was remembered most vividly as the medieval home of the *Meistersinger*, the master singers who had organized their lives into a seemingly flawless guild society. Richard Wagner glorified Hans Sachs and the Mastersingers of Nuremberg in his famous opera of the same name. Wagner re-created a total, organic world, where craftsmen and shopkeepers were men of culture; they moved easily in the social circles of nobility to whom they paid homage—and were in turn respected. With its populist pageantry, its parade of proud shoemakers and milkmaids, *The Mastersingers of Nuremberg* helped bolster the egos and rationalize the insecurities of Germany's lower middle class. But its appeal was broader, for this class and its perceptions had become a paradigm for the whole nation. Not surprisingly, it was one of Hitler's favorite operas.

The city of Nuremberg itself was a swath of red-tiled roofs huddled along narrow, winding streets, nestled beneath the protective flanks of a massive Romanesque and gothic fortress. This medieval city provided the Nazis with a marvelous stage set—but its picturesque roofs were not enough. In keeping with the Party's grandiose schemes, the spirit of National Socialism would have to be created in the city's outskirts, in the form of gigantic arenas, halls, and neo-Roman stadia. Within these vast spaces—constructed partly with stone quarried by concentration-camp inmates—the Party faithful would gather, lending flesh and voice to this newest model of Germany's greatness.

Among these edifices, some of them designed by Albert Speer, was the Zeppelinwiese, or Zeppelin Field. For the 1936 rally it was enlarged and flanked with grandstands until it had the capacity to hold 400,000 people—only 20,000 less than the entire population of the city of Nuremberg. The grandstand consisted of 170 stone pillars and 34 evenly spaced towers; atop each tower were 6 flagpoles of imposing size; 150 powerful spotlights were installed to create a nighttime operatic spectacle, consuming 40,000 kilowatts of electricity in one evening. Additional klieg lights were strategically placed to light up all architectural features and the field itself.

The result was colossal. Albert Speer himself had designed the special lighting effects: each of the 150 spotlights surrounding the grandstand were aimed into the heavens; columns of blinding white light shot skyward, extending the already massive structure vertically in a "cathedral of light." The illumination emanating from this enormous arena was so bright that the reflection it made in the South German sky was seen as far away as Frankfurt.

The spirit of National Socialism was captured in Leni Riefenstahl's famous cinematic vision of the Nuremberg rallies, *Triumph of the Will*. Hitler's private airplane is seen droning above the cloud cover. Through a break he sees below him the old clustered buildings of Nuremberg, and like Odin descending from Valhalla, he lands to greet his minions. Thousands have gathered, from every party formation and every walk of life, including the Hitler Youth. Riefenstahl's camera follows the line of young Nazis at attention, sweeping past to trace the curve of their aquiline noses, their shocks of blond hair, the jut of their chins in profile.

On September 13, 1936, Hans Scholl marched with these youths as they streamed past their Führer through the winding streets in an unending trail—a river emptying into the great arena on the Zeppelin Field. Walking to the side of each formation was a standard-bearer; for his Ulm company, it was Hans Scholl. The sky was a brilliant blue that day, the sun shone; it was inevitable that some Germans in the reviewing stands were commenting on the "*Hitlerwetter*" (Hitler-weather)—somehow the Führer had mysteriously regulated the climate for the benefit of his people.

The *Lower Bavarian Daily* reported on the Youth segment of the 1936 rally in the breathless, portentous style of the Third Reich:

YOUNG GERMANY IN NUREMBERG FLOODS THE FÜHRER
WITH CHEERS . . . 50,000 BOYS AND GIRLS PRESENT

This morning Germans are gathered again in the stadium before the Führer, to show him what they are made of, that they belong to him, that they are a part of him. . . . The broad oval of the stadium is one solid brown surface. . . . It seems as if youth does not want to be silent ever again, for the Führer—their Führer—stands before the microphone to speak to them. Every time Adolf Hitler tries to begin, the endless cheers of *Heil* roar again, subsiding only after minutes. Then the Führer speaks. . . .

They were words like those that had often been heard before:

Everything that we demand of Germany in the future, *that*, boys and girls, we demand of you. . . . In you will Germany live on, and should there ever remain nothing more of us, then you will have to bear in your clenched hands the flag which we raised on high out of the chaos. . . .

You could not be other than bound to us, and when the great columns of our movement march singing through Germany, then I know you will join these columns, and then all of us will know: *Before us is Germany! In us marches Germany! And behind us comes Germany!*

Once Hitler's words had rung out, the German newspaper reporter wrote, the youths, spectators, and the Führer himself were overcome by "an exhilaration and a fervor for which there are no words. Everything else is forgotten. One thought only, one fire has consumed us all."

But unaccountably, something had been happening inside of Hans Scholl during these days of endless speeches, marches, and fervent displays. We do not know precisely how and why, but at some point during the course of this great spectacle, Hans no longer felt himself to be in step with those around him, a "living cell" in the great "racial body" of the German *Volk*. Instead he began to feel like an insignificant cog in the mechanism of a giant, faceless machine. At first he would challenge that machine lightly from within; next, less tentatively, he would try to turn his back on it and search for alternatives. But eventually he would come to the decision that there were no alternatives, and he would confront the machine face-on—this time with resistance in mind.

FOUR

THE STRONG PERSONALITY that had led Hans Scholl to leadership in the Hitler Youth also contained a strain of nonconformism. Inevitably, this meant conflict with figures of authority, and with their ideological positions. Although the full details of his Nuremberg experiences are not known, Hans did tell his sister Inge later that there had been no room at the rallies for a single "sensible conversation." All he had experienced, he told her, was a continual attempt by those in power to brew enthusiasm, however mindless.

Hans's nature was outspoken and sometimes volatile; however, he also had a tendency to hold back his feelings in a dejected, even sullen silence until he had fully worked them out. When he returned from Nuremberg, his sisters and brother sensed that a subtle transformation had occurred within him, but they did not understand it at first. Perhaps Hans didn't either—but several events rapidly brought it to fuller consciousness.

The leader of Hans's own Hitler Youth company found him one day reading quietly by himself. The book was not one of the limited volumes in the local Hitler Youth library, but Stefan Zweig's banned *Sternstunde der Menschheit (Mankind's Stellar Hours)*. Despite state censorship, Robert Scholl had seen to it that the family bookshelves remained stocked with the German literature that he considered significant, and almost as a matter of course, all of his children continued to read these books. This particular work was one of Hans's favorites, a set of essays in which Zweig rhapsodized about great moments in human achievement, from Balboa's discovery of the Pacific to the laying of the first transatlantic cable, from Handel's

Messiah to the defeat of Napoleon at Waterloo. Above all, Zweig wrote of individuals following their own consciences and the idiosyncratic needs of their own creativity, not in the name of any one tribe or nation, but as expressions of universal accomplishment.

The book was torn from Hans's hands. This filth is forbidden, he was told; the author is a Jew. Whatever Hans's earlier attitudes might have been toward Jews in the abstract, he knew these people not as stereotypes but as actual human beings, colleagues and friends of the family whom Robert and Magdalena Scholl continued to see. And he found Stefan Zweig's book far more compelling and thought-provoking than all of the countless speeches and Party lessons that he was coming to realize had not been designed to help him think, but to keep mind and body too busy to reflect.

A more crucial disillusioning event came a bit later and was to cost Hans his position of leadership in the Hitler Youth. Shortly after returning from Nuremberg, Hans did something he knew was prohibited: he decided to help his squad design their own unique banner: The symbol they chose was a mythical animal, colorful and rare; it would say something special about them, how they differed from every other squad in the Jungvolk. By going against the rules in this manner, Hans was compensating, perhaps, for some reprimand he had received at the rallies from a Party superior for one of his irrepressible actions or comments. And surely he was testing, trying to see just how constraining the Hitler Youth was, how far he could go. While he had his boys dedicate their banner to the Führer, he also had them swear personal allegiance to this new flag, symbol of their own small community.

The reactions to this flag taught Hans that there was no room for alternate communities in the Hitler Youth, or in the Third Reich as a whole. One evening, the boys of Hans's squad marched through the streets of Ulm beneath the glorious griffin leaping across their banner. But when they arrived at an assembly before a higher group leader, their pride was attacked as insolence. The youth leader was outraged at their banner, a clear deviation from principle, and even more so by the brazen manner in which it seemed to be flaunted in his face. Hans's personal leadership was being challenged; this was not another example of Aryan élan, but of insubordination. The Hitler Youth leader ordered the twelve-year-old bearing the banner to hand it over immediately. But the boy, shocked and torn between loyalties, stood paralyzed. Furious, the youth leader strode up to him and began to rip the banner from his hands. And then Hans Scholl gave the boys perhaps the most important lesson he had ever offered them, one which they were unlikely to see repeated. Acting, as he would again later, without concern for consequences, he dashed to the defense of his bullied charge and struck the youth leader, knocking him down.

The 150 boys in the squad then watched their revered young leader stripped of his rank before their eyes. Hans could not have felt this a humiliation. It was one of those dramatic moments that make things clear in a flash; it was natural, inevitable, part of his new and rising opposition.

At first it may have seemed that Hans was only shifting the focus of his teenage rebelliousness from his father and the older generation to the enforced conformity of the Hitler Youth itself. But once this shift had taken place, and as Hans's judgment matured, his disillusionment and disgust with National Socialism grew rapidly, now aided and abetted by Robert Scholl.

After this, events that previously Hans had ignored or dismissed began to have new meaning. A young Ulm teacher had recently disappeared; later the Scholls learned that he had been forcibly placed before a band of Storm Troopers, each of whom marched past him and on order spat in his face. Afterward he was hauled off to a concentration camp and never heard from again. The Scholl children asked the young teacher's mother what he had done to deserve such treatment. "Nothing, nothing," she told them in despair. "It's just that he was not a National Socialist, he simply couldn't go along with it—that was his crime."

Once disillusionment had occurred, no matter how or why, its effects became an inevitable part of daily life. With each passing day, Hans could not avoid noticing things about National Socialism that distressed him, things that corresponded to his father's warnings and the whole tenor of his humanistic upbringing. Suddenly, Robert Scholl's children were asking him about concentration camps, and whether the Führer could truly be aware of their existence. They were echoing the tendency of most people, whenever a new sign of Party corruption or brutality was revealed, to repeat the phrase, "If only the Führer knew!"

"Could he *not* know of them," Robert Scholl replied, "if they have already existed for years, built by his closest associates? And why hasn't he used his power to disband them immediately? Why have those released been forbidden to talk about their experiences, under threat of the most terrible punishment?

"This is war," he told Hans. "War against the defenseless individual, war against the happiness and freedom of his children—a terrible crime."

Inge Scholl had the feeling, she reported later, of having lived in a clean and beautiful house, only to discover that unspeakable things were taking place in the cellar, behind locked doors.

For every question the children asked him, Robert Scholl had an answer ready. Hadn't Hitler kept his promise to eliminate unemployment? "No one contests that," he told them. "But don't ask, by what means! He has created the war industry, he's building barracks. . . ." The quality of the relationship between father and children was changing. If their discussions took place after dinner, Robert Scholl might say, "Now, if you'll excuse me, I'll go and earn a jail sentence." Hans and the others knew what he meant: their father was about to tune in to a forbidden radio station—perhaps Beromünster in Switzerland, or the BBC, both forbidden after the outbreak of war, in 1939—to get the kind of news that the Nazi media never reported.

Walking along the banks of the Danube with his children one spring evening, Robert Scholl suddenly turned to them. "All I want is for you to walk straight and free through life, even when it's hard," he whispered harshly.

Although nearly three years separated Sophie Scholl from her older brother Hans, their relationship was special, enriched by a tacit understanding. What they experienced together was not so much a meeting of like personalities as of complementary ones; their rapport became one of the givens of their lives.

When Hans joined the Hitler Youth, it was in keeping with their relationship that Sophie should follow suit. Her love of nature had also seemed compatible, at an early stage, with the BDM, the Hitler Youth's female auxiliary: she enjoyed the camping-out and the hikes; she loved to watch the flicker of burning logs at night. Although she could write of nature in a lyrical manner not all that unusual for German youth, her descriptions also could reveal a sensuality and a desire for independence that deviated considerably from the social conventions established for women of the time:

I could shout for joy that I am so alone, with the wild, rough wind drenching my body. I'd like to be on a raft, standing upright above the gray river, whose hurrying water the wind cannot disturb. . . . The sun comes out and kisses me tenderly. I'd like to kiss it back, but I forget that immediately because now the wind has leaped on me. I sense the wonderful firmness of my body; I laugh out loud for joy because I can offer the wind such resistance. I feel such strength in me.

Sophie could sense, even at an early age, that she was not meant for a life dominated by marriage and motherhood; her letters to Fritz indicate an avoidance of such a role, which others probably assumed for her without question. By following Hans's example, Sophie would soon participate in a life that offered greater meaning to her, a life in which her actions had effect in the world.

And yet brother and sister differed from one another. While Hans seemed an impetuous if dark-haired version of the Aryan model, Sophie was thoughtful, even reserved at times, and her appearance was not quite right. One of the sayings of the day was "German girls wear braids!" It was consistent with the ideologically crucial role the Nazis had given the peasant, and was in keeping with their criticism of "decadent" female interest in cosmetics and elegant hairdos.

Sophie's hair was dark, like Hans's, but she also sported a *Bubikopf,* a short, boyish bob. And she did not show the ready conformity of a girl being raised ultimately for Aryan motherhood; she was too firm in her own convictions, and quick to pick up inconsistencies in the attitudes of others. At times she tried to disguise her seriousness, but friends and family often noticed that certain look on her face, when she thought no one was observing her. It was a troubled look, withdrawn and concerned; it put frown lines in her forehead. It seemed to suggest depth of character, a wisdom that is surprising in one so young.

Not that Sophie was morose. One of her teachers had even once called her frivolous—a misreading of Sophie's laughter when she heard what she considered to be an absurd ideological comment intoned solemnly in class. She could not help but laugh—there were often contradictions that she found impossible to ignore. Even at the age of twelve, Sophie was already aware of anomalies that would take Hans years to recognize. "Why," she asked her sister Inge about a favorite Jewish friend, "isn't Luise Nathan allowed to be a BDM member, with her blond hair and blue eyes, but I am, with my dark hair and eyes?"

Sophie's relationship with Robert Scholl held a depth of mutual understanding similar to the rapport she shared with Hans; it continued to exist despite the pain she caused her father by joining the BDM. Although he made his position on National Socialism clear—she could observe his distress when he watched Party displays on the cathedral square outside their Ulm window, or when he argued with Hans—her father had not tried to prevent her from joining. He knew that opponents to tyranny could never be created by force, only by personal experience.

To Robert Scholl, his youngest daughter Sophie remained "the wisest of my women," even when she had become a member of the movement. She must have begun to sense the truth very early, because indoctrination did not seem to have an impact on her. One time she went on a BDM field trip with Inge; it was State Youth Day, which meant songs and marching in uniform. After some of the festivities were over, Sophie and Inge took a walk through the woods on their own. In a secluded spot they came across a tent of boys not in uniform. Intrigued by the sight of youngsters who were not a part of the brown-shirted crowd, the girls struck up a conversation, which they turned to the subject of National Socialism, hoping to learn more about these boys by being provocative. But one of the boys suddenly grew silent. Sophie realized the reason in a flash: he was Jewish. Apparently he wouldn't talk for fear that these girls in uniform would tell their leaders about an "underground" Jewish youth group located nearby.

On another occasion, after Hans had returned from Nuremberg, an important BDM leader arrived from Stuttgart to conduct an evening of ideological training for the girls in Ulm. When the members were asked if they had any preferences for discussion, Sophie suggested they read poems by Heinrich Heine, one of her favorite writers. But the leader and her BDM comrades were aghast at the suggestion, and shocked by the personal revelation that she had unwittingly made: her suggestion meant that she still had on her bookshelf "degenerate" Jewish writings that had been burned and banned by Propaganda Minister Joseph Goebbels in 1933. Despite the pressure and the possibility of repercussions, Sophie's uncanny sense of self came through.

"Whoever doesn't know Heine," she said in a whisper, as all eyes turned to her, "does not know German literature."

It was exceptional for long-standing members of the Hitler Youth to turn against the movement in which they were earning recognition and prestige. Still, Hans and Sophie Scholl were not the only German teenagers who felt a distaste for National Socialism that slowly matured into opposition.

In the same year as Hans's turning point, in 1936, when membership in the Hitler Youth had become compulsory, gangs of hostile young men began to appear in the cities of Germany and especially in industrial districts. Among them were the children of workers with some degree of class consciousness; Communists were to remain the firmest opponents of the regime, suffering extreme torture in the hands of the Gestapo and in the concentration camps. But most of the young people seem to have been consciously "unpolitical."

Sharing a contempt for playing soldier, these groups would gather in pubs to drink alcohol, smoke, and play cards with their elders. Or they would behave like the "punks" of a later era, dressing in simple, almost ragged clothes to express their rejection of the stifling hypocrisy around them: they wore long hair, checkered shirts, old hats, and signet rings with skull and crossbones. Calling themselves the Navajos, the Black Gang, or the Edelweiss Pirates, they listened to so-called degenerate swing music, and jeered at the smug obedience of Hitler Youth stalwarts.

Some of these groups did more than jitterbug and look dangerous. Having been forced into the Hitler Youth, these youngsters played double roles: after-hours they gathered occasionally with criminal elements and tried to disrupt Hitler Youth meetings. In Munich a band calling itself the Red Anchor was said to have appeared in Haidhausen, the same working-class district from which Hitler had launched his beer-hall putsch. Their targets were not people in elegant furs and top hats, but anyone alone and wearing a Hitler Youth uniform. In Leipzig in 1937, the police carried out a major action against a group that had spread to Berlin and Cologne as well. According to the Gestapo, 1,500 boys had banded together in 1936 to attack youth leaders at night; their explicit goal was to recruit more members in Leipzig than were in the Hitler Youth. Their two seventeen-year-old leaders were eventually caught and sentenced to three years' hard labor.

By the time the Hitler Youth became compulsory, perhaps only 10 per cent of its members were diehard National Socialists; the rest were a mixture—some bored, some annoyed, some seething on the inside, but most of them willing to go along with whatever their society seemed to demand. And yet, like the White Rose to come, there were those few who took a stand, not only as teenage rebels, but consciously, as political dissidents. Between 1940 and 1945, 1,807 inmates were executed in the Brandenburg prison alone for political reasons, some after years of forced labor. Of these, 75 were under twenty years of age; 22 were high-school pupils or university students. In Hamburg between 1933 and 1945, of all those sentenced for political "crimes," 11 per cent were youths.

While the Hitler Youth marched tirelessly and proudly to songs like "The Rotten Bones of the World Are Trembling" or "When Jewish Blood Spurts from the Knife," these other German young people, few as they were, changed the words of these songs and sang altered versions of their own, perhaps in the loneliness of their cells or on their way to the scaffold:

> We are criminals in your state
> and proud of our crime.
> We are the youth of high treason
> And we shall break this servitude.

FIVE

SOMETIME in 1937, Hans Scholl took a small but serious step into opposition, joining an underground youth group that still managed to operate, despite Gestapo attempts at surveillance. They called themselves the "d.j.1.11," the German Youth of November 1, 1929, the day their founder had arrived back in Germany from wanderings abroad, and decided that another anti-Nazi youth group was needed—before the Hitler takeover—to counter the growing influence of the Hitler Youth.

These young men—girls were not accepted as members—maintained a tight organization, protecting their identities through the use of Germanic runes and nicknames. Although they did not take effective action against the Hitler Youth, their very existence was an act of defiance.

The group's members developed attitudes and styles that would set them clearly apart. They were not nationalistic; and unlike the earlier *Wandervogel,* they preferred hitchhiking to tramping. For their group name and in their writings they used lowercase letters, a modernist style reminiscent of the Bauhaus movement in art and architecture, and one that was reviled by the Nazi establishment. They sang Balkan folk songs, even American cowboy laments, played the Russian balalaika, and devoured banned literature. Finally, as an act of nonconformity, they rejected the military-style tents of the Hitler Youth and used one of foreign ethnic origin, the Lappish *Kothe.* This tent, shaped something like a wigwam, had a hole at the top through which smoke could escape. Tucked deep in the woods to avoid Nazi vigilance, camps made up of such *Kothe* looked like primitive forest villages.

Everything was politically controversial in the Third Reich, including art; its appreciation was an important component of the Scholl family life. Among the family friends were a number of artists critical of National Socialism, including Otl Aicher, who helped Sophie with her sketching and later married her sister Inge.

In the summer of 1937, Hans and Inge went to Munich to visit the premiere exhibit of the new Haus der deutschen Kunst (House of German Art). The two eldest children shared an enthusiasm for the great German expressionists who had flourished in Munich only twenty years before, especially Franz Marc. Hans admired Marc's dynamic blue horses, an arrangement of sensual curves and arcs, galloping across rose-colored canvases. And Inge felt an affinity for the architectural designs of the Bauhaus; to her the heroic new art museum, a rather severe neoclassical edifice over endowed with bare Doric columns, was unoriginal and uninspired.

Everything they saw in the museum that day profoundly disturbed their esthetic sensibilities: idealized Germanic families, their faces dour and emotionless; a crusty old peasant reading the official Nazi newspaper with delight; nude statues of men, meant to indicate "action in repose," and of women, in stances that were supposed to suggest fertility and grace but which instead seemed passive and sterile. Every work in the vast halls was representational with a vengeance.

At the opening of the exhibit, Adolf Hitler had said that these works had finally put an end to the "artistic lunacy and pollution of our *Volk*"; one of the exhibit judges announced that the most perfect shape ever created in the new Germany could be seen all the time at Party rallies: the steel helmet.

To complement this exhibit of Germany's new artistic awakening, Propaganda Minister Goebbels gathered together examples of the "degenerate art" that it had replaced. Hans and Inge also walked over to this counterexhibit in a Munich gallery a few blocks away. They found these paintings far more stimulating and incisive than the ideologically derivative works they had looked at before. Many of their favorite modernists were represented, but the paintings were now given new captions: "Thus did Sick Minds View Nature" and "Peasants Depicted in the Yiddish Manner." Next to the modern works were pictures painted by the mentally ill in German and Austrian asylums, implying that both types of creativity had the same inspirational source.

The "Degenerate Art" exhibit backfired for the Nazis by attracting greater crowds than the exhibit at the House of German Art.

At about this time, the Scholl children began to take part in a clandestine reading circle, made up mostly of friends with whom their family had always maintained contact. "We have a large circle—all of them anti-Hitler," the wife of a local artist told Inge. "And each of these friends has his own separate circle which is anti-Hitler, and so on and so forth: a great underground network against Hitler. If only one could somehow get them to act collectively. . . ." This circle was to become especially important for Sophie and Inge, who could not be members of Hans's d.j.1.11 group. They circulated forbidden literature and even printed their own modest newsletter, *Windlicht* (Storm Lantern), in which seemingly harmless articles contained disguised references to current political ills. They also began to receive anonymous writings in the mail, critical of the regime.

After 1937, the pressures in Nazi Germany diverted Hans from d.j.1.11, but he nonetheless remained in contact with his comrades. Hans now began his required six months with the Reichsarbeitsdienst, or National Labor Service, where he worked on the building of Germany's new highways, the autobahns.

Afterward, Hans entered military service, something he wanted to get over with as quickly as possible. Since his base was not far from Ulm, he was able to receive occasional visits from his youth-group friends. But the Gestapo had decided once and for all to put an end to all illegal youth activity. When the crackdown came, it was swift and affected the entire Scholl family. Hans was arrested one day at his base and taken to the Gestapo prison in Stuttgart.

Meanwhile, security agents burst into the Scholl home in Ulm. Mrs. Scholl overcame her shock quickly; she quietly went upstairs to the children's rooms with a basket under her arm; she put any potentially incriminating material she could find into the basket. Downstairs, she walked past the Gestapo agents and out the door, saying in the brisk manner of the German hausfrau, "The gentlemen will excuse me—I have to hurry to the baker's."

It was a wholesale arrest. Inge and Werner were taken, transported in an open truck to Stuttgart. Sophie too was hauled off. She was sixteen at the time, wearing her hair bobbed so short that the family decided the Gestapo must have thought she was a boy. Although released later that day, Sophie was jolted by this first direct encounter with brute force. Her home would never be quite the same again: the doors and windows that kept the hostile world at bay could never be sealed. For a sensitive, intelligent adolescent, deeply attached to her parents and family, it must have seemed that all certainty had been swept out of her life.

Inge and Werner were released after a week of confinement in a cold Gestapo cell. Hans was detained three weeks longer while the Gestapo tried unsuccessfully to pump him for information. In Ulm, Robert Scholl watched helplessly as the other children tried to comfort their mother, who had become lifeless and depressed. He paced like a caged bear, wondering what was happening to Hans. "If they do anything to my children, I'll go to Berlin and shoot him!" he shouted. There was no question whom he had in mind. In school, Sophie had to endure the harassing questions of her classmates, who wanted to know what crimes her family had committed.

Hans was finally released at the personal behest of his cavalry officer. By then, the experience of the arrests had transformed their home into a precarious island and the outside world was now a vast, limitless region of confinement. Now the impact of other events—the triumphal march of German troops into Austria, the destruction of Jewish shops and homes and synagogues on Crystal Night, and the invasion of the Sudetenland—rocked their home. They were living in a Nordic tempest that was growing more savage and wild every year.

On September 1, 1939, the German armed forces invaded Poland, unleashing the Second World War. Sophie wrote to Fritz Hartnagel expressing her bitterness. "Now you'll surely have enough to do," she wrote. "I can't grasp that now human beings will constantly be put into mortal danger by other human beings. I can never grasp it, and I find it horrible.

"Don't say it's for the Fatherland."

Once war started, Hans had to continue in military service, with alternating periods of university study at Tübingen and then Munich. In 1940, during the invasion of France, he was ordered to the front lines as a medic. Although he observed little of the actual fighting, he saw a good deal of its results: working at a field hospital where four hundred wounded soldiers were being treated, he had to assist during leg amputations and other operations. He despised his own occupying army for requisitioning the most lovely houses in the town of

Saint-Quentin, in Picardy, where he was stationed for a time. "I liked it better when we slept on straw," he wrote. "What am I—a decent person or a robber?" In Ulm, Sophie was depressed by the rapid collapse of the French forces. "If I didn't know that I'll probably outlive many older people," she wrote in a letter to Fritz on June 28, 1940,

> then I'd be overcome with horror at the spirit that's dominating history. . . . I'm sure you find what I'm writing very unfeminine. It's ridiculous for a girl to involve herself in politics. She should let her feminine feelings dominate her thoughts. Especially compassion. But I believe that first comes thinking, and that feelings, especially about little things that affect you directly, maybe about your own body, deflect you so that you can hardly see the big things anymore.

The last years of high school had become difficult for Sophie; National Socialist ideology pervaded every lesson, and she felt alienated from most of her classmates. "Sometimes school seems like a film to me," she once wrote. "I look on but for all intents and purposes I'm excluded from performing." At least one of her teachers seemed to agree; she evaluated Sophie's classroom behavior as "totally uninvolved." Yet whenever she was asked a question, she had the answer; she paid enough attention to fulfill the requirements for her *Abitur*. But she did not participate. For Sophie, the difference between observing and participating had become a conscious choice.

Her behavior did not go unchallenged. As the time of her examinations approached, the school principal called her to his office several times with warnings; if she didn't change her attitude she would not graduate. He could not have used a better weapon. Sophie had always yearned to go to university; she wanted to specialize in biology and philosophy, perhaps to invest the former with more human truths than Nazi racialist ideology had done. University study was also a means to avoid service to the regime more than was necessary. And it meant a chance to develop herself in a time when women were discouraged from any productive career outside of their procreative one.

But Sophie did not change her attitude. It must have been a large personal triumph when she passed her *Abitur*, despite everything, in March 1940.

But now the delays began. "Wouldn't it be wonderful," she wrote in her diary early in 1941, "if Hans and I could study together for a time? We're already bursting with plans!" But the state required that all female high-school graduates serve at least six months in the National Labor Service. Hans tried from Munich to get an exemption for Sophie and a university placement, without success. As a girl, Sophie would have to do either housework in a "child-rich" family, or as was more usual, some form of manual labor. To avoid these two unappealing options, she tried to substitute kindergarten studies at the Fröbel Seminar in Ulm, along with some practice-teaching.

Sophie experienced her months in the Fröbel Seminar as a kind of reprieve. Susanne Hirzel, the daughter of an Ulm pastor and one of Sophie's close friends, enrolled as well; they provided each other with moral support. Once, as BDM girls in the days after membership had become compulsory, Sophie had confided a fantasy of hers to Susanne: "Really, one ought to try and infiltrate their highest offices, and then reveal all of their hypocrisy."

Fräulein Kretschmer, their inscrutable seminar teacher, had managed to keep her job despite the fact that she was not a convinced National Socialist; this made life a bit easier for the two girls. During one ideological training session, when the interns were supposed to listen attentively to a speech by Hitler on the radio, Sophie and Susanne sat reading quite openly. The only response Fräulein Kretschmer made was to signal quietly to them; with most other teachers this could have meant serious trouble.

These months in Ulm, working with children and sketching children at play, were probably the last relatively untroubled ones Sophie was to have. She had managed to avoid mandatory service and still had a chance to work and learn without being involved in the war effort. She still had time for an occasional bicycle excursion into the countryside around Ulm. "Even when you're sure everything is falling to pieces," she wrote after one such respite, "the moon is always right back in its usual place the next evening; the birds are still singing the next day as sweetly and eagerly as ever. And whether or not their singing is of any use, they never give that a thought." But she couldn't escape the ugly daily realities: "I think I would be much happier if I could," she wrote, "but the way things are now, everything else has to take second place."

Despite Sophie's hopes, her work at the Fröbel Seminar was not deemed an acceptable substitute for the National Labor Service. She would still have to do a six-month manual job; she would be delayed yet again in joining Hans at the University of Munich.

In March 1941 she was ordered to a run-down castle that had been turned into a work camp for young women. By this time, there were two thousand of these camps across Germany, housing young women between the ages of eighteen and twenty-five, conscripted for labor sometimes so fatiguing that they felt themselves to be beasts of burden. But their reaction often depended upon their political orientation. One young woman who made a career for herself in the BDM as a zealous propagandist described her own Labor Service experience as bone-wearing. And yet she could sing aloud for joy in the fields: "Our camp community was a model in miniature of what I imagined the *Volk* community to be," she wrote later in her memoirs.

For Sophie it was terrible. The girls wore uniforms and had ideological training sessions run by fanatic women leaders. The rooms in the castle were huge, cold, and damp—she was always cold—and the meals consisted mainly of boiled potatoes in their skin. Surrounded by young women of her age, she wrote in her letters that she never felt so alone in her life. The others obeyed, they submitted, they asked no questions; in their free time they talked about nothing but boys and sex, giggling interminably.

Sophie felt uncharitable, snobbish; she loathed them. And even more, she was enraged by the women leaders who exploited the power they never would have gained in any other society. They barked orders, they made their charges jump like marionettes. She seethed each time they ordered her around, and once wrote, "We live like prisoners; not only work but leisure time is turned into duty-hours. Sometimes I want to scream '*My name is Sophie Scholl! Don't you forget it!*'"

Her bunkmate snored and never took a bath; even bed was no sanctuary, except after lights-out when she took her flashlight and read Thomas Mann's *Magic Mountain* under the covers. The book was on the banned list; the very act of reading it must have given her a feeling of communion with ideas and values that transcended time and place. Mann's lofty mountaintop in the Swiss Alps may have become more real to her than the daily rounds in the fields or the gray-brown coldness of the castle.

One visiting day Inge and Otl Aicher came to the castle, managing to visit Sophie despite the machinations of the camp leader, who tried to detain her until the very last minute. It was a beautiful day and the three of them picnicked in a nearby meadow. But the joy of reunion was shattered by a radio announcement: Germany was invading the

Soviet Union: it was June 22, 1941. Although the Third Reich was at the height of its victories that summer, the announcement shocked and frightened many Germans, even those with confidence and pride in Hitler. The idea of a war on two fronts, especially in the vastness of Russia, where no European ever seemed capable of winning, was a staggering one. To Sophie it now seemed that the war, and the viciousness of those who conducted it, would go on forever.

Not long after, she wrote to Fritz. "If one believes in the victory of might, one also has to believe that men are on the same level as animals." And to Inge she wrote, "I go on, neither sad nor particularly happy, trying to hold on to my own values."

There had to be a meaning, a significance beyond this world she lived in that had become a grotesque perversion of itself. There had to be a deeper truth. She read Saint Augustine under a tall tree on the castle grounds when the weather had become warm and the days were longer. In her recorded reflections of that time, she described the peace that settled over her as she read. She felt herself merging with the leaves, the branches, the trunk of the tree, the birds who chirped companionably. At these moments she knew there was a meaning beyond what men had done to the world.

Sophie had grown up in a middle-class milieu in which the perspectives of the far left seemed alien and hardly accessible; National Socialism, calling upon youth to become part of a cause greater than themselves, had seemed a more immediate alternative at first. If she had followed the route open to her, she might very well have carved a career for herself in the BDM, assuming along the way the tools of Nazi oppression. But she did not.

Rejecting this course, she might still have remained inconspicuous in her society; she might have led a quiet life of bicycle trips and chores and studying for exams, like so many German girls around her, who kept their eyes closed whenever possible to the ugly contradictions of their world. But there was something in Sophie Scholl that made her different from these girls; it had to do with the sharpness with which she saw these contradictions, and how she must live if she was to remain true to her values, her inner self.

Once, in her diary, she wrote: "After all, one should have the courage to believe only in what is good. By that I do not mean one should believe in illusions. I mean one should do only what is true and good and take it for granted that others will do the same."

SIX

IN JANUARY 1943, about five weeks before he was seized by the Gestapo, Hans Scholl wrote a long letter to Rose Nägele, a young woman he had known since childhood, one of several with whom he had developed an intense and intellectual relationship. The friendship seemed to be loosening its grip on Hans by this time, and in the letter he explained, gingerly, his gradual withdrawal:

> I love transitional periods. They make demands on the spirit, hard as they may be to take. It's the same drive in me that makes a stopover in a huge railroad station so appealing. I know a man who, wherever he goes, never takes off his coat, who is always a guest. . . . When you speak to him you think that after every sentence he'll suddenly pull a watch out of his pocket and say, "Time to move on." That man appeals to me very much.

The image is interesting; it reflects Hans's intellectual and literary interests as well as his restless personality. Like the creative efforts of many young, aspiring intellectuals, it also has the whiff of the poseur, making himself terribly mysterious and important. Even so, there is something strikingly modern about the man-in-the-overcoat; he seems to embody the spirit articulated in the 1940s, although there already were subterranean attitudes and values developing in the 1930s on both sides of the Rhine, in France and Germany, which were later to be expressed by writers like Camus and Sartre, whom Hans Scholl had almost certainly never heard of. Hans's image of himself was not dissimilar to theirs: the alienated man in the mantle of anonymous gray, without possession or home, alone, seeking and creating his own world.

It was therefore an original image, and considering where he grew to manhood and his earlier adolescent nationalist fervor, it was both a daring and comprehensible one. Wandering without itinerary around the world, looking at one's watch, moving on: these are images that strike directly against the tedious and blaring *volkishness* of his own nation; they were a blow against all those roots-in-the-soil tentacles that were encircling and stifling his spirit.

But the essence of exile, of uprootedness, was more profoundly exemplified in Hans's friend Alexander Schmorell, torn apart by his two heritages, Russia and Germany. His German grandfather had settled in Russia as a fur trader without giving up his German nationality. Alex's father, Hugo, was born in Russia but considered himself German; he went to Munich to study medicine, although afterward he settled in Russia and married a Russian woman, the daughter of a Russian Orthodox cleric.

During the First World War, Hugo Schmorell was sent to the Urals from Moscow; there he ran a hospital for German civilian internees and prisoners of war. Alex was born there in 1917, a time of turbulence and civil war. He was barely two when his mother died during a typhus epidemic.

In 1921, three years after the Russian Revolution, Dr. Schmorell took the last train out of Russia that was evacuating German civilians and POWs; he took along his four-year-old son and his old Russian nurse. Hugo Schmorell settled in Munich, married again—a German woman also born in Russia—and established his medical practice.

Some say it was his Russian nurse—who never learned to speak German and talked incessantly to her Shurik about his lovely mother and her radiant world—who implanted in Alex a longing for his homeland, for the endless steppes, the birch-tree forests, and the glowing icons, that he would never lose. Accounts of his life in Germany give the impression that he was a happy child who had an easy and comfortable life, but there were two children who were born of the new marriage in Munich and who felt completely German. Perhaps he was happy, but he was also homesick for a faraway land he didn't remember.

He spoke fluent Russian, and cultivated a Russian style as he grew older by reading Dostoevski, Gogol, and Pushkin. The Schmorell family, living in a villa in Harlaching, an affluent suburb of Munich, seemed to have tolerated Alex's "Slavic soul" but did not have much sympathy for it. He was a talented boy; he loved music, the tragic and gay folk songs of Russia as well as the great classics; he played the piano and the balalaika. He learned to paint and sculpt; he wanted to become a sculptor, although that was not a vocation his father could easily accept. Hugo wanted his sons to be solid middle-class professionals; he wanted them to become doctors.

Alex reluctantly went along, and was lavishly rewarded with allowances and the freedom to use his leisure as he pleased— indulging his tastes in art, in travel, in horseback riding, skiing, and mountain climbing, activities of the privileged youth of Munich.

He was raised in the Russian Orthodox church, an acknowledgment of his mother's faith, and from his early youth there was a strange mix of gaiety, light humor, and melancholy in Alex's personality. He always had friends, also girlfriends, was always involved in the creative as well as the performing arts and in sports, was always on the move. He truly belonged to the youthful elite of Munich; it was an enviable place to be if one was young, educated and fairly affluent.

But there was something else in Shurik: a love to wander off into the countryside or alone in the city, to spend time with hired hands on farms, to talk to farm-women, to gypsies and vagabonds. He was attracted to tramps, to the marginal men in the fiercely homogeneous *Volksgemeinschaft*, or "racial community," that was Nazi Germany. Marginality became his expression of freedom, a freedom blending in with every book of Russian literature, every song and chant of Russian music.

Instinctively, he profoundly despised the values and precepts of the Third Reich. It was not a rational disgust; it seemed to go much deeper. It was not even a question of ethics and justice; it was simply unbearable to live and function in a gray, regimented world inhabited by men and women in uniform, marching in lockstep. Alex was in the Scharnhorst Youth, a right-wing youth group, just before the Nazi takeover, but he was never enthusiastic, and after his group was integrated into the Hitler Youth in 1933, he gradually stopped showing up for meetings. He never experienced the existential sea-change of Hans Scholl after the 1936 Party Rally; his life was dominated not by convictions but by gut feelings.

One gets the impression that Alex was a bit spoiled, as if lavishness and material gifts could replace paternal understanding. He was stylish and elegant; he looked like a young English country squire, especially in his riding breeches and boots, with turtleneck shirts. There are hints of him being a bit of the family problem—the boy who gets into trouble and has to be rescued with his father's money or influence. In one case, when he was serving as a medic in the Wehrmacht, he was caught wearing civilian clothes instead of the despised uniform. His father and uncle—who had contacts in high places—were able to get him out of trouble.

He could be inconsiderate, he could be reckless, he was prodigal in his energies and talents and affections, and there was no sense of caution in him; he simply did not understand what it meant to play things safe.

By the time Alex met Hans in the fall of 1940 at the University of Munich, he had lived through the early stages of Hitler's conquest of Europe. After the obligatory National Labor Service stint in 1937, doing road construction on one of the autobahns, he became a medic and was in the German units that marched into Austria to bring that country "home into the Reich." He also served in Czechoslovakia in 1938, and in France in 1940, as did Hans, although they did not meet at the time.

At the beginning of his army career, Alex had a severe emotional crisis. He was to take the oath of induction, swearing absolute loyalty to Adolf Hitler. He could not do it; he completely broke down. Finally he went to the commanding officer and told him that he was unable to take the oath—incredible as that seems—and asked to be released from military duty. His request was turned down, but, amazingly, there were no repercussions; perhaps the officer was an understanding sort. In fact, there were many more congenial souls tucked away in medic units than in other military outfits, which is one of the reasons the eventual conspirators were able to find one another.

After proclaiming his refusal to take the oath, Alex felt better. Even though he was forced to serve, he felt absolved from obeying the words of the oath. Later, when the war with Russia began, he vowed to his friends that, never, as long as he lived, would he shoot a Russian. Fortunately, on the front he never had to face that decision.

By the fall of 1940 he was back in Munich, studying for his *Physikum*, the premed exams at the university. He could live at home again, take classes in sculpture, attend concerts. He met Hans during this period; they were attached to the same medic unit. With their similar wide-ranging tastes and interests, they were immediately attracted to one another; they both loathed the military and the Nazis, and their personalities, so unlike in many ways, complemented one another—the man in the overcoat and the vagabond, both passing through on a stage they found absurd and barbaric.

Together they crammed for the medical exams, which they passed, and the Schmorells gradually accepted Hans into their home, inviting him to the "reading evenings" that Alex would hold intermittently in the family residence. It was through Alex that Hans met two other key members of the White Rose. At one of those Schmorell evenings, Shurik introduced Hans to Christoph Probst—known as Christel—an old friend from gymnasium days in Munich; and he brought him together with Traute Lafrenz—Alex had met her when he studied briefly at the University of Hamburg—after bumping into her at a performance of the Brandenburg Concertos.

By the spring of 1942 these friendships had solidified. Hans and Traute had been conducting a passionate and tumultuous relationship that had so worn them down that Hans would soon look elsewhere. Russia had been invaded a year earlier, air raids on German cities were intensifying, and life in those cities was becoming drab and dispirited.

The decision was made at this point by Alex and Hans, perhaps with the knowledge and agreement of Christel Probst, that the time had come to act.

Willi Graf was a latecomer to the group, the last to join before Sophie arrived. He was also the outsider; no matter how deeply he was to become involved in the conspiracy, no matter how perilous the acts he was to commit, there always remained a sense of distance between him and the others.

Unlike the others, Willi was an intensely devout Catholic, a silent, brooding young man who put his faith to test constantly. His taciturnity and lack of social grace disguised the fact that he was tormented by doubts—in himself, in the notion of resistance in wartime, and sometimes, perhaps, in some secret and terrible place in his heart, even in God himself.

Willi was raised in Saarbrücken, a city on the French border; in 1942 he was twenty-four years old. His father was a wholesale wine merchant who demanded correct and pious behavior from his children; it was his mother who provided the warmth and tenderness that softened this severity. The church played a primary role in Willi's life from childhood on; religion was his major interest even in school, along with the arts, poetry, and music. He never became interested in public affairs or politics: his revolt, when it came, was not a political one.

The true *Einzelgänger* of the White Rose, Willi Graf yearned more than any of the others for deep and lasting friendship. There was something terribly exacting and painful about his expectations of friends. When Hitler took power, he had just turned fifteen. He made a list of all his friends; then he crossed out the names of those who had joined the Hitler Youth; he never associated with them again.

Like the others, on school holidays he went on week-long hikes in the country or abroad, and was a member of the Gray Order, one of those "unauthorized and illegal" Catholic youth groups that was rounded up in 1937 and 1938. He was arrested while studying at the University of Bonn, interrogated, and released several weeks later. The experience strengthened his revulsion for the regime, and convinced him that Hitler and his men were the embodiment of evil.

By 1939 Willi was a medic; he served in Poland and then in Russia after the 1941 invasion, and was treating the wounded right in the midst of battles. What he saw seared his soul: it was not just the blood and agony of the wounded that profoundly disturbed him, it was the unspeakable cruelty and brutality of his fellow soldiers in dealing with unarmed conquered people. "I wish I never had to see everything I've watched in these past days," he wrote to his sister Anneliese from Russia.

His structure of the universe, the theological foundations, grew shaky: What was one to do? How was one to behave in a tidal wave of butchery and terror? "To be a Christian," he wrote, "is perhaps the hardest thing to ever become in life. We never *are* Christians, and only in death perhaps can we become Christian to a small measure." His diaries are laconic, almost cryptic, but filled with inarticulate anguish. He watched Russian women and children and old men driven out of their homes by German troops; in one village only a cat and some flowers remained. He took care of them.

Stricken by his experiences and sharing them with no one but his sister and his diary, he was furloughed to Munich, to the Second Student Company at the Bergmann School, where he met

Hans and Alex, and through them, Christel Probst, whom he particularly admired.

Life became much easier for Willi in Munich. He took fencing lessons, read constantly, sang in the Bach choir; and most important, he had friends—old comrades from the Gray Order, but the new and livelier group around Hans and Alex as well. But he remained haunted by the scenes in Russia.

The torment never left him, and when Hans and Alex, sometime around Sophie's arrival, broached the subject of conspiracy, of producing underground leaflets, he could not bring himself to decide. Everything in him cried out to destroy the tyrant and the evil he was witnessing, but another side of him spoke about the ethics of illegal and perhaps unchristian acts when his own friends were fighting for their lives.

It took weeks for Willi Graf to decide. That time must have been another siege of spiritual torment; he was fundamentally so alone. Even after he assented and joined in the clandestine work, even after sharing another posting to Russia with Hans and Alex and other friends—this time, mercifully, he was not alone—and even when he took upon himself the greatest risks, he never stopped doubting.

Crossing over the line was an act Willi Graf had to repeat again and again—and it was never easy.

SEVEN

THE "LEAFLETS OF THE WHITE ROSE" began to appear in Munich in mid-June 1942. Four of them came out, one after another, like a staccato burst of fire—filled with rage, brimstone, and literary citations. And as quickly as they came, they were gone.

The city had seen nothing like it in years; perhaps only in the early months after Hitler's takeover had such lengthy and passionate anti-Nazi tracts been circulated. The leaflets were typed single-spaced on both sides of a sheet of paper, duplicated, folded into envelopes with neatly typed names and addresses, and mailed as printed matter to people all over the city.

At least a few hundred of the leaflets were turned in to the Gestapo by individuals who received them. The police began to discern a pattern: the leaflets had been scattered around the university, but not in large numbers. Most of them were mailed individually to academics, civil servants, and—oddly, from the Gestapo viewpoint—such non-intellectuals as restaurateurs and pubkeepers. For the state security services, the leaflets were an unwelcome manifestation in Munich, "Capital City of the [Nazi] Movement"; they were a symptom of ebbing morale, and in addition showed some strategic planning on the part of the authors. It was not easy to track down printed sheets in the mail, not easy to find the mailboxes where they were posted; it was much simpler for the Gestapo to pluck people out of phone booths where they were pasting up posters, or spot them in public toilets painting anti-Nazi graffiti on walls.

After some weeks of investigation, the authorities concluded that the leaflets were designed to reach "the educated classes"—which in itself was unusual—and that their author or authors remained "unknown."

From the authors' point of view, the situation was rather more complicated. Although the timing of the release of the leaflets did seem skillfully planned, it was really more a matter of organization that reached the operational stage, rather than a clever attack on the depressed German psyche.

At that point in the summer of 1942, Germany was still winning battles; the thrust into Russia was deepening, and Rommel was scoring success in North Africa. But it was clear that the war was going to last. To help prepare the population, Propaganda Minister Goebbels produced a major new film, *Der Grosse König* (*The Great King*). Ostensibly about Frederick the Great of Prussia, the film actually presented a new image of Adolf Hitler, no longer as a populist spokesman but as a tragic, unapproachable hero; it suggested that he shouldered the burdens of war alone; it also helped explain his increasing absence from public view. "The year will be hard and difficult," film posters said, "but . . . every man who loves and honors his country must stake his all."

But at the end of May, over one thousand silver-winged airplanes of the Anglo-American forces—they made a spectacular display for those watching below—had destroyed almost all of the city of Cologne, and not just the industrial sections and railheads. Other cities—Hamburg, Lübeck, Düsseldorf—were being savagely hit in air raids, and the streaming silver formations kept moving to the south, ever closer to the city of Munich.

Meanwhile, fear of denunciation had increased; this kept people from sharing their disaffections with one another in any form other than the widespread *Flüsterwitze*, or "whisper jokes." "Do you know that in the future teeth are going to be pulled only through the nose?" one joke went. "Why? Because nobody dares open his mouth anymore." The joke was partly in response to Hitler's speech at the end of April calling for harsher punishments and threatening to remove from office "any judge who manifestly does not know what the time calls for."

The appearance of the leaflets showed that Hans Scholl and Alex Schmorell had begun to act, possibly after planning and discussion with Christoph Probst. Each of the medic-students earned 250 reichsmarks a month (more than the average German worker), and by pooling what they had with some of the allowance Alex got from his father, they were able to buy a secondhand duplicating machine in an out-of-the-way shop—at an outrageous price. Alex also bought the typewriter and got special printing paper, stencils, envelopes, and stamps—always in inconspicuous amounts. An acquaintance, an architect named Manfred Eickemeyer, gave them access to his studio in Schwabing, letting them use his cellar for printing and storage.

Everything was in place: now it was time to write "The Leaflets of the White Rose." The choice of the name White Rose is still obscure, although it was obviously intended to represent purity and innocence in the face of evil: it is a poetic or artistic symbol rather than a political one. Later, under Gestapo interrogation, Hans would say that the name was taken from a Spanish novel he had read. Actually, a novel about peasant exploitation in Mexico had been written by the mysterious German author B. Traven (the author of *The Treasure of the Sierra Madre*), and was called *The White Rose*. It had been published in Berlin in 1931, and there is a chance that Hans and Alex read it; nevertheless, ambiguity remains.

Hans and Alex would each write a draft of a leaflet individually, then come together to read each other's efforts, discussing them aloud, and then, finally, Hans made the editorial decisions. Most of the prose usually turned out to be from Hans's pen.

The first leaflet appeared, in mailboxes all over Munich, bellowing with anger.

> . . . every individual has to consciously accept his responsibility as a member of Western and Christian civilization in this last hour; to arm himself as best he can to work against the scourge of humanity, against fascism and every other form of the absolute state. Adopt passive resistance, *resistance*, wherever you are, block the functioning of this atheistic war machine before it is too late, before the last city is a heap of rubble like Cologne, and before the last youth of our nation bleeds to death because of the *hubris* of a subhuman. Don't forget that each people gets the government it deserves!

The leaflet goes on to cite Schiller's work on the codes of Lycurgus and Solon, and Goethe's "Awakening of Epimenides" at some length, ending with the call: "Freedom! Freedom!" and a note to the reader to please reproduce the leaflet and pass it on.

This first effort changes keys from rage to admonition, to lofty poetry about the individual and the state, to the final call for freedom. It is unstructured, confusing, rambling, and touching.

The ripples began.

Sophie knew nothing about the White Rose and their new campaign. A little over a month after she arrived in Munich, rumors began to circulate that anti-Nazi literature had appeared at the university; reading such a leaflet without reporting it to the Gestapo was a crime. Among the students there was a flurry of tension and excitement; some of them did turn the leaflets in, but most did not.

While attending a lecture, Sophie noticed a mimeographed sheet lying under a desk; she picked it up. "Nothing is more unworthy of a cultured people," she read, "than to allow itself, without resistance, to be 'governed' by an irresponsible ruling clique motivated by the darkest of instincts." She felt a sudden thrill; darted a look about her. "The state is never an end in itself. It is important only as a means by which humanity can achieve its goal, which is nothing other than the advancement of man's constructive capabilities."

Now she saw clearly that there were others at the university who felt as she did; they called themselves *Die Weisse Rose*, "The White Rose," and they were taking action. But there was something about the words . . . She folded the leaflet quickly into her notebook and left for her brother's room, to show it to him.

Hans was not there; she began to leaf through the stack of books on his desk. An old volume of Schiller fell open to a page full of pencil marks: ". . . if a particular state hinders the progress of the spirit, it is reprehensible and corrosive. . . . The longer it exists, the more corrosive it becomes." Turning the pages further, she found the passages cited in the leaflet, word for word, underlined.

She was gripped with shock.

When Hans came in, she confronted him; he denied any involvement, as he already had to Traute Lafrenz. Alex and Christel arrived, and the confrontation became the moment of truth for Sophie Scholl.

Her thoughts, as always, revolved around the war—concern for her younger brother Werner and her friend Fritz, both at the front. But she was also experiencing a quickening self-criticism for standing by and doing nothing but "feeling." Not long before, she had shocked Fritz by refusing to contribute sweaters and gloves to the Winter Relief fund for men at the front: "It's all the same if it's German soldiers freezing or Russians, and it's equally tragic," she had told him. "We have to lose this war. If we donate woolens now, we only contribute to extending it."

Now she was facing her intense and determined older brother, who had crossed the invisible line. Her inner turmoil must have been nearly unbearable. She spoke to Hans, in front of Alex and Christel, about the terrible risks he was taking; she reproached him for adding extra weight to the family's impossible burden: Werner in Russia, their father awaiting a prison sentence, their mother's heart condition deteriorating under the strain. And by now their entire family had at least some sort of Gestapo record.

Hans tried to shrug it off, and his friends defended him. Alex told Sophie that their actions were not reckless, that the choice of people to receive the leaflets was more or less random, and that there was no way to link Hans or Alex to the operation. Christel spoke about acting for a higher good, and Hans, too, finally said that in the name of the German intellectuals whose moral spines had been broken in 1933, they had to act.

She saw, in spite of her fear, in spite of her terror, that there was no turning back. "Be performers of the word," her favorite epistle said, "not just listeners." They had crossed over; they had chosen the only way they could. She would now join them.

EIGHT

MUNICH was—and still is—a deeply Catholic city. Churches are everywhere, reconstructed Gothic, baroque, rococo, neoclassicist, bearing witness to the curves and bends in the river of Catholic history. While strolling down a narrow medieval lane, one suddenly encounters them, looming above—like the Frauenkirche, its twin domes still dominating the city of which it is the symbol. Or one comes upon a rococo jewel of a chapel, ornate and delicate amid the cars screeching and the pedestrians running in the heart of town. Churches are in profusion—in the downtown commercial district, in residential neighborhoods, in the vast and sprawling suburbs, and in every town and village in the Upper Bavarian countryside. Their interiors are alight with Bavarian rococo altars and gilded Virgins, in gleaming contrast to their cold, white walls. They are bedecked with fresh flowers on the bleakest days of winter, offering silence and fragrance and color to the pious and to the passerby seeking rest.

The church permeates the air of Munich, whether one is Catholic or not. Most of the White Rose members were not Catholic, or at least not seriously practicing ones, but the intellectual and emotional currents of protest against the Nazis associated with Catholicism played a significant role in the shaping of their resistance.

The Roman Catholic church, as most institutions in Germany, had an ambiguous relationship with the men of the Third Reich from the very beginning. Hitler signed a concordat with the Vatican on July 20, 1933, about half a year after taking power. It was considered a most essential diplomatic breakthrough at a moment when he was still being viewed as a pariah among world statesmen. The agreement, a marriage of convenience on both sides, permitted German Catholics to practice their faith unmolested, but forbade any activities that intruded on the functioning of the state. It stripped Catholic youth organizations like the New Germany, the one that Willi Graf belonged to at that time, of the right to wear their own uniforms, plan and carry out excursions into the countryside, print or distribute their own journals, or undertake any program not directly controlled by state and Party authorities.

The church consented to the agreement in order to protect its clergy from harassment and arrest—which in fact it was unable to do. Thousands of priests, nuns, and lay workers were arrested for "immorality," or for "smuggling foreign currency," a trumped-up charge often used by the Nazis in their crazed hunt for dissidents. But the agreement with the Nazis had a deeper, more fervent motive: the official hierarchy was offering Hitler tacit support for his avowed anti-Communist policies both inside and outside of Germany.

The National Socialists did not make for smooth and ingratiating partners. As their power waxed at home and abroad in a crescendo of diplomatic, economic, and psychological triumphs throughout the thirties, the latent contempt in the Party for religion and clerical institutions became more overt and crude. Outspoken priests were hauled off to prison, the sanctity of the confessional was violated by the Gestapo, Catholic publications were no longer merely censored but closed down, and monasteries and convents were forced to shut their gates.

Michael Cardinal von Faulhaber, the archbishop of Munich-Freising, embodied the ambiguities of most ecclesiastical figures toward the Third Reich. A conservative nationalist and an ardent believer in the justness of the German cause in the First World War, he had been named Munich's archbishop in 1921. As most prominent church, intellectual, and military leaders in Germany, he never supported the Weimar Republic or its efforts at building democratic institutions; in fact, his was one of the persuasive voices that brought the deputies of Pope Pius XI to the negotiating table with representatives of Adolf Hitler.

It was also a fact that the cardinal tried to use quiet diplomacy to ease Nazi excesses, that he pleaded in behalf of victims in concentration camps; and there were times that his voice was heard. But persecution of Catholics persisted. About four years after the Nazi takeover, on November 4, 1936, the Bavarian cardinal was received by the Führer at his awesome Alpine retreat at Obersalzburg. The three-hour meeting was actually a warning: "The Catholic church should not deceive itself," Adolf Hitler told the cardinal. "If National Socialism does not succeed in defeating Bolshevism, then both the church and Christianity are finished in Europe. Bolshevism is the mortal enemy of the church as much as it is of Fascism."

Even though the church hierarchy was in fundamental agreement with this point of view, by March of 1937 they felt impelled to speak out. Pope Pius XI issued an encyclical, *Mit brennender Sorge* (*With Burning Concern*), charging Nazi Germany with violating the concordat and threatening to unleash "destructive religious wars."

Kristallnacht, November 9, 1938, or what has also been called the Night of Broken Glass, had a disturbing impact on members of all churches in Germany as they saw civic order disrupted and watched Jews being herded into the streets, beaten, spat upon, and taken away; they watched as SA and SS men in civilian clothes smashed Jewish shops and homes and set houses of Jewish worship to the torch. The police looked away. The Scholl family recalled that night with numb, impotent horror: the beast in man had lifted its mask and the time of euphemistic niceties and rationalizations was over. Cardinal Faulhaber sent a van to the chief rabbi of Munich when he heard that the temple was in flames in order to help salvage the sacred relics.

Although conflicts between the Catholic leadership and population, on one hand, and the Nazi state, on the other, were to emerge intermittently throughout the twelve years of the Third Reich, the major energies of the Nazis were directed toward the propagation of a new state church, to be created out of the majority confession in Germany, the Protestant, or Lutheran, church.

The German Christians, as they were known, rejected the Old Testament's "Hebrew" values, and called for the reawakening of the "Nordic spirit," a rebirth of ruthlessness and strength. Traditional Christianity was the religion of the "sick and the weak." With Adolf Hitler as the new messiah, they saw their faith as identical with their nation. "Either we have a German god or none at all," a spokesman for the German Believers' Movement proclaimed in 1934. "We Germans have been forsaken by the Christian God. He is not a just, supernatural God, but a political-party God of the others. It is because we believed in him and not in our German God that we were defeated in the struggle of nations."

The new church de-Christianized the rituals of birth, marriage, and death, and tried, not too successfully, to transform the deeply ingrained Christmas customs into a celebration of the winter solstice.

The antithesis of this primitive and clumsy effort to create a Nazi religion was the Bekennende Kirche, usually called the "Confessing church," but perhaps more accurately translated into English as the "Professing church." This group of Lutheran pastors met for the first time in March 1935 to express their revulsion for fascist "theology."

Among its leaders, and indeed its moving spirit, was Martin Niemöller, minister in the wealthy Dahlem suburb of Berlin. He too had been a staunch conservative, and was actually a U-boat captain during the First World War. He and another young pastor, Dietrich Bonhoeffer, member of a distinguished Prussian family, were to become the driving force in this group, this perilously eroding rock of Protestantism in a sea of hate.

The Confessing church stated unequivocally and publicly that "the new religion demands belief in an eternal Germany in place of the belief in the eternal kingdom of our Master and Savior, Jesus Christ . . . This insane belief creates a god from man's image and being . . . It is anti-Christian . . . In the face of temptation and the danger of this religion . . . we must bear witness to our country and people."

Five hundred Protestant ministers who read these words from their pulpits were arrested. By 1939, by the time Hitler was ready to go to war, the stubborn band of pastors had almost completely been silenced. Martin Niemöller had been arrested, tried, and imprisoned. Upon his release, he was taken by the Gestapo and put into the Sachsenhausen concentration camp and then the one at Dachau; he was freed after the Allied invasion in 1945. Dietrich Bonhoeffer was to end up in the German resistance movement; his clandestine effort to negotiate peace with the Allies, provided that the military would be able to assassinate Hitler, ended in his arrest in April 1943 and his execution in April 1945, shortly before the Allies entered the concentration camp where he was imprisoned.

So it was that in their years of adolescence and early maturity the members of the White Rose had witnessed the choking off of all voices of moral protest. They had seen their own churches grow silent and rigid as the spirit animating them departed under the aegis of brute force.

One of the next significant attacks on the churches came at a time when the Nazis were at the pinnacle of victory at war and popularity at home: from June 1940 till the invasion of Russia in June 1941. It was in this heady year of unrelieved triumph that the Nazis struck at Catholic Bavaria—a move that even ardent believers in the Führer agreed was counterproductive. In April 1941, Gauleiter Adolf Wagner of Upper Bavaria and Munich—who also held the post of Bavarian minister of culture—announced that all crucifixes were henceforth to be banned from schools. The reaction, for Germans under National Socialism, was violent. Schools in rural areas struck, meetings were held by enraged parents who had never before visited their children's schools, and petitions and protest letters were written and signed without hesitation. People were not afraid to speak up. In some alpine villages farmers strode into schools and threw the mandatory picture of Adolf Hitler out of classroom windows.

Everyone agreed that it had been a stupid move made by an exceptionally stupid and insensitive gauleiter; Wagner was tolerated by Hitler and his cronies mainly because he was one of the loyal "old fighters," a participant in the legendary moment of creation when the Nazi brownshirts in Munich had battled with Socialists, Communists, and even occasionally with the police, back in the "decadent days" of the Weimar Republic. Adolf Wagner was so loyal he even sounded like Adolf Hitler; when he spoke on the radio, listeners were not sure if they had unexpectedly tuned in on the Führer. And in spite of Hitler's reciprocal feelings, he did countermand Wagner's crucifix decree. One thing had been made clear during this episode: Bavarians might accept persecution of Jews and all political opposition, or at least look the other way when it happened, but when their own deeply felt religious traditions were at stake, they were prepared to fight.

Toward the end of this period, in the summer of 1941, rumors began to spread throughout the country about special secret programs that were going on in mental hospitals and other institutions: rumors concerning murder. The idea of purifying the race, of preventing physical malformations through heredity and "cancerous growths" in the *Volk* community, were certainly not new in the Third Reich. One of the first laws passed by the National Socialists was called "The Prevention of Offspring with Hereditary Diseases"; it went into effect July 14, 1933, six days before the Vatican signed the concordat with Hitler. Among those to be sterilized were manic depressives, cripples, epileptics, and those with hereditary forms of blindness. Decisions to sterilize were made locally, and appeals could only be forwarded to special "eugenics courts." But until the outbreak of war, the killing of the mentally and physically "defective" had not been fully instituted. While German troops were overrunning Poland and Russia, people at home were gradually becoming aware that "useless eaters" were being "weeded out"—this vocabulary had already become a part of school curricula and bureaucratic life, referring to Jews, Gypsies, and homosexuals, as well as the mentally ill, the physically handicapped, the incurably ill, and the old.

Families all over the Reich related incidents to one another about friends or neighbors or colleagues who had close relatives in nursing homes and hospitals, and who had received official letters about the "sudden death" of the patient. In the usual peremptory tone, the bureaucratic message told the families to come immediately to collect the urn of ashes "or else it would be destroyed." And as usual, the letters implied that the bureaucracy, the state, was doing the families a favor.

By August 1941, as many as eighty thousand Germans had been murdered in the euthanasia program. In many cases they had been experimented on by physicians who had been trained in traditional medical schools and universities; these doctors tried a variety of poisons, gas, and injections to see which worked most quickly and effectively—this was the "humane" aspect of the program. The SS provided sealed "gas-vans" in which the exhaust from the engine was pumped into the van's interior. This program was to serve as a model for Hitler's genocide of the Jewish people.

The Scholl family in Ulm heard more details about the euthanasia program from a Protestant sister, a friend of Mrs. Scholl's who had herself been a religious nurse during the First World War. This sister worked in a nearby home for mentally retarded children. In agony she related what happened at the home to Magdalena Scholl. One day the SS came with a convoy of trucks, entered the building, and began pushing all the children out to the open vans. The sisters stood dumbstruck, utterly at the mercy of the armed men in black. The children did not understand; they were confused but not afraid. They asked the sisters where they were going. The head nurse said in despair, "You are going to heaven." The children laughed with delight and waved as they disappeared down the road.

The provincial bishop of the Lutheran church in the southwestern state of Württemberg, a Dr. Wurm, wrote an angry letter to Reichsminister of the Interior Wilhelm Frick. He said that the local population saw smoke rising from the crematorium near the nursing home in Marbach. He noted that wounded veterans of the First World War, epileptics, and "other people capable of working" were "involved." The Catholic bishop of Limburg also protested to the minister of justice, sending along a copy to Minister Frick; he talked about the killings at Hadamar, a nursing facility, where the death toll had reached about ten thousand. He said the children in the area would stand and watch the hospital buses go by their villages in the direction of the home and would comment, "Here come the murder wagons." They taunted each other while they played, saying that if they did not behave, they would be taken to "the baking ovens."

The Catholic bishop of Münster, Clemens August (Count von) Galen, could bear no more. He had long been a critic of the Nazis, and as far back as 1934 had spoken out against their racial policies. That July, in 1941, he stood up in his church and thundered his outrage at a program that was "against God's commandments, against the law of nature, and against the system of jurisprudence in Germany." He roared at his congregation, "These are our brothers and sisters!" and asked them how they expected to live if the measure of their lifespan was economic productivity. No one's life was safe any longer, he said, and he then asked who now could have confidence in his doctor.

The bishop inveighed against the seizure of monasteries, convents, and churches, and warned the people that "an enemy at home"—meaning the Gestapo—existed. But, he added, nothing must be done by force. The only way was "spiritual and moral opposition." The people must "remain strong, be steadfast."

Bishop Galen's sermons, transcribed and duplicated, began to circulate all over the country, appearing in home mailboxes—and not only those of Catholics. A copy arrived at the Scholl home one day with no return address on the envelope. It was an incredible voice of courage in the darkness: that a churchman dared to speak up and that others dared to take down his words and disperse them throughout the land was an event whose significance cannot be fully comprehended out of its time and place. Hans Scholl happened to be home in Ulm at the time, after serving with the occupation army in France; he was, at that point, already a medic-student at the University of

Munich. He read the sermon over and over again. "Finally someone has the courage to speak," he said to his family, and then added, "and all you need is a duplicating machine."

The Nazis had a choice: arrest Galen and the few others who protested, or stop the killing. They chose the latter. "Euthanasia" was officially halted, although throughout the war years persons with "defects" continued to disappear, including the babies of Polish and Russian forced laborers. Galen was left untouched—for the moment: Joseph Goebbels promised his friends that the bishop would be hanged as soon as final victory was achieved.

As victory did follow victory in the plains of Russia, somehow there still remained small pockets of anger and niches of dissent in the Third Reich, and not least of all in Munich. Young men like Hans Scholl and Christoph Probst—neither of them Catholic—had begun to turn to theological and philosophical writings in their quest for means to cope with the ever-growing barbarism. They could not understand how their country had fallen into this chasm of terror and butchery; the heritage of another Germany was still strong in them. They found some guidance—and in some ways were able to identify with the authors—in Augustine's *Confessions*, in the works of Thomas Aquinas, who obliquely justified the "murder of tyrants," and in French Catholic writers like Pascal and Claudel. Perhaps if they had lived in Prussia they would have turned to other writers and confessional perspectives, but in Munich and in the south it seemed natural to seek answers in the body of Catholic thought that was most immediately available.

Hans's rage, and Willi's terrible confusion, and Christoph's sense of helplessness had been growing steadily for years. The war had not yet started, Kristallnacht had not yet taken place, when Hans expressed his deep revulsion for the people in Vienna, at their ecstatic jubilation as Hitler's forces marched into their city on March 12, 1938, to attach Austria to the Reich. "I don't understand people," Hans wrote in his diary after listening to the howling roar of the masses over the radio; he was nineteen at the time. "I want to go out to some huge and empty plain and be completely alone."

Perhaps in ordinary times these young people would have remained unaffected by religious beliefs—with the exception of Willi Graf. But the times were extraordinary; the world was going straight to hell; no one, inside or outside of Germany, seemed able or willing to stop it, and they strained with every fiber of their beings to find a meaning to life. Without a religious structure it was difficult; without God it was becoming impossible.

Christoph Probst was not born a Catholic, although he was to be baptized one, minutes before his execution. His short life seems like a terribly abbreviated Tolstoy biography. He moves from a world of urbane sophistication, from a family of freethinkers and sensitive intellectuals into an atmosphere of rustic simplicity, rollicking babies, and an austere faith in the Christian God. His father, Hermann Probst, came from a merchant family and had inherited private means. He was able to devote much of his time to scholarly pursuits; he was an esthete who did not want to be tied down to academic or civil-service posts. In his last years of life, he was particularly attracted to Eastern religions, and studied Persian and Sanskrit in order to be able to read classical testaments in the original.

The Probst home was filled with friends, books, and ideas that were to be driven out of Germany after 1933. The bookshelves were filled with volumes concerning the Mahabharata and the Bhagavad Gita. Among Hermann Probst's friends in Munich were artists like Paul Klee and Emil Nolde—whom he introduced to each other. Both were later to be banned, with Klee hounded into exile. Nolde painted young Christel with his sister, Angelika; the portrait of the two children who were so deeply attached to each other was prominently displayed in the Probst living room.

Christoph's parents were divorced when the children were small; both remarried and they remained on good terms. Christel and Angelika were sent to progressive and liberal boarding schools around Bavaria, and to gymnasium (humanistic high school) in Nuremberg and then Munich—where Christel first met Alex Schmorell. In the twenties, these schools had kept aloof from the enthusiasms and conformities of the various youth movements that were becoming raucously nationalistic. Even in the mid-thirties, when Christel was at school, many of these institutions managed to evade linkage with the Hitler Youth or the forced feeding of their pupils with Nazi ideology.

Christel was formed not so much by crushing disillusionment, as was Hans, or by anarchistic revolt, as was Alex, but by humanistic Western values that were part of his everyday life as he grew up; until 1936 he was insulated in a direct, personal way from Nazi brutality and terror. But then, when he was seventeen, his father, in a depression, committed suicide. We cannot fathom Christel's innermost reactions, but regardless of his own feelings and grief, he did try to comfort his stepmother. Her life was now in serious danger; she was Jewish and no longer had the protection of an "Aryan" husband. Mrs. Probst continued to live in their home in the rural community outside Munich; the villagers must have had high regard for her, for they tried to make sure that she was not molested or harassed by the Nazis.

Christel loved both sets of parents. At no time did he express anger or resentment at the divorce or at the boarding-school existence he led, although it was by no means an ordinary childhood and adolescence by German middle-class standards. Unlike the British, the Germans have traditionally preferred to mold their children at home. The reality was that his home consisted of dormitories almost all his life, and that he and Angelika clung to one another as if holding on to a life raft. He never had a real and lasting home till he married Herta Dohrn when he was twenty-one.

He passed his *Abitur* at the relatively early age of seventeen; he was then required to serve in the National Labor Service before entering university. He chose to study medicine, a choice made at least partly as an act of rejection of the Nazi sterilization programs, and he served simultaneously, as did Alex, Hans, and Willi, as a medic in the military—in his case, in the Luftwaffe.

A tall, good-looking, and athletic youth, Christoph radiated an essential sweetness and kindness that was combined with intellectual curiosity, introspection, and an astounding maturity. He was never afraid to show tenderness and love. He believed that "the life of the mind," or *Geistesleben* (which can also be translated as "life of the spirit"), was the focal point of a man's being. His interests in literature, music, and the arts began to expand into philosophical regions as the years of Nazi power wore on. Learning and knowledge had meaning only if they related to ethical behavior; for Christoph there never seemed to be a cleavage between the word and the deed.

"It's a mistaken conclusion that the intellectually developed person can take less because of his greater tenderness," Christel wrote his half brother in 1942. "My viewpoint is that the intellectual can take more—even if he is physically handicapped and is suffering. Precisely because he is part of the kingdom of the spirit can he live fully and completely."

In 1940, Christel married Herta Dohrn. At first the young couple lived with Christoph's Jewish stepmother in Zell bei Ruhpolding. Children came quickly: by 1942, at the age of twenty-three, he had two sons, and a daughter would follow shortly. He was completely paternal; he adored his children. Through them he had found a haven, a place of warmth and laughter and predictability—one that seemed to have been lacking all his life. On weekends when he was off duty, he spent a great deal of time with his children and with his father-in-law, Harald Dohrn, an educator and scholar, and a passionate convert to Catholicism. It was during this period that Christel met Hans Scholl; they were introduced by Alex, who had known Christel for years and considered him his closest and dearest friend.

Clean-cut, with a wide grin, pipe-smoking (as was in vogue among all the young men), Christel seems like the quintessential Lancelot: supple and strong, kindly, virtuous, and fervent—but without the need to prove himself. If one dares speculate who among the White Rose was truly loved by the others, then Christoph's face appears, caught in a snapshot, head lifted in semi-profile, laughing up at his little son slung on his shoulder: he is the unanimous focus of a deep and genuine affection.

In the summer of 1941, Hans Scholl introduced himself to the distinguished Catholic editor Carl Muth; Hans appeared at the door of his home in the Munich suburb of Solln carrying a letter of introduction provided by Otl Aicher, who had become acquainted with Muth not long before. There was an immediate attraction between the fragile, white-haired scholar and publisher of seventy-four and the darkly intense student of twenty-three. This friendship and the relationships catalyzed by it were crucial in the evolution of the White Rose.

Carl Muth lived without a family in a small house nearly bursting with books, journals, and manuscripts. He had founded the journal *Hochland* (*Highland*), as a voice of Catholic progress, in 1903. It was totally banned by the Nazis in 1941, shortly before Hans met Muth. It must have been a cruel blow to a man who had managed, since 1933, never to mention the name of Adolf Hitler in his publication, and in all those years had gotten away with it. Now and then issues had been confiscated, but his right to publish had not been challenged. By focusing on historical subjects like Hellenic Greece, the Middle Ages, and the Enlightenment—as did those few serious anti-Nazi publishers still functioning in Germany—he had made indirect and adroit attacks on the regime; its intellectual capacities were generally too limited to even notice—until 1941.

Muth's home, with its small garden, was to become a sanctuary for Hans, as well as for Sophie and Inge Scholl, who were introduced to Muth by Hans soon afterward. Hans was utterly fascinated by him, undoubtedly having heard about his reputation for integrity, depth, and wisdom before finding a way to meet him. Muth had struck a chord in *Hochland* that echoed: its circulation, which was never large-scale or intended to be, had risen from five thousand in 1933 to twelve thousand in 1939.

The Scholls came by to see the old publisher regularly. They all felt about him as Hans did, regardless of their Protestant affiliations, and they seemed to cling to him and his private world of inner exile as if it were their whole anchor to sanity. Muth's magic was not only his philosophical sweep of knowledge or his deep hatred for National Socialism, but his youthful, almost playful sense of ethical and metaphysical exploration. He not only listened to young people, he wanted to live and share their experiences; he wrote letters in detail to explain his point of view when doubts seemed to arise. As Inge Scholl later put it, Muth swung "between excommunication and sainthood." Hans meant a great deal to the old scholar too, perhaps more than any other young person: he represented the "other" Germany, the young Germany that had miraculously remained uncorrupted. The Scholls' presence in his home was a deep source of satisfaction and even joy.

It was not long before Hans, after discussions over ersatz coffee in the garden, began ordering and cataloging Muth's library. He came to Solln every day between classes and hospital duty and read Plato, Claudel, Bernanos, and even Marx for hours. Inge Scholl came and stayed with Muth for a week or two at a time, bringing him food from Mrs. Scholl in Ulm, taking care of him, lifting his spirits. Sophie stayed at his house for a week when she first arrived in Munich in May 1942 and was looking for a furnished room.

Muth introduced Hans to various friends; one was Pater Rumuald Bauerreis, archivist of the Monastery of Saint Bonifaz in Munich. Muth wrote him a note in the spring of 1942, asking the father to look after his young protégé. Hans was given access to the vast and rich library of the order. Saint Bonifaz, Hans quickly learned, was in danger of being shut down by the Nazis; he and Alex, who sometimes came along, decided to smuggle out some of the most precious tomes from the monastery library before the arrival of the Gestapo. They came back with rucksacks the same day they heard the news of the impending closure; they had found a "simple man" who owned a wagon and who, as Hans said, "understood what the Nazis are better than the generals and professors do." The books were put on the wagon and taken to the Schmorell residence on Benediktenwandstrasse in Harlaching.

It was at Muth's home that they met Theodor Haecker one day in the winter of 1941. He had been a collaborator on *Hochland*, but had been under a speaking and writing ban since 1935. He suffered dreadfully from the imposed silence and the separation from his audience, and was unable to be subtle or evasive in expressing his contempt and rage for the Nazis. Haecker was sixty-three years old, a widower, a man with penetrating blue eyes under bushy eyebrows, with closed, unreadable features. He was tormented by what was happening to Germany and Europe, obsessed with the notion that Germany would be destroyed by God for its deeds against the Jewish people. In his diary, known in English as *Journal in the Night*, he wrote: ". . . a time may come when Germans will have to wear a swastika on the left side of their clothing, sign of the Antichrist. They are crucifying Christ a second time, as a people!"

Haecker was a converted Catholic, and was a nationally distinguished translator and explicator of Kierkegaard into German; his life's goal was to reconcile and harmonize existential concepts with Catholic dogma and thought.

What pulled Hans to Solln and to men of the stature of Muth and Haecker went deeper than the affinity of the young for the old and wise, or their mutual anti-Nazi feelings. These Catholic thinkers, particularly Haecker, were struggling to use existentialism in a world that had gone mad. Existentialism has always been a formidable stream, if not the major current, in modern Catholic and Protestant reflection, but at that point in 1941 and 1942, it was crucial in helping Hans and his friends to come to a decision, to cross the line.

Pascal, a Catholic, and Kierkegaard, a Protestant, had expressed the fundamental assumptions behind all existential thought. "There is no permanence for man: it is a condition which is at once natural to mankind, yet most contrary to his inclinations," Pascal had written.

"We burn with the desire of finding a secure abode, an ultimate firm base on which to build a tower which might rise to infinity; but our very foundation crumbles completely, and earth opens before us unto the very abyss." In this manner, in the seventeenth century, did a young Frenchman come upon the dawning crisis of Western civilization, the crisis that led Kierkegaard two centuries later to make a desperate "leap into faith"—an acceptance of God, a belief that he exists—after enduring a near-fatal siege of angst.

These ideas were part of the essential bond between Haecker and the young men in the White Rose. In a universe where all values have been shattered, where religions and histories and literatures and social structures have lost their meaning, man has to stand up again, accept his condition, accept that he is alone and has no protection, and proceed to create his own world, his own values, his own decisions, his own actions—and be willing at all times to pay the consequences, to be responsible for everything he thinks, says, and does. This is the existentialism of Martin Heidegger—which tragically led to his temporary submission to the will of the Leader, Adolf Hitler, as the quintessential spokesman for "a complete revolution of German existence"—and the existentialism of one of Heidegger's most renowned admirers, Jean-Paul Sartre.

For others who thought along this line, self-creation, this acceptance of aloneness, was not possible, at least not without help—from God. And God has to be accepted totally on faith, without rational proofs, and without his being immanent in grandiose and heavy Hegelian-like metaphysical systems.

Existential thought can be seen as the last and only response possible to German romanticism and Russian nihilism. The modern world is alienated, cold, unacceptable; we no longer know where we belong, we are no longer in harmony with the universe. But instead of turning back, as the romantics and nationalists did, to a perfect past, the existentialist proposes that we walk on, that we accept this unbearable condition, that we create ourselves anew and make "authentic choices" even if we are alone and can expect neither help nor mercy from anyone. This kind of thinking that forces man to choose, to act in order to be, and to accept the responsibility of action, was profoundly part of the intellectual and ethical current animating men like Dietrich Bonhoeffer. He also believed that to act—in this case, to resist Hitler, perhaps even to kill him—was to become free.

There is no question that existentialist thinking was an undercurrent among serious intellectuals in the Third Reich and was a crucial factor in the resistance that developed.

Theodor Haecker, one of its primary exponents, would read aloud from his journal and from his banned or unpublished works at Muth's home and, later, at the studio where the White Rose gathered. His need to be heard was greater than his fear of arrest. The inner tension must have been enormous; his hands shook as he read. A sample from his journal in May 1940, the kind of extract he would read to the young people:

> The fate and thus the task of the German Christian is without an example which he might follow. . . . He is alone! Everything that he feels, thinks and does has a question mark to it, questioning whether it is right. The leadership of Germany today, and of this there is not the slightest doubt and it cannot be evaded, is consciously anti-Christian—it hates Christ whom it does not name. . . . From the very beginning, the successful trick of these people sent to plague Europe has been to combine the special interests of their basely impulsive and greedy natures, intellectually speaking, soulless and half-educated, with the true and genuine wishes and claims of the German people . . . The German people will be beaten, but not struck down and wiped out. The one ray of light in my mind is this: it is better for a people to be defeated and to suffer, than to sin and apostasize.

This was more or less the way Haecker addressed the students, and their response, their interchange, must have been of the utmost importance to him. He never overtly encouraged anyone to resist: it meant near-certain death. In fact, he told the young people that evil, the Antichrist, was in some way part of God's plan. But he transmitted two levels of messages: one of choices and creation, and the other of resignation; Hans Scholl could never accept the latter. "Where are the Christians?" Hans shouted after hearing an "enemy broadcast" reporting that German Communists and Social Democrats had resisted the Nazis and been caught. "Should we stand here with empty hands at the end of the war when they ask the question: '*And what did you do?*' " Sophie Scholl expressed this same emotion when she wrote in her diary, "I want to share the suffering of these days. Sympathy becomes hollow if one feels no pain."

The names of the White Rose did not appear in Theodor Haecker's journal, for obvious reasons. He was taken for questioning—as was

Carl Muth—by the Gestapo after the White Rose arrests and executions in February 1943. But more than a year later, on June 9, 1944, there is an odd, cryptic entry in Haecker's diary:

> Friday morning towards 10 o'clock. High explosive bombs. The house and my flat destroyed. Unbelievable destruction. Some good helpers who console me by being what they are and by helping! Scholl! And also some *crapule*. Upright souls. And miserable souls. God is merciful! God is great! God is precise but magnanimous.

It is a cry at the brink of obliteration, the cry of a man utterly and truly alone in the universe, the involuntary cry of a man sliding into physical and mental chaos; at that supreme moment of crisis, out of the black night of his soul, it seems that Theodor Haecker cried out for Hans Scholl.

NINE

"WHERE BOOKS ARE BURNED, they will ultimately also burn human beings." The poet Heinrich Heine's warning, no matter how often it is cited, remains chillingly apt. In 1933, in Germany, the books were burned—the heritage and humanity of a nation consumed in flames as the fierce, exulting shouts of university students filled the night.

The universities remained as shells, deceptive facades of normalcy as hundreds of professors were thrown out and forced to flee the country. The University of Munich had a "brown" reputation for years before Hitler had taken power, mainly because of the vociferous agitation of the Nazi movement in the city and its strong student auxiliary at the university. But all the universities in the Reich, whether they had a liberal reputation, like Freiburg, or a conservative one, like Munich, were "coordinated" or "integrated" into a centralized system of control and conformity.

The German universities, distinguished and respected as they were in the world intellectual community, particularly in the fields of natural, physical, and the social sciences and in philosophy, had been hotbeds of nationalistic fervor since early in the nineteenth century. The spirit of academic freedom in these institutions did not necessarily mean an atmosphere of universalism, objectivity, or tolerance for other people's—or nations'—points of view. Nationalism—and the surging, craving hunger for unification of all the petty German states without a common political identity—burst forth when the foreign conqueror, Napoleon, strode over German lands. To unify meant to be strong, to be strong meant a refusal to submit to alien invaders; ultimately, the refusal to submit was to become the need to conquer and dominate others.

This outpouring of national emotion, this surge of self-discovery and self-glorification originally came not from the masses of working people in the cities or from the artisans and peasants in the country-side. It came first from the intellectuals, the artists and the professors who occupied a fairly exalted role in their society.

But in spite of the wave of nationalism that in the nineteenth century swept Germany—and Russia and Italy, among other countries—there were always German voices speaking out against xenophobia, against prejudice, against blind passions and national apotheosis. Friedrich Schiller, toward the end of the eighteenth century, in giving his inaugural address as professor of history at the University of Jena, reminded his audience that "the first law of decency is to preserve the liberty of others, the second is to demonstrate one's own freedom." Even those who bitterly opposed the Napoleonic conquest of their native regions, like the Catholic Rhinelander Joseph Görres, who later was named professor of history at the University of Munich, spoke out loudly and openly against "Prussian and Protestant" waves of aggression coming from the north to conquer German lands, now that Napoleon was destroyed.

The universities in the Rhineland and southwest Germany, like the general populace in these areas, often expressed a spirit of opposition to the forced unification of Germany under Prussia. The University of Freiburg stubbornly maintained the traditions of the French Revolution, and in the 1820s helped in the experimental development of local parliaments and other democratic institutions.

It is in this region, southwest Germany, that most of the members of the White Rose were raised, and it was at the University of Freiburg that a small circle of academics also formed a resistance group against Hitler. Southwest Germany—and, to a lesser extent, Bavaria and its capital, Munich—have always felt themselves to be the "true" cultural heart of Germany, an independent force between calcified, pompous, and Catholic Austria, and the aggressive, Spartan, Protestant upstart, Prussia. Generations of professors in this region disseminated protest against the hegemony of Prussia and against what they saw as false nationalism and a fraudulent sense of security this nationalism offered; for them, after Prussian soldiers arrived and wiped out their vestiges of democracy in 1848, Prussia represented "the peace of the grave and the order of the cemetery."

The University of Berlin was founded in 1810 as part of a reform movement in Prussia, but it quickly became a bastion of Prussian nationalism, "the intellectual bodyguard of the Hohenzollerns," the Prussian ruling dynasty whose scion later was to crown himself kaiser, emperor of the Germans. It became clear as Napoleon rose and fell, that freedom, in Prussian terms, meant acceptance of and obedience to the state, in Prussia itself and in the German territories it began to annex. Men like Hegel and Fichte at the University of Berlin, mighty figures in the world of ideas, began to ennoble Prussia with almost religious reverence; a new messianic feeling for Germany and the German language began to sweep the land, although at that point, Fichte, in his addresses to the German nation as rector of the university, spoke about Germany as a "Fatherland of the mind," rather than as a warrior-folk.

But as early as 1813 the spirit of conquest, of parades and marching armies, had permeated the air. One of the great intellectuals of the era, Ernst Moritz Arndt, described his feelings about a military parade in words that cannot differ significantly from the testimony of spectators at a Nazi demonstration of armed might. "When a great crowd was before me," he wrote in 1813,

> when a band of warriors passes by with flowing banners and sounding trumpets and drums, then I realize that my feelings and my actions are not an empty illusion, then it is that I feel the indestructible life, the eternal spirit, and eternal God. . . . Like other men I am egotistical and sinful but in my exaltation I am free at once from all my sins, I am no longer a single suffering individual, I am one with the *Volk* and God. In such a moment any doubts about my life and work vanish.

The social sciences as developed in German universities later in the nineteenth century expressed this idea of aloneness and community in a more "objective" and rational manner. Ferdinand Tönnies delineated ideal types of social organization —*Gemeinschaft*, or community, and *Gesellschaft*, or society. Gemeinschaft was born of deep, unconscious factors in a people; it grew organically; it was a part of nature; it existed independent of man's choice; it expressed a will that was larger than any one human being. Gesellschaft was the alienated, industrialized, and modern world we know today. It grew out of contract, not out of nature; it could be changed; it was based on compromise and superficial changes in the body politic.

As the Prussian state moved its armies across Germany and its process of annexation seemed inexorable and overwhelming, the movements of resistance began to fall apart even where they had been strongest, as in southwest Germany. At the University of Karlsruhe, in the state of Baden, Professor Hermann Baumgarten, a liberal and an advocate of the values of the Enlightenment, wrote a tract in which he expressed the intellectuals' surrender to military force. In 1866, after Prussia took Schleswig-Holstein from Denmark and annexed Frankfurt and Hannover, Baumgarten wrote "Why Citizens are Incapable of Political Affairs," a notion with an astounding resemblance to the ideas later to be expressed by Thomas Mann during the First World War when he was still a devout German nationalist; Mann's essay is called "Reflections of an Apolitical Man." The citizen and the intellectual, these great representatives of the mind believed, were unable to make political decisions and were incapable of understanding the real flow of history and politics. The proof of this lay in the martial victories of Prussia; before victory and power all men must bow. There was also an element of vulgarity in politics; intellectuals were actually above such day-to-day trivia as making political decisions; discussion, negotiation, and compromise dirtied one's hands.

National decisions were left to the warrior caste and its advocates. The soaring sense of triumph, of a world waiting to be conquered and tamed—perhaps not so different a feeling from the one experienced by the proponents of manifest destiny in America and imperial expansion in Britain—was most clearly enunciated by the renowned Prussian historian Heinrich von Treitschke. "No nation in the world can think so greatly and humanly of its state as Germany," he wrote toward the end of the nineteenth century. "None strives as seriously as the Germans to reconcile . . . the power of the state and the liberty of the people, well-being and armed strength, science and faith. And because the foreigners know it, they hate us."

The First World War inflamed national passions to a raging fever that did not end with defeat. The Treaty of Versailles, with its "humiliating" conditions, became the red flag that set off the nationalist frenzy. The First World War was the crucible for Adolf Hitler; without it, he would have no historical existence. Its great harvest was the

Bolshevik Revolution in Russia, an earthshaking upheaval that sent the child Alexander Schmorell and his father back to the German homeland. The First World War was the testing ground for the convictions of Robert Scholl; he remained a pacifist in spite of the massive pressure of the gemeinschaft around him.

To have lost a war was the supreme disaster—to endure the imposed demilitarization of German lands, to suffer the enemy's demands for economic reparations, to experience inflation, unemployment, and anarchy in the streets—this was more than the German nation could bear. Each disaster sped up the process of infection, of rage and the desire for revenge. The national right loomed larger and more powerful as the Weimar Republic slipped from crisis to crisis in an almost unending plummet. Writers like Ernst Jünger and Moeller van den Bruck, the foremost German translator and interpreter of Dostoevski, spoke grimly of the great crisis of the spirit, the existential zero-point of man, and envisaged the rise of a superman to lead the extraordinary chosen people, the Germans, to a new world of humanity over which they would rule.

Through all this the German universities were never really bastions of free spirit and free inquiry, apart from the natural and physical sciences. In virtually all of the universities, however, the voices of liberalism, moderation, and self-criticism could be heard, but they were usually lone voices, not expressing the will of the community—the community, of course, being defined by believers in the concept of the *Volk*, and not by the labor movement, the Socialists, and the artistic anarchists on the left.

But no matter how "conservative" the universities were, they had never experienced the siege of repression that came with the takeover of power by the National Socialists in 1933. Although nothing came of most of their plans, the Nazis had grandiose schemes about what to do with the university, the "ivory tower," and "the weaklings" that resided in it. Even though the German university had never been a home to leftist or liberal thought, it was detested by the men of the radical right.

Some of the Nazi theoreticians on the national level, themselves professors in the New Order, made some daring proposals when they gained power. Ernst Krieck, for example, suggested that the universities be dissolved entirely—this was to be made a constant threat to faculty and students throughout the twelve years of the Third Reich.

He wanted to turn them into technical and vocational schools. Alfred Bäumler, a philosopher and expert on Nietzsche for the Party, proposed that the universities be made "houses for men," eliminating all "feminine-democratic" elements.

By the time the members of the White Rose enrolled at the University of Munich in the early 1940s, virtually all vestiges of pluralism in thought and quality in scholarship had vanished. To be sure, the university looked the same as it had for decades. It was situated at the edge of Schwabing, the artists' section of town. This was an appropriate place for it to be, squatting between the worlds of the bourgeoisie and the bohemians. It consisted of a low-lying series of neutral-colored edifices on both sides of the austere Italianate thoroughfare called Ludwigstrasse, which was Sophie Scholl's favorite street in Munich.

The university blends in architectonically with the grand design of the street, which is one of the most noteworthy in the city. Ludwigstrasse is long, severely straight, treeless, and awesomely classicist. It has the naked and endless perspective of a surrealistic painting, but it is neatly parenthesized on both ends. On the northern end, just beyond the university, is the Siegestor, a smallish victory arch of the Bavarian army, and on the southern end, near midtown Munich, it is enclosed by the Feldherrnhalle, a copy of the Florentine loggias, replete with Bavarian lions and generals; it was the scene of Hitler's infamous 1923 putsch.

Ludwigstrasse, the university, and much of Munich was designed deliberately to seem a part of the Latin and Mediterranean world. This was a decision made by the Wittelsbachs, the royal family of Bavaria that had become known throughout Germany—and Europe—for its Louis XIV pretensions as builders of castles, palaces, plazas, and long avenues, all in the grand manner.

The university, with its simple pseudo-Renaissance lines, fits comfortably into the physical and social map of the city. Its horizontal plainness is softened somewhat by two large fountains facing the entrance of the university that splash languidly as soon as spring arrives each year; they announce in sight and sound the arrival of balmy weather and easier living. Munich is a city that loves fountains and clearly prefers the summer heat to the dark days of a Gothic winter.

Like the city itself, the university has attracted a strange assortment of people over the years. One of them was Rudolf Hess, a veteran of the First World War who enrolled as a student of economics after the armistice but spent most of his time passing out anti-Semitic leaflets and fighting the modest forces of the short-lived Bavarian republic. He had become acquainted with Karl Haushofer, professor of geopolitics at the university, whose concept of *Lebensraun*, or "living space," for the German people had become so inspiring to Adolf Hitler; it was Hess who introduced Haushofer, a former general, to the Austrian corporal in the early days of "struggle" for the Nazi movement. Munich was also one of four or five universities where Joseph Goebbels dabbled in philosophy and the arts before receiving his doctorate in Heidelberg in 1921.

In 1933, like all universities, it was taken over by National Socialist personnel. The new rector, Professor Dr. Walter Wüst, an *Oberführer* in the SS, was known as one of the leading experts on "Aryan culture." By 1942, when the White Rose had assembled there, the university was thoroughly "integrated" into the Nazi system. The students were imbued, to the point of boredom and apathy, with Nazi clichés from their days in the Hitler Youth, and all classrooms and lecture halls were infested with spies from the National Socialist Student Association, zealously scribbling notes, their antennae groping for heresy while professors uneasily lectured. Academic freedom had become, in the words of Walter Schultze in a speech to the Scientific Assembly of the National Socialist Association of Professors, "a notion of freedom that is specifically our own, since we know that freedom must have its limits in the actual existence of the *Volk* . . . Ultimately freedom is nothing but responsible service on behalf of the basic values of our being as a *Volk*."

A sampling of courses offered at two universities, Berlin and Munich: "Geography in the Service of the National Socialist State"; "The Life of the Soul in its Racial, National and Historical Forms"; "*Volk* and Race (including legislation on racial improvement and eugenics), with slides and field trips"; "Birth, Marriage and Death: The Role of Race in the *Volk*ish Character (with slides)"; "Retrogressive Peoples, Primitive Races, Ancient Cultures, 1st part (with slides)"; and "The Sociology of War (open to the public)."

Academic scholarship and publications had reached the nadir; professional and scientific journals produced in Germany were now barely read in the international community of scholars. An extract from the journal *Deutsche Justiz* (*German Justice*)—an article by

Supreme Party Judge Walter Buch, published October 21, 1938—indicates the level of the scholarly press of that era: "The Jew is not a human being. He is an appearance of putrescence. Just as the fission fungus cannot permeate wood until it is rotting, so the Jew was able to creep into the German people, to bring on disaster, only after the German nation, weakened by the loss of blood in the Thirty Years' War, had begun to rot from within."

Despite the descent into mindlessness and terror, pockets of knowledge and decency somehow went on existing here and there, scattered among the different institutes and faculties, attracting as little notice as possible. Students with anti-Nazi sentiments were able to find like-minded *Kommilitonen*, or "fellow students," through a kind of secret rejectionist vocabulary and by observing unguarded expressions on people's faces when a cryptically subversive remark was made. Sophie Scholl, as a new student, was guided by Hans's girlfriend and fellow medical student Traute Lafrenz through the labyrinth of evasion. At Traute's and Hans's suggestion, Sophie took a course in philosophy that met twice a week, in the morning, in the large auditorium; it was the most popular course offered in the summer semester of 1942—the semester ran from May through July—and the lecturer was Dr. Kurt Huber.

Evasion had not been the only form of protest at Munich University, however; in 1935, for example, a distinguished author named Ernest Wiechert had given a series of talks on "The Poet and His Times." His lectures were enormously popular and crowded; what he said stunned his listeners. He told them bluntly that the "art" fabricated by the Nazis was "murder of the soul." He also admonished the students "not to allow yourselves to be seduced, if your conscience orders you to speak." The lecture was reproduced as a leaflet and circulated at other German universities. Ernest Wiechert was taken away by the Gestapo and put into prison; some time later he was detained in Dachau for a brief period.

Professor Fritz-Joachim von Rintelen lectured on ancient Greek thought. He was one of the most superb manipulators of double meanings at the university, and his lectures were subtle but devastating critiques of Nazi thought and practices, as viewed through the prism of the civilized Hellenic past. His classes were also packed, but one day he simply didn't show up. Nor did he appear at his next scheduled lecture. One of Rintelen's students—Jürgen Wittenstein, a fellow medic and friend of Hans, Willi, and Alex—recalled the episode later. He and about fifty other students dared to go to the *Rektor* himself to ask what had happened to their teacher. Rector Wüst actually came out of his private office to meet the delegation, probably because the idea of students demanding to see him was incredible. When they told him what they wanted, he simply stared at them in disbelief for a moment, wheeled around, went back into his office, and slammed the door. The students then staged a protest on Ludwigstrasse, in front of the university, and in a final and dazzling display of defiance, they walked over to Rintelen's flat and stood under his window in a show of solidarity. It was courageous, it was incredible; nevertheless, Rintelen was not seen at the university again.

Even in 1942, after nearly a decade of Adolf Hitler, these amazing acts, these pockets of decency persisted, daring, isolated, near-inexplicable. Professor Heinrich Wieland, director of the university's Chemistry Institute, had made his domain a sanctuary for *Mischlinge* —for half-Jews, usually children of mixed marriages who were now living in a twilight limbo between the New Order and transport to a concentration camp, which is what was happening to their Jewish parents since the summer of 1941. Hans Leipelt, from Hamburg, was one of those students enrolled at the Chemistry Institute; later he was to try to carry on the activities of the White Rose after their executions.

To this day no one is quite sure how and why professors like Wieland were allowed to continue functioning. Another major exception that doesn't fit into the picture of bland, brown-shirted dullness was Kurt Huber.

Since 1926, Huber had been lecturing as the equivalent of an associate professor, without tenure, in philosophy, psychology, and musicology. Some 250 students would attend his classes, and the university administration begrudgingly assigned him the largest hall, the Auditorium Maximum, to accommodate his audience.

In 1942 Huber was forty-nine years old, a smallish man, about five feet six or seven, with graying hair. He was pale and looked tired and worn, older than his years. He walked with a heavy limp, dragging his right leg behind him. He had suffered acute diphtheria as a small child, and his larynx had had to be slit to save his life; the aftereffects never completely disappeared. His hands trembled, sometimes his head would shake violently, especially when he was upset. He would limp up to the podium, wait for silence, and then begin. Sometimes it took painful seconds and even minutes for his voice to clear and become comprehensible. But when it did, the experience was splendid. He prepared each lecture painstakingly but spoke extemporaneously. The development of his ideas, the way he shaped them, gave the students a glimpse into the world of the mind, into the enormous and powerful history of ideas that was so vital a part of their national heritage.

His lectures in philosophy mainly centered on the German idealists—Kant, Hegel, Schelling, and others, and on the works of the seventeenth-century philosopher and mathematician Gottfried Wilhelm von Leibniz. Huber was writing a definitive work on Leibniz during this period. He was an interesting choice for Huber to make: Leibniz is considered a singularly modern thinker, and his influence on the nineteenth-century idealists, particularly Hegel and Fichte, was profound. He tried to reconcile the concepts of substance and form, to find a middle point between the processes of reason and the methods of science. Mathematics provided a means for this: in the late 1660s Leibniz posited a model to demonstrate that all ideas, verbal or nonverbal, can be reduced to an ordered combination of numbers or words, and in the external world, to a combination of sounds or colors. But this reductionism of the world to logical calculus remained insufficient for him; in his *Théodicée*, published in 1710, he reflected on the necessity of including God in an analysis of the cosmos. By that time of his life he was deeply concerned about the existence of evil in a perfect, mathematically ordered universe. He resolved the problem by declaring that each creature in the universe is finite, and therefore imperfect; since each creature has its special place in creation, in the cosmic hierarchy, it is part of nature and part of the expression of "universal harmony." Leibniz was expressing thoughts that were to recur in Enlightenment thinking of the eighteenth century. In his view, evil is like "dissonance in music"; it is a lack, a flaw, but ultimately, because it is an integral part of the whole, evil, too, increases the "beauty" of the universe and God.

When Professor Huber lectured on subjects like these, he could not resist tossing in an occasional ironic or barbed remark. He had a dry wit—not a very academic trait in Germany, and certainly not under the Nazis. The unexpected remark just seemed to leap out of him, as if he could not do otherwise, as if there were some deep need to throw down the gauntlet. He would mention Spinoza and say with a wry smile, "Careful, he's a Jew! Don't let yourselves be contaminated." There would be restless and fearful murmurs in the hall, but the students came back in droves, and somehow there were no repercussions.

Kurt Huber's political and social attitudes were conservative, and precisely because he viewed the Nazis as a mass movement of revolutionaries did he loathe them. He was an authentic representative of German philosophical and historical nationalism—but he never advocated war or conquest as a method to further the German spirit. At one time, early in the Nazi regime, he had tried to get a full professorship, which he undeniably deserved: he was considered one of the more brilliant, universal, and articulate younger figures in the academic world. He was turned down by a National Socialist university bureaucrat who said: "We can only use officer material."

That casual and brutal remark may have been shattering to a man who had spent his life overcoming pain and affliction by sheer self-discipline and intelligence. In addition, he was deeply committed to the German cause and a fervent admirer of the military as a pillar of a moral German order. His own inability to serve his country in uniform must have been among the sorest of his trials; he had been of age during the First World War and had missed sharing the legendary bonds of comradeship that grew out of the trenches and that were so extolled later by nationalist writers. Now again, in the thirties and early forties, he was living in a society that prized everything he was not. Nevertheless, he went on admiring Prussia and the military for their discipline, steadfastness, and code of honor. He hated the man who would soon send these brave and strong young men out to die without purpose or reason.

Huber was born in Switzerland but raised in Stuttgart, in southwest Germany, in a cultivated middle-class home. Both his parents were educators and scholars. His mother taught him to play the piano; his father, harmony and counterpoint. He was a brilliant pupil, and had perfect pitch. Beyond music, he had that rare kind of mind that spans the "two cultures," the sciences and the arts. He completed his doctorate summa cum laude at the University of Munich in the fields of music, philosophy, and psychology. His great love was folk music, and his studies and writings in this field were international in scope. Among other musicological pursuits, he analyzed the chants of Burmese women working in the rice paddies; he made speculative investigations into the tonalities and rhythms of other cultures.

His brief moments of recognition as a scholar were barely noticed at the University of Munich. He was chosen in 1936 to represent Germany at the International Folk Music Congress in Barcelona, before another fascist, Francisco Franco, launched his drive to seize power from the Spanish republic.

Kurt Huber could have used his folk-music talents and reputation to carve out a niche for himself in the Third Reich. Because of the "folk" aspects of his musical interests, he was invited in 1938 to take over a new folk-music institute at the University of Berlin. He eagerly grasped the opportunity after the years of disappointment.

But the Berlin year was a disaster; the university administration and the Nazi student organization expected him to produce blood-and-soil marching songs based on folk tradition. He refused to cooperate; he was a scientist, not a propagandist. The situation became tense and almost unbearable. At the end of the year, the contract was not renewed, and the Huber family, more reduced in circumstances than ever, returned to their spartan life in Munich.

In his mid-thirties, Huber had married Clara, a robust and healthy woman much younger than himself. By 1942 they had two children: Birgit, who was eleven, and Wolf, two. The family lived frugally—they had to; no matter how hard the professor worked, drove himself, and struggled to get along with his more compliant colleagues, he could not achieve recognition or reward in this society. He seethed inside—his personality has been described as "choleric." He was a man full of indignation, full of the injustices and degradations—personal and national—that he encountered every day outside of his home, and it was only in his home that he could let go.

He was a demanding, authoritarian family man, with a good-natured and worried wife. He was precise, judgmental, impatient; his goal was perfection. He could make his children tremble when he lost his temper or supervised his daughter's piano lessons. But he could be gentle; he would caress them when he came home in good spirits, stroking their heads and trying to guess, with a smile, what meal Mrs. Huber had prepared, just from the lingering odors in the children's hair. He loved them with every fiber of his passionate hidden being, and they knew it. When he thought about the Nazis or about the bombing of German cities or about the destruction of German culture, he would get carried away and begin to shout. Clara Huber would run frantically around the room shutting windows, whispering intently: "Kurt, stop it! They'll take you to Dachau!"

Apart from his family, Huber really cared about one other group of people: his students. They were the hope of the future, the only one he had left. He would transmit to them, as a professor, as a mentor, the German values that mattered; they would not totally be destroyed by barbarians and bombs. He loved his students in a distant, intellectual way, not with intimacy. But some, like his doctoral student Katharina Schüddekopf and Hans Scholl, would be invited to share coffee and cake with the family. But he never called anyone outside the family *Du* the intimate form of "you."

Kurt Huber was to come into contact with the White Rose through Hans Scholl. Although Sophie, Willi, Traute, Alex, and Hans all heard him lecture, none of them had met him personally. Although he was different from them in age, temperament, and in political and social outlook, he shared with them the rich heritage of the German intelligentsia. Kurt Huber and the others in the White Rose would undoubtedly have agreed on the definition of the perfect human being—a German definition, perhaps the one written by the nihilist-existentialist poet-philosopher Friedrich Nietzsche in the year before he vanished into madness.

Nietzsche held up as the standard of perfection that Olympian figure of German letters, Johann Wolfgang von Goethe. Given their backgrounds, their middle-class values and education, each member of the White Rose would have affirmed that Goethe was the model they would strive to emulate, however imperfectly.

Nietzsche had written that Goethe was a man who

did not desert life, but placed himself at its center. He was not faint-hearted but took as much as possible upon himself, into himself. What he aimed at was totality; he fought against separating reason from sensuality, feeling, will. He disciplined himself into wholeness, he created every gesture, self-controlled, having respect for himself as a creature who might dare afford the whole range and wealth of being natural, of being strong enough for such freedom, the man of tolerance, not from weakness but from strength, because he knows how to use to his advantage what would destroy an average character. Such a mind, having attained real freedom, lives in the very center of things with a joyful and confident acceptance of fate, lives in the faith that only the particular in its separateness is objectionable, and that in the wholeness of life everything is affirmed and redeemed. He no longer negates.

In June 1942 Kurt Huber was invited to a reading evening at the home of a Frau Doktor Mertens. Perhaps to get his mind off the war and the bombing raids, perhaps in the diminishing hope of finding some like-minded colleagues somewhere, he decided to go.

A publisher was present, Heinrich Ellermann, and a writer and former actor named Sigismund von Radecki, a convert to Catholicism who was extremely adept and witty when he read prose aloud; it was almost as if one were at the theater. Some medical students had also somehow gotten themselves an invitation.

After discussing the literary theme that had been read aloud, the talk, to the chagrin of the hostess, turned to politics. No one present knew each other well; the subject was dangerous.

There was a general consensus that German culture was decaying. Someone ventured the opinion that the only way to cope with the situation—the Nazis—was not through protest but simply by hanging on, tending to one's cultural obligations and tasks as scholars and just waiting out the nightmare.

At that point a medical student broke in with a caustic remark. A dark and scowling Hans Scholl said, "Why don't we rent ourselves an island in the Aegean and offer courses on world-views?" Considering his lowly status in relation to the academics and professionals who were present, one gets a glimmer of Hans's enormous self-assurance and also of the passion that made him break out of the usual docile-student role required in traditional German society.

The atmosphere must have turned glacial after such an impertinence. But Kurt Huber was becoming flushed. He was not offended by what Hans said; on the contrary, he was suddenly galvanized. He spoke loudly: "*Something must be done, and it must be done now!*"

The silence was earsplitting. Hans stared at the older man with admiration. Their eyes met; neither would forget. When the evening ended they spoke to each other briefly, introduced themselves, and said they would meet again.

The circle had been formed. Although Kurt Huber knew nothing about them, he was now almost a member of the White Rose.

TEN

BEHIND THE SCENES that summer, the creative and the logistic aspects of the White Rose operation did not go smoothly. The contents of the leaflets were stringently criticized by the few people who knew the identity of their authors.

One such person was Manfred Eickemeyer, who lent Hans his atelier on Leopoldstrasse in Schwabing. Eickemeyer worked as an architect for the German *Generalgouvernement* in occupied Poland, with offices in Cracow. He had seen the deportations that were taking place all over the country, and had watched the mass shootings of Jews. He described to Hans and Alex how special squads of the SS had rounded up men, women, and children, loaded them into trucks, brought them to the outskirts of town, ordered them to dig trenches, and then shot them in groups—one group after another, falling in layers on the bodies underneath. He told them that the Wehrmacht stood by and did nothing to stop it.

He was shaken and appalled. On his intermittent trips to Munich, he would talk about it; he wanted the world to know what was going on—especially the German people. Informing people, he thought, was the only way to stop it.

Eickemeyer was in town when the second leaflet appeared, during the third week of June 1942. Among its passages:

> ... since the conquest of Poland 300,000 Jews have been murdered in a bestial manner. Here we see the most terrible crime committed against the dignity of man, a crime that has no counterpart in human history. ... Is this a sign that the German people have become

brutalized in their basic human feelings? . . . that they have sunk into a terminal sleep from which there is no awakening, ever, ever again?

It seems that way . . . if the German does not arouse himself from this lethargy, if he does not protest whenever he can against this gang of criminals, if he doesn't feel compassion for the hundreds of thousands of victims—not only compassion, no, much more: *guilt*. . . . Everyone shrugs off this guilt, falling asleep again with his conscience at peace. But he can't shrug it off; everyone is *guilty, guilty, guilty!*

The leaflet ends with some aphorisms by Lao-tsu and the request to circulate the information.

Apparently Manfred Eickemeyer was quite disappointed in what he read. No detailed descriptions of the atrocities, no names or places, no specifics were given. The "Jewish Question" was summed up in a few sentences. He told that to Hans, told him that the leaflets were not informative or pragmatic; he wondered why precious space was given to Lao-tsu instead of to the brutal facts. It might not have been an easy critique for Hans to accept; he was pouring his heart out with every word.

Nevertheless, the cranking out of the pages, the procurements and the mailings, still went on, now with the help of Sophie and Traute. Eickemeyer himself still had sympathy enough for the enterprise to contribute a few hundred marks and to continue allowing the White Rose to use his atelier, a not inconsiderable danger to himself.

It may have been the third leaflet that was sent by the group to Professor Kurt Huber. It arrived in the mail at his home a few days before he received an invitation to a reading evening at the residence of Alexander Schmorell, whom he did not know.

What he read must have shocked, upset, and provoked him; words like these had not been circulated or spoken aloud in the last ten years of his life.

"Our state is the dictatorship of evil," the leaflet began; it went on to describe the Nazi leadership as "criminals and drunkards." The language got rather violent, almost out of control, and then subsided a bit in order to discuss how to fight back. The only means of opposition, the leaflet said, was "passive resistance"—an expression the authors must have heard in relation to Mahatma Gandhi and the independence movement in India.

The leaflet continued, obviously now trying to be more precise about means and ends. The goal of the White Rose:

to bring down National Socialism, and in this struggle we can't shrink from any means, any act. . . . A victory for fascist Germany in this war would have inconceivable and terrible consequences. The first concern of every German is not the military victory over Bolshevism, but the defeat of National Socialism.

Some of the "means" then suggested:

> . . . *sabotage* the armament industries, *sabotage* every assembly, rally, ceremony, and organization sponsored by the National Socialist Party . . . *sabotage* in every scientific and intellectual field involved in continuing this war—whether it be universities, technical colleges, laboratories, research stations or technical agencies.

These were dangerous, if still imprecise, suggestions. Kurt Huber's mind must have been agitated and confused as he set off that evening in June to Harlaching, to the Schmorell villa. Hans Scholl had come by to invite him personally, and even though he did not know what to expect, he could not refuse the opportunity to join his students.

He was met at the streetcar stop by Hans and Traute Lafrenz; they stood with bicycles, waiting to escort him to Alex's house. As they walked into the quiet residential area, its homes surrounded by trees in bloom and high walls that hid lavish gardens, Traute abruptly turned to Huber and asked if he had received a White Rose leaflet. He must have paused; the question, so pointed and direct, from a young woman he had never met before, must have startled him. He undoubtedly was put on guard: Kurt Huber was a man who did not find independent, sophisticated, and intellectual women sympathetic. He was comfortable with women who accepted the role that "nature" had given them: the comforter, the nurturer, the provider of sanctuary for the struggling man in a hostile world. As he saw it, women were there to pour coffee for the men as they talked over the serious issues of the world; women were not there for intellectual companionship or friendship, but for spiritual succor.

He replied to the young woman that yes, he had received a leaflet. He didn't say much beyond that, except that he doubted the impact of the leaflet was worth the terrible risks.

They had by now arrived at the Schmorell home. Since the winter of 1941, with his parents' consent, Alex had been hosting "reading and discussion evenings" at their home. Now it was summer; the garden was in bloom, and before entering the living room, the guests were clustered about the open veranda. After a few minutes, they entered the elegant salon. Tasteful and comfortable couches and armchairs were set in a semicircle for the discussion; a grand piano glistened on one side of the room, and the gold of an enormous icon, illuminated with special lights, gleamed in the pale evening.

It may have been difficult for Kurt Huber to reconcile the affluence, the glowing good taste, and the young, handsome people now surrounding him, with the austerity of his own life and the grim issues of war and destruction that tormented him day and night.

Huber's guardedness continued during the evening; he contributed little of significance to the discussion. Talk turned to politics, to the endless apocalyptic prognoses of the future, to the latest outrage at the university or on the war front. All the White Rose members, among others, were present: apparently they were waiting for Kurt Huber to open up and express his real feelings; perhaps he would join them.

But he was put off. Often an incautious man in the open arena of the lecture hall, now he was distant, holding back, sitting amidst these young and lively students in the quiet elegance of a private home. He finally did speak, lamenting the decline of intellectual standards in the schools and the universities, and about the suppression of real scientific investigation in virtually all fields, but he lapsed again into silence, and left the gathering early.

The others were disappointed, probably Hans most of all; but determined as he was, Hans Scholl would try again.

The fourth and last leaflet in the short explosion of printed fireworks in Munich appeared in mid-July, just before the group disbanded for the more than three months' semester break.

Practical measures were put aside for the time being; the authors talked at length about Christian obligations to resist, and quoted extensively from Novalis, a romantic writer. The leaflet assured its readers that "the White Rose is not in the pay of any foreign power," and added that recipients should have no fear that their names appeared on any secret lists, for they had been chosen randomly from telephone directories.

The last line of this leaflet was to become the summing-up, the distilled essence of what the Munich group was all about: "*We will not be silent.* We are your bad conscience. The White Rose will not leave you in peace!"

ELEVEN

WHILE THE LEAFLETS were being cranked out at night, life went on as usual during the days of a languid Munich summer. The city looked drearier than before; the facades of the buildings were dingy in the sunlight, and the streetlamps were blacked out at night in the event of air attacks.

But the ostensibly casual, if hectic, life of the medic-students continued. They attended lectures, went to their clinics, met at the Lombardi for a cheap but good Chianti after a concert or a stroll in the English Garden. All of them played instruments and were quite good at it; occasionally some of them came together as an informal chamber-music group. Some weekends they took trips into the mountains; the long hikes and fresh air helped relieve the tensions and exhaustion. On the way back to Munich, they might make a stopover at Christel's home in Ruhpolding.

The easy and pleasant student life they led was only apparent; their nerves were crackling with tension. In reality, there was only pretense and secrecy and lying to their families and friends, and never enough time to sleep and still show up at all the places they were supposed to be.

Alex Schmorell turned to his first love, art, to distract himself from medical studies, the tedious routine at the base, and the terrible nighttime stress. He took courses with his friend Lilo Ramdohr, in drawing and sketching. Often the two of them would invite a Munich tramp to Lilo's flat to pose for them in exchange for a hot meal and a bath. Alex's penchant for bums and vagabonds, although he didn't know it and probably never would, had already turned into a grotesque nightmare: much later it was revealed that the posing tramp was a Gestapo informer. The young man-of-the-world with the Russian soul and the light charm could no longer smile so easily; the pressure was taking its toll. He turned to sculpting as his true vocation, spending hours alone, creating form and life out of masses of clay. "Without work (and by work I mean only sculpting)," he wrote about this time, "Germany is the most unbearable situation I can imagine for myself. A terrible restlessness is my most stubborn companion. . . . Only work is peace."

Alex's restlessness was to end soon enough; before the end of July he was sent to Russia, along with Hans and Willi and their friends Jürgen Wittenstein and Hubert Fürtwangler from the medic-student company. At last Alex was going home; as a medic in a German uniform, he would finally see the ravaged and suffering land he considered his real home.

Rumors that the company would be posted to the front during the semester break coursed through the Bergmann School early in the month; they were confirmed by mid-July.

It was time to dismantle the White Rose operation; depression overcame the small circle of friends. They had finally begun to act, and the entire painstaking and difficult process had to be stopped before they had gotten anywhere. The machine had to be taken away, all vestiges of the project hidden or destroyed. Hans, Willi, and Alex were going to Russia.

A date of departure was announced, then changed, then a new one issued. They had to pack, see families, store books, and say farewell— temporarily, one hoped—to friends.

They decided to throw a farewell party, and with Manfred Eicke-meyer's consent, it was held at his atelier. About fifteen people were invited to the studio in Schwabing on the evening of July 22. The men were due to leave at seven the next morning on a troop transport train.

Among the guests were Kurt Huber and all the members of the White Rose. Pillows and chairs were scattered around the large, open studio; tea, cake, wine, and schnapps were served. As night fell, the blackout curtains enhanced the intimacy and bohemian atmosphere.

As usual at these kinds of affairs, art and literature were discussed by the group at large. As the evening wore on, the talk turned to polit-ics. Alex, perhaps flushed with wine and the idea of Russia, was more voluble than expected; he said that passive resistance was the only way to deal with the present realities. Suddenly Kurt Huber spoke up, loudly and nervously; he agreed with Alex that "active" resistance was impossible, that they were not "industrial workers who could go out on the streets and strike." No other means were available, he said, except for intellectuals to boycott Nazi functions and wait out the death of fascism. He was beginning to tremble all over.

Hans disagreed with Kurt Huber. The bitter isolation of individuals from one another would not prepare the ground for an overthrow of the regime. The only way, he said, was working together, in groups, cooperatively.

The discussion heated up, talk turned to the destruction of German cities in the air raids. What would be left of that great cultural tradition they wanted to save from the Nazis if they were bombed into the ground?

At this point Manfred Eickemeyer was angry; he didn't care about the German heritage, the canvases of great paintings; maybe the German people deserved what they were getting, and should drink the cup "to the bitter dregs."

Kurt Huber was shaking all over, almost writhing in his chair, his face flushed. Yes, he said loudly, maybe there is only one way, clandestine propaganda, sabotage and . . . "*assassination.*"

They stared at him, not believing what they had heard.

The silence was broken when Hans Hirzel, a young high-school student from Ulm, dropped in unexpectedly to say goodbye to Hans. He was the brother of Sophie's close friend Susanne Hirzel. Before the evening ended, Hans and Sophie would give the boy eighty marks to buy another duplicating machine, hide it in Ulm, and help them prepare for the new round of activities when the three medics returned from the front.

Kurt Huber was leaving the party now, shaking hands with the tall young men off to the battlefields he would never see. He asked them to drop him a line, give their impressions. Hans said they would.

Hans and Alex would have exchanged quick glances, affirming that they would not tell Huber that they were the White Rose, at least not yet.

They watched the older man leave through the courtyard, escorted by Christoph Probst to the streetcar stop. They would have waved; the professor would wave back.

He must have looked small, tired, and very lonely.

TWELVE

SOPHIE, Traute, and other friends gathered outside Munich's Ostbahnhof to see the young men off. They waved energetically as the train moved out toward the east, and went home to face the empty rooms of a suddenly colorless summer.

It took three days for the military train to reach Warsaw. The student company had a few hours between trains and took a stroll through the city, which was baking in a fierce heat wave. Conditions had grown far worse in Warsaw than they were the last time Willi had passed through on the way to the front, and he noted in his journal: "The misery stares us in the face. I hope I never see Warsaw in these conditions again." Hans, in a letter he wrote later to Professor Huber from Russia, mentioned that the friends went to the Jewish ghetto. "The city, the ghetto, and everything related to it made a decisive impression on everyone" was the rather guarded way he put it.

By the time the medics arrived in Warsaw, in July 1942, starvation and epidemics had wiped out much of the Jewish population, which had been driven into the Jewish quarter's walls and barbed-wire fences. A few weeks before, the SS had launched the deportation drives from the Warsaw Ghetto to the extermination camps of Auschwitz, Treblinka, and Maidanek.

The decision to destroy the Jewish people completely—the "Final Solution to the Jewish Question," as it was called delicately in the corridors of power of the Third Reich—had been made about one year earlier. The implementation of the long-awaited program actually began on June 22, 1941, the same day that Hitler's armies overran Russia, in spite of a mutual treaty of nonaggression.

Jews from all over the occupied territories, and even some from the Reich itself, had been herded into the Warsaw Ghetto, as they were in ghettos throughout occupied Poland. When Hans, Alex, and Willi arrived there, pouring out of the gates of the ghetto, prodded by men in gray uniforms, emaciated and blank-eyed men, women, and children were marched in disheveled rows through the sizzling hot streets of Warsaw down to the railway station, to be thrust into sealed cattle-cars.

There were Germans in uniform who taunted and gratuitously tormented their victims—some sent snapshots home to display their licensed sadism—and there were also Germans deeply shaken by what they saw, but who seemed unable to put their experiences and feelings into words, except to say that "the situation is beyond description," or as Willi did, "misery stares us in the face," or that they were "depressed" or feeling "extremely low."

It took more than a week for the train to reach Wjasma, the gathering point for the central front and for the 252d Division to which they were assigned. Wjasma, a small town, was almost completely destroyed; there was nothing there, as Willi noted, "but dirt, misery, and German marching music," and, on a hill amid the ruins, an intact wooden church.

They moved on to the town of Gzhatsk, some sixty miles west of Moscow, actually the farthest penetration point into Russia made by the Wehrmacht. It was here that the great eastern offensive stalled and gradually sank into the mud and snow.

In spite of the misery and devastation, the young men lifted their eyes beyond it and were intoxicated by the huge expanse of the steppes, the open skies, the mystery of Russia. "Beyond the border begin the wide, the endless steppes," Hans wrote in his diary soon after their arrival, "where every line dissolves, where everything solid disintegrates and becomes a drop in the sea, where there is no beginning and no middle and no end, where man is homeless and only melancholy fills his heart."

It was not only the naked and limitless landscape that captivated them; they found themselves in an exceptional position because of Shurik's presence. With him they were able to enter the wooden doors of cottages and hovels and huts that were barred to Germans. Willi wrote simply: "The land opened itself up to me through Alex."

One can imagine the shock, the terror, and then—slowly, incredulously—the smile lighting up the faces of the peasants when they met Shurik, this tall young man in a dusty gray enemy uniform, speaking their language easily, offering them vodka, putting out his hand in friendship. He would tell them, as Willi, Hans, and perhaps Hubert Fürtwangler stood by a bit awkwardly, that he was born in Russia, that he felt it was his homeland and that someday he would come and stay forever. He was charged up, nearly ecstatic; his childhood memories and fantasies were fulfilled: Russia was what he always knew it would be; in spite of what people in Germany might think or say, he experienced no disappointment.

He wrote a warm, emotional letter to his parents in Munich on August 5, 1942, shortly after arriving in Gzhatsk.

> We traveled a total of twelve days to arrive, and here we'll stay. The front is about ten kilometers from here. Gzhatsk is almost completely destroyed and the Russians are still firing, sometimes by day, sometimes at night. But our camp is in the woods and is completely out of danger.
>
> I speak often and much with the Russian people, with simple people and with the educated, especially with physicians. I am extremely impressed. If you compare the present Russian generation to the German or French, you reach an amazing conclusion: they [the Russians] are so much younger, fresher and more appealing.

At this point Shurik may have wanted to reassure his father that his love of Russia was untainted by Communist indoctrination:

> And oddly, all Russians have one opinion about Bolshevism: they hate nothing more in the world than that, and most important: even if the war does not end well for Germany, Bolshevism will never return here. It is over, done with, and the Russian people, the peasant as well as the worker, hate it totally.
>
> I have to end now and go to the surgical station where I work.
>
> If possible send wooden matches,
>
> > Greetings to all,
> > I kiss all of you,
> > Your Shura.

Soon the young medics were invited into farmhouses, sang folk songs, joined in the dancing, and provided the local people with schnapps and medicine. Shurik reported home later in August that these twenty years of Bolshevism have not made the Russian people forget how to sing and dance, and everywhere you go, you can hear Russian songs. New and old ones are sung. Played on balalaikas and guitars and so beautiful. . . . Regardless of their poverty, the people are terribly hospitable. The samovar and everything else they own are put on the table when a guest arrives.

All of this fraternization, of course, was strictly forbidden by the German military, and went on mostly in the evenings, a good distance away from German installations. Summer nights are white, long, and sultry on the Russian plain, and the spontaneous festivities took on an almost bacchanalian aspect, with cannons booming and crimson rockets shrieking through the air and spattering the sky a few kilometers away.

Hans felt himself "ripped apart," singing and dancing in a kind of frenzied way by night, and tending the wounded and dying by day. He had wild and restless dreams when he finally was able to sleep. Willi too, in spite of a far more contained temperament, was caught up in the intoxicating world of the steppes, the songs, the cannon fire, and the vodka: "In the early morning hours it is wonderful outdoors," he wrote in late August.

Pity that we're in the forest where you can't see the horizon. The encircling trees narrow the view. In the evening we listen to Russian songs at a woman's house. She works in the camp. We sit in the open air, behind the trees, the moon comes up, its rays falling in the spaces between the rows of trees, it's cool, the girls sing to the guitar, we try to hum the bass part, it's so beautiful, you feel Russia's heart, we love it.

A few days later, Willi made an entry that offers a rare glimpse of his deep shyness and utter naïveté regardless of what he had observed being done by his own army in the burnt-out villages. The entry concerned a visit to the house of a Russian girl, Sina, who spoke some German and apparently worked in his camp; he had mentioned her offhandedly several times previously.

In the afternoon I visited the house where Sina lives; actually I came to ask for eggs. On a record player I hear Russian music, songs. We begin to talk about everyday life. I am shocked by the enormity of the rage against the Germans. A real aversion. They talk about Moscow, the city is supposed to be beautiful. It's actually easy to find your way to the Russians if you want to make the effort. I feel very good being with them.

In their bunker at night, they read Dostoevski's *Crime and Punishment;* Willi commented that he was reading it for the third time. The feverish power of the story of a man exploring the limits of a world where there is no God expressed their own spirits, their dizzying thoughts about the meaning of good and evil and freedom and Russia.

"At this point in my life," Willi wrote,

> Dostoevski has been important, and that's because I have gotten to know some Russians better in the last few weeks. Being together with Alex opened up this land for me, a land that was almost unknown or at least incomprehensible. . . . We sit with peasants and sing together and they sing wonderful old songs. You forget for a whole moment all the sadness and the horror that is happening around you. Wonderful afternoons and evenings we have with the Russians—while the cannons and guns rarely stop roaring and we take care of the sick and the wounded. Two worlds around us. . . .

"It's interesting," Willi goes on,

> that the simplest people: peasants, fishermen, craftsmen, know Dostoevski and are involved in what he writes—not superficially but in the deepest sense. You can't say the same about Germany, the people that truly know Goethe are not numerous. Here poets are really part of the people and are understood by the people. I deeply regret that I don't know more Russian. It would have been so indescribably beautiful to have been able to really talk to certain people!

The experience in Russia was undoubtedly one of the highest peaks of their young lives. It was unique—because of Shurik—and it was brief, lasting less than three months. Hans's, Alex's, and Willi's exalted and almost mystical reaction to Russia may seem an enigma, but it grew out of German attitudes toward the Slavic East.

Settled stolidly if sometimes insecurely in the central plains and valleys of the European continent, relatively unprotected by seas and mountains, the German people have looked eastward with interest, suspicion, and desire for over eight hundred years. Across their own uneasy and shifting eastern borders, they have kept watch on the Slavic world up to the Urals and Siberia, regarding themselves as constituting a kind of bulwark against primitive hordes, against the dangerous and mysterious world of the Orient.

Russia, the Orient, the East—these words seem almost interchangeable in the German vocabulary of the nineteenth and first half of the twentieth century. Feelings about "the East," about Russia, this land of czars and peasants and onion-domed churches, were always ambivalent, much in the same way Westerners regard the countries of the so-called Third World: a place to acquire raw materials and food-stuffs cheaply, to relieve population pressures, to colonize, to experience adventure, and to carry one's own religious, commercial, or patriotic mission to lesser breeds, or a place simply to expand to—for the sake of expanding.

In the medieval period, in the thirteenth century, the Teutonic knights moved into the East, conquering and colonizing northern Slavic peoples and the Baltic regions. Later, in the early eighteenth century, Peter the Great and subsequent czars called German "experts" into their undeveloped country, considering them dull but reliable and well-trained technicians from an advanced society; they could help modernize and unify a Russia vastly swelling beyond its Muscovite borders into a mammoth multilingual and multinational empire.

Over the centuries, Russia had been seen as a kind of frontier for Germany. As do all frontiers, it meant both menace and freedom. Along with this came a certain contempt for Russia's inhabitants, society, and state. As Germany struggled in various ways to unify itself into one political order out of an array of princely states and duchies in the nineteenth century, the tides of Bismarckian nationalism and militarism won out and crested in a wave of national arrogance and a feeling of superiority in relation to other peoples and cultures. With it, the contempt for the Slavic East inevitably waxed. It was to wane briefly after the First World War, at least for some Germans, with the advent of the October Revolution in Russia and the dawn of a new world under "scientific socialism." But even this short-lived dream was shattered for the German left, after a decade of Stalinism ate away like acid at the portrait of the Russian Utopia.

The quest for German *lebensraum* in the East—the belief that the Russian steppes existed for German needs, and that the Slavic peoples were inferior races to be used as brute labor to work the soil—never fully disappeared from German thought. It was to spring full-blown into life as national policy when Adolf Hitler and his associates began to promulgate their vision of the future of the Eurasian continent after 1938.

But, as with all beliefs, there had always been a countermotif to this point of view in Germany, the other end of an almost purely black-and-white spectrum of opinion about Russia—the motif shared and deeply felt by Alex, Willi, and Hans.

"The Russian soul" is an expression heard often in the German language, and it usually has generally positive connotations. It refers to depth of feeling, artistic sensibility, an expansiveness of heart and a spontaneous generosity; however, it also has undertones of unbridled passion and orgiastic experience. It is associated with wild swings of mood from the pinnacle of exaltation to the chasm of nihilism and despair, from the tenderest gesture of kindness to drunken brutality on the rampage: in short, all the aspects of humanity—except the disciplined, or measured, and Apollonian ones—are contained in the throbbing vessel called the Russian soul. It has nothing to do with the Russia of Lenin, Trotsky, Brezhnev, or even Sakharov, although perhaps it does have something to do with Solzhenitsyn. The idea of the Russian soul seems to tap some deep need in the German psyche; its values are primeval and free, both repellent and thrilling to a controlled, work-oriented people. In the nineteenth century, the Russian soul was an expression of longing in both cultures, Germany and Russia, for true freedom and true community, contradictory as those ideas may seem. Anarchy and unity, obedience and freedom, are defined and invented and imagined on page after page of literary and philosophical tomes in both countries.

The hunger for national unification, for national importance, and the desire for a special "spiritual" kind of freedom unknown in the West, were not the only traits that the two most autocratic societies in Europe had in common: in the post-Napoleonic era, they both rejected the values and body of beliefs of the Enlightenment coming out of Western Europe; both turned ferociously against the French Revolution with its emphasis on the leveling of classes and the *fraternité* of equal men; both rejected the idea of parliamentary democracy, which they saw as a triumph of numbers over values, of quantity over quality. Indeed, for both Germany and Russia, Western Europe was a marketplace that destroyed integrity and principles for the sake of compromise and gold (the word they used for this notion was "corruption"). And both societies turned away from the idea of the private man, living anonymously in the city, freed from the moral pressures of community, village, and town (they saw this as "alienation").

German and Russian intellectuals and literati regarded the emerging industrial bourgeoisie as a threat to the true orders of noble, artisan, and peasant, and both groups saw their respective nations as the civilizing—if retrogressive—vanguard that would bring the truth back to Europe, the truth lost in the centuries of exploration and modernization since the Renaissance, the truth of a pure and "whole" life as in the preindustrial world of peasants and priests.

The intellectual systems of both countries nourished one another. German philosophical idealism, embodied in the works of Hegel and Schelling, made an enormous impact on the Slavophiles of Russia, and in turn, Russian writers like Dostoevski, Gogol, even Tolstoy and Turgenev—but especially Dostoevski—struck a deep chord in the German romantics and their youth movements.

"Has anybody ever understood the human meaning of nationalism in a more German way than the great Russian moralist?" asked Thomas Mann, referring to Dostoevski, in a work he was writing in the midst of the First World War, when Russia and Germany were enemies. "If spiritual affinity can form the foundation and justification of political alliances, then Russia and Germany belong together."

Categorizing feelings or attitudes toward other nations tends to water down the complexity of ambivalence: till the present day it would be unjust and inaccurate to present German views on Russia in a purely negative or purely positive light. But there is no question that the Russian people, literature, and landscape already existed in a romanticized, idealized, and dreamlike form in the minds of the members of the White Rose before any of them set foot on Russian soil. And by 1942, with their regimented nation at war with Mother Russia, their longings and their beliefs about "the enemy" undoubtedly were factors in stiffening their resistance to the Nazi cause—and to every value associated with technology, efficiency, modernization, facelessness, and so-called progress.

After the summer semester ended, there was nothing to keep Sophie in Munich. It was a relief to go home, but her spirits were low. Fritz and both her brothers were at the front, her mother was in poor health, and now she had to face two months of work in an armaments factory over the summer vacation—another new requirement in a society now made up of nothing but proclamations and orders.

This train trip from Munich to Ulm brought no exhilaration. Not long after she arrived, her father was tried and sentenced to four months in prison for an anti-Hitler remark. She made a hurried trip back to Munich. With Traute's assistance, she cleared out Hans's room and her own to make sure that no incriminating scrap of evidence could be found by the Gestapo now that the entire family was in danger of *Sippenhaft*, or "clan arrest."

Magdalena Scholl was shattered by her husband's arrest. Although it was probably not mentioned in the Scholl home, the knowledge hung in the air that many prisoners served their terms, were released, and emerged from the prison gates only to find a Gestapo official waiting with the appropriate signed and stamped papers of "transfer"—to a concentration camp.

Sophie requested a postponement before checking in at the factory in order to help her mother at home; she was turned down.

It was a grim and lonely time. The family was allowed to send Robert Scholl a letter every fourteen days; he could write once a month. Sophie's letters to her father were filled with words of encouragement and poorly concealed defiance. Her manual work at the factory began in August. Sometimes in the evenings she would go out to the grounds of the prison, as close as possible to the barred windows where she hoped her father might be.

She took her flute along and played the melody "Die Gedanken Sind Frei" ("Your Thoughts Are Free"), an anonymously written song of the 1848 revolution, part of the accepted liberal and anti-despotic heritage of Germany. A sample of one of its verses:

> *Your thoughts are free,*
> *No one can guess them,*
> *They flee right by*
> *Like shadows in the night;*
> *No man can know them,*
> *No hunter can shoot them*
> *With powder and lead,*
> *Your thoughts are free.*

She loathed the work at the factory. It was not only the idea of making parts for Hitler's machines of war that oppressed her, but also, as she wrote to a friend,

this spiritless, lifeless work, purely mechanical, these tiny little pieces whose whole we don't know, whose purpose is horrible. The work affects you not so much physically as mentally. The constant noise of the machines, the shocking howl of the sirens at the end of the shift, the degrading image of human beings at the machine, as if wholly in the power of the machine . . . how beautiful is a farmer's work, a craftsman's, yes, even a street cleaner's.

Her daily thoughts often turned to Hans, Alex, and the others in Russia—even her dreams did. "I went walking with Hans and Shurik," she recorded in her diary one morning upon waking.

> I walked in the middle . . . half the time jumping, so that the two of them could lift me in the air and swing me forward a bit. Then Hans began: "I know a perfectly simple proof for the existence . . . of God. People breathe so much that after a while the entire heaven must become polluted from man's used-up breath. But, to make sure that people don't lose this nourishment for their blood, from time to time God puffs a mouthful of his own breath into our world . . . and renews the air. That's how he does it." And then Hans lifted his face up to the dark, melancholy sky, drew a deep breath and blew it all out. His breath streamed upward in a blue shining column, becoming larger and larger, going far up into the heavens, pushing aside the dirtied clouds, and there above us and before us and around us was the purest, the bluest sky. It was beautiful.

At the factory she started a private slowdown strike. She was rebuked by the foreman; she shrugged and told him she couldn't help it, she was clumsy.

When she looked around at her fellow workers, all women, she realized that she was relatively lucky. Most of the girls and women were forced laborers from Russia, living in barracks behind barbed wire in a compound adjacent to the factory. They were treated like cattle, barely surviving on watery soups, working seventy hard hours a week (the Germans worked sixty).

Gradually she made friends with a few of the Russian women, not with many words, but with a few friendly smiles when no one was watching them. She tried out a few phrases that Shurik had taught her; the Russians' warm response touched her. She gave them some of her bread and rations furtively; her contact with them—their smiles, their warmth, their simplicity and innocence—was one of the few positive experiences in those months of uncertainty.

The news of Robert Scholl's arrest had reached Hans in Gzhatsk almost as soon as he got there. His mother wrote, asking Hans and his brother Werner, who, by coincidence, was stationed in Gzhatsk with a regular unit, to submit a plea for clemency for their father. She thought that the fact that the Scholl sons were on the front lines might have some impact on the judicial authorities.

Hans rode over on horseback to Werner's unit. He had made up his mind as soon as he got his mother's letter: there would be no petition for mercy. Werner went along with Hans; they wrote their mother that they felt they were acting in the spirit of their father. As Hans put it in his diary, "I know false pride, but I also know real pride." But his father's arrest deeply upset him. As he wrote home on September 18, 1942: "Here I think so much about father, and in the way it can only happen in Russia, I shoot up the whole tone-scale of my personality to the highest tone of rage, and then, just as quickly, I sink back into an expectant, confident and calm state."

The activity on the front near Moscow was gradually dying down as more men and munitions were poured south by the German High Command in the direction of the Volga River, concentrating for an offensive against a major industrial city called Stalingrad.

In October 1942, word seeped into their unit that they would soon be recalled to Germany. Shurik had contracted diphtheria and then lapsed into depression. He didn't want to go back; he wanted to stay in Russia. But if he did—that is, if he deserted, as he said so often he would—what would happen to him in Russia? He could not shoot a Russian, but he would also never fire a gun at a German. Shurik had always envisaged his goal in life as being a bridge between the two countries and cultures, a reconciler, a man of harmony and peace. Now he was plunged into a limbo between them; he belonged suddenly to neither; he was alone.

It was probably the second severe emotional crisis of his life. He stared moodily at his mud-caked boots; he said he would never wash them clean, never wash off the soil of Russia.

Autumn was settling in on the Muscovy plain. Hans wrote in a letter home:

> Alex is almost in good health again, but still not ready to leave the barracks. So I still have to go fishing by myself. But the fall is beautiful here. Can you imagine what it looks like when the endless birch forests gradually change into all the colors of late summer, from soft gold to purple-red. The sun is always shining, the autumn wind chases the clouds— just now a staff doctor got me angry, complaining about my unmilitary haircut. *Jawohl, Herr Stabsarzt* . . . the time will come when we will experience Russia in a different way, when

we'll let our beards grow as long as we can, till they touch the earth, if we enjoy doing it.

They were all obviously depressed about the continuing German encroachments into Russia, and even about going home; but there was nothing to do, for Alex or for themselves, except to discuss "the plan" (as Willi put it cryptically in his diary): the restructuring of resistance activities once they got back to Munich.

As the day of departure from Russia grew close, their emotions were at fever pitch. Willi's notation for that day: "The last morning, preparations, saying good-bye to Sina, to the children. It's very hard for me. . . ." And the intensity of their friendship was heightened and exalted too, even with friends left at home, like Christel Probst. He wrote Hans at the very end of the Russian interlude; he too was affected by Russia. His words expressed feelings in a form far more open and free than was expected among young German men.

In a letter dated October 18, 1942, from Ruhpolding, Christel said:

> It's strange that now the first letter from you has come; just in the past week I have experienced such a strong feeling of missing you. It's true; I've experienced and seen everything as if I'd been with you, and I've often felt the pain of separation. More and more I sense how my life demands true male friendships, the intellectual exchanges—but even more, those of the heart.
>
> I've rented a room for Herta and Mischa in Ruhpolding and go there often. I play toccatas and fugues by Bach. And then, after breakfast, the children come down. *Ach*, Hans, when you sit like that, in the warmly heated room, the small one playing with a car, the other crawling up your lap, then it really goes straight to the heart, and you doubt if you've earned the right to so much happiness and grace. To be together with the children is such a joy that I am often filled with the sense that this could not be permanent. . . .
>
> Now, Sunday morning, I've read your letter and got the answers to questions in the discussions I've been having with you in my mind. Your dear words have deeply moved me and I understand so well what all of you have experienced in Russia.
>
> I am looking forward to a joint skiing and mountain-trekking winter with you, dear Hans and Alex. We'll also go on sharing our common interests and obligations in the city.
>
> I think of you often and am deeply convinced that nothing can happen to you in Russia.

The men at the front had now seen and experienced much; they could no longer brake themselves as they had done so long at home. They began to use their fists. A few days before they left Gzhatsk in October, they had a brawl with Party officials visiting the front who were sitting at a nearby table in a tavern. Somehow they got out of that without being caught.

At one stopover on the train journey home, Hans told his sister Inge later, he saw a young girl with the Star of David on her breast; she was repairing tracks on the line, along with other people with yellow badges on their clothes. Her face was pallid, sunken in; her eyes, beyond grief and terror. Impulsively, Hans thrust his rations in her hand. She looked up at him, then at his uniform. She threw the packet of food to the ground.

He scooped it up, wiped off the dust, and picked a daisy growing by the side of the tracks. He placed the package, with the daisy on top, at her feet. He said, "I would have liked to give you a little pleasure." He boarded the train.

When he looked back, the girl was standing there, watching the train disappear, the flower in her hair.

Defying orders was now their way of life. Instead of standing patiently in a long line waiting to be deloused in Wjasma before going on to Germany, they took off and went into town for a last splurge. They used all the money they had left and bought a collective samovar; it served them well on the long train trip—they had hot tea day and night.

Not only did they bring back lice and a samovar; they smuggled in a few weapons. The three of them were spoiling for a fight. At the Polish border, they were almost arrested. Again the train had stopped, and this time they watched as German guards abused, beat, and stamped on Russian POWs. Their rage exploded. Alex and Hans and Willi jumped off the train and, cursing, fell on the guards. The train began to move, and before the stunned guards could react, the three of them had swung aboard.

It was November when they came back to Germany. They passed through Berlin and went directly to Munich to their unit—and then were dismissed for a few days to go home before classes began again at the university.

Like Manfred Eickemeyer, they had seen for themselves; they had passed through a universe beyond their ability to describe or express. Hans wrote a few days after his return to Germany:

F l u g b l ä t t e r   d e r   W e i s s e n   R o s e .

I

    Nichts ist eines Kulturvolkes unwürdiger, als sich ohne Wider-
stand von einer verantwortungslosen und dunklen Trieben ergebenen
Herrscherclique "regieren" zu lassen. Ist es nicht so, dass sich jeder
ehrliche Deutsche heute seiner Regierung schämt, und wer von uns ahnt
das Ausmass der Schmach, die über uns und unsere Kinder kommen wird,
wenn einst der Schleier von unseren Augen gefallen ist und die grauen-
vollsten und jegliches Mass unendlich überschreitenden Verbrechen ans
Tageslicht treten? Wenn das deutsche Volk schon so in seinem tiefsten
Wesen korrumpiert und zerfallen ist, dass es ohne eine Hand zu regen,
im leichtsinnigen Vertrauen auf eine fragwürdige Gesetzmässigkeit der
Geschichte, das Höchste, das ein Mensch besitzt, und das ihn über jede
andere Kreatur erhöht, nämlich den freien Willen, preisgibt, die Freiheit des Menschen preisgibt, selbst mit einzugreifen in das Rad der
Geschichte und es seiner vernünftigen Entscheidung unterzuordnen, wenn
die Deutschen so jeder Individualität bar, schon so sehr zur geistlosen
und feigen Masse geworden sind, dann, ja dann verdienen sie den Untergang.

    Goethe spricht von den Deutschen als einem tragischen Volke, gleich
dem der Juden und Griechen, aber heute hat es eher den Anschein, als sei
es eine seichte, willenlose Herde von Mitläufern, denen das Mark aus dem
Innersten gesogen und nun ihres Kernes beraubt, bereit sind sich in den
Unergang hetzen zu lassen. Es scheint so - aber es ist nicht so; viel-
mehr hat man in langsamer, trügerischer, systematischer Vergewaltigung
jeden einzelnen in ein geistiges Gefängnis gesteckt, und erst, als er
darin gefesselt lag, wurde er sich des Verhängnisses bewusst. Wenige
nur erkannten das drohende Verderben, und der Lohn für ihr heroisches
Mahnen war der Tod. Ueber das Schicksal dieser Menschen wird noch zu
reden sein.

    Wenn jeder wartet, bis der Andere anfängt, werden die Boten der
rächenden Nemesis unaufhaltsam näher und näher rücken, dann wird auch
das letzte Opfer sinnlos in den Rachen des unersättlichen Dämons gewor-
fen sein. Daher muss jeder Einzelne seiner Verantwortung als Mitglied
der christlichen und abendländischen Kultur bewusst in dieser letzten
Stunde sich wehren so viel er kann, arbeiten wider die Geisel der Menschheit, wider den Faschismus und jedes ihm ähnliche System des absoluten
Staates. Leistet passiven Widerstand - W i d e r s t a n d - wo immer
Ihr auch seid, verhindert das Weiterlaufen dieser ateistischen Kriegs-
maschine, ehe es zu spät ist, ehe die letzten Städte ein Trümmerhaufen
sind, gleich Köln, und ehe die letzte Jugend des Volkes irgendwo für die
Hybris eines Untermenschen verblutet ist. Vergesst nicht, dass ein jedes
Volk diejenige Regierung verdient, die es erträgt!

    Aus Friedrich Schiller, "Die Gesetzgebung des Lykurgus und Solon";

"....Gegen seinen eigenen Zweck gehalten, ist die Gesetzgebung des Lykurgus ein Meisterstück der Staats- und Menschenkunde. Er wollte einen
mächtigen, in sich selbst gegründeten, unzerstörbaren Staat; politische
Stärke und Dauerhaftigkeit waren das Ziel, wonach er strebte, und dieses
Ziel hat er so weit erreicht, als unter einen Umständen möglich war.
Aber hält man den Zweck, welchen Lykurgus sich vorsetzte, gegen den Zweck
der Menschheit, so muss eine tiefe Missbilligung an die Stelle der Bewun-
derung treten, die uns der erste, flüchtige Blick abgewonnen hat. Alles
darf dem Besten des Staates zum Opfer gebracht werden, nur dasjenige
nicht, dem der Staat selbst nur als ein Mittel dient. Der Staat selbst
ist niemals Zweck, er ist nur wichtig als eine Bedingung, unter welcher
der Zweck der Menschheit erfüllt werden kann, und dieser Zweck der Menschheit ist kein anderer, als Ausbildung aller Kräfte des Menschen, Fort-

Facsimile of the First Leaflet of the White Rose

Sophie Scholl, born May 9th, 1921, Forchtenberg am Kocher, executed February 22, 1943, Munich

Hans Scholl, born September 22, 1918, Ingersheim, executed February 22, 1943, Munich

Christoph Probst, born November 6, 1919, Murnau, executed February 22, 1943, Munich

Alexander Schmorell, born September 16, 1917, in Orenburg, Russia, executed July 13, 1943, Munich

Willi Graf, born January 2, 1918, Kuchenheim, executed October 12, 1943, Munich

Professor Kurt Huber, born October 24, 1893, Chur,
executed July 13, 1943, Munich

Farewell at Munich's East Station before leaving for the Eastern Front, July 23, 1942.
L-R: Hubert Furtwängler, Hans Scholl, Willi Graf (back to the camera), Sophie Scholl,

Sophie sniffs a white rose.
& Alexander Schmorell (far right)

July 23,1942, at Munich's East Station. L-R: Hubert Furtwängler, Hans Scholl, Sophie Scholl, & Alexander Schmorell (far right)

Jürgen Wittenstein leaving for the Eastern Front

Hans Scholl & Alexander Schmorell aboard the troop train enroute to the Eastern Front, July 1942

Hubert Furtwängler, Hans Scholl, Willi Graf, & Alexander Schmorell at the Russian Front, summer, 1942

Alexander Schmorell & Hans Scholl

Christoph Probst &
Alexander Schmorell

The Gestapo Headquarters in Munich where members of the White Rose were interrogated

Roland Freisler, President of the People's Court, 1942-45, "Hitler's Hanging Judge"

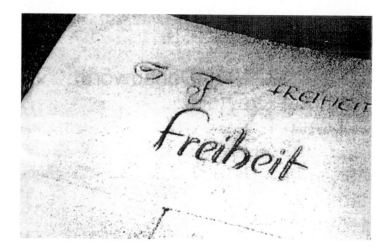

The back page of Sophie's indictment, where she had inscribed, "Freiheit": "Freedom"

NAZI SLUR STIRRED STUDENTS' REVOLT

Official Was Jeered When He Told Girls It Was Duty to Bear Children Without Marriage

THREE WERE GUILLOTINED

Woman, Brother and Another Soldier Beheaded for Issuing Anti-Nazi Tracts

By GEORGE AXELSSON
Wireless to THE NEW YORK TIMES.

STOCKHOLM, Sweden, April 17—The pictorial weekly Veckojournalen reports that a woman was among the three Munich University students who were executed last February for spreading anti-Nazi tracts. The others, it says, were soldiers, one a Stalingrad Sixth Army survivor who had been decorated with two Iron Crosses, —first class and second class.

The weekly asserts the victims were a medical student, Sergeant Hans Scholl, veteran of Stalingrad and son of an official of Ulm; his sister, Maria Scholl, a philosophy student, and another medical student, Private Adrian Probst.

They were guillotined after Gauleiter Gieseler of Munich had demanded that they be publicly hanged on the campus.

Details Are Reported

The background of the incident was reported as follows:

Gauleiter Gieseler in a speech at a university festival Feb. 11 denounced women students for using studies as a pretext to escape war service and declared in an insulting fashion that if they did not want to work in munitions factories they ought at least to bear children, without marriage.

The women students retorted with jeers. Men students formed lines protecting the girls when policemen charged. A riot ensued in front of the university.

The following day Munich house walls bore the inscription: "Revenge for Stalingrad! We want our liberty back!"

The student body issued two tracts, one an appeal to men and girl students, protesting against Nazism and its suppression of individual thinking and the free expression of opinion and also against the attempt to force uniformity on students.

The tract praised the men for protecting the girl students and called for a fight to recapture the right of the individual to decide his own destiny "without which no spiritual values can be created."

The tract concluded with a call to battle against the Nazi party by resigning from Nazi organizations and by refusal to attend lectures by pro-Nazis. The war was condemned and German youths were urged to establish a new Europe.

"A new faith in liberty and honor dawns," it said.

The university was occupied by the police and. Scholl and Probst were arrested for distributing the tracts. They were tried the next day on charges of "favoring the enemy."

When Sergeant Scholl was accused of Communist activities he replied, "I am not a Communist; I am a German." To Judge Freisler he said, "You will soon stand where I stand now."

The executions were carried out immediately after the sentence. For several ensuing nights the city walls bore inscriptions: Scholl lives! You can break the body but never the spirit."

Facsimile of *The New York Times* article of April 18, 1943

A packed memorial service in Munich University Atrium on the fortieth anniversary of the first White Rose arrests and executions, February 1983. On February 18, 1943 Sophie and Hans Scholl were caught dropping leaflets from one of the balconies

Far from all political thought (which is not that strange to me, but rather is closer to me than ever; more about that later), I am grateful to God today that I had to go to Russia. There I finally learned not to take myself so utterly seriously, but to turn the aimless reflections upside down, and direct the mind outward, toward concrete reality.

What they had seen and done in Russia and en route back to Germany is still clouded over, but the Gestapo may have been aware of them even then. Willi's enigmatic diary entry of November 11, 1942, has never been fully explained. He wrote, after they arrived exhausted in Munich from Berlin, that "the *Kriminalpolizei* [the criminal police] visited us, but after that I went on sleeping."

What is known, though, is that their rage, so muted and coolly expressed in letters and diaries, had taken on new dimensions. The fight was only now really to begin.

THIRTEEN

ALTHOUGH Sophie had some grounds for rejoicing in the early days of October 1942, she seemed to remain depressed.

The good news was that Robert Scholl, after serving two of his four months in prison, was released without explanation, although prohibited from practicing his profession. Sophie had also completed the eight weeks of work for the war effort, and now, as she wrote Fritz Hartnagel, who had been transferred to the Stalingrad front,

> Hans is coming back from Russia. Now I really should be happy that he is back with us, and I am, and I'm already sketching out the days we'll be able to spend together in our small flat in Munich ... and yet, I can't be completely happy. The insecurity we live in constantly casts its shadow; it won't allow any positive planning for tomorrow and all the coming days. It hangs over me day and night and never leaves me for a minute. ... When will the time finally come when we won't need to clutch on with all our strength and alertness to things that are not worth the effort? ... Every word, before it's uttered, has to be considered from all sides to see if the slightest shimmer of ambiguity exists. Trust in other people has to give way to suspicion and watchfulness. Oh, it's exhausting and discouraging.

Sophie was grappling with a desperation that appears to have had personal aspects beyond her concerns about her family and the war. It seems that she had been strongly drawn to Alex Schmorell since she had arrived in Munich, and the attraction may not have been reciprocated. In her diary during the period when Alex, Hans, and Willi were in Russia, she referred often, if obliquely, to Alex. Then, on October 10, 1942, she wrote:

This morning I was at the Schmorrels' [in Munich] in Shurik's room, looking for books. What false dreams people can create for themselves! Months ago I was still thinking my feelings for Shurik were greater than for anyone else. But this was such a false delusion! It was only my vanity that wanted to possess a person who had value in the eyes of others. I distort my own self-image in a ridiculous way.

It was not a time for auspicious beginnings. The atmosphere in Germany had become grimmer. Winter was coming, coal for heating was getting scarce, and the air raids over Munich and South Germany were stepping up. The prospect of spending winter nights in unheated black cellars while bombs whistled down was bringing out a bleak despair in the population.

Munich suffered its first direct air raid the night of October 30, 1942. An aristocrat living in the country outside Munich described it in his diary:

> . . . a hideous red glare, transforming the autumn night and its full moon. I heard in the distance the muffled booms. . . . It had taken three minutes for the sound to carry, three minutes during which the victims at the scene had been gasping and gagging and dying. Finally, the whole of the sky to the west was a gigantic sheet of fire.

Anti-Hitler whisper jokes were making the rounds more than ever before. They were not particularly funny, but they were dangerous; the more Germany's leaders felt themselves embattled, the harsher the sentences for these utterances.

When the White Rose met again in Munich in early November for the start of the winter semester at the university, national morale was plummeting. The German offensive at Stalingrad had not only been stopped in its tracks, but the Russians had launched a massive counter-offensive.

In spite of the incessant blaring of Goebbel's propaganda apparatus about victory piling on victory, Hans and Willi and Alex had seen for themselves that the German troops were exhausted, that they had no adequate clothes or supplies for a Russian winter, and that the logistical pipelines were operating chaotically—if at all. The news reports on the "people's" radio was a pack of lies; from listening to "enemy broadcasts"—Swiss Radio and the BBC—they also knew that Anglo-American forces had landed in North Africa, and that the American industrial machine, now totally geared to war, was delivering an endless supply of munitions, fuel, and machinery to the Russians and the British.

The Allied invasion of Europe, they believed, was drawing near.

At Franz-Joseph-Strasse, the discussions were daily vehement affairs. Hans and Sophie's landlady had left them the flat and fled to the countryside as the bombing raids became frequent. The friends came and went at all hours, and the "plan" was the major if not the only subject of conversation when they were alone. But the program was never discussed if a relative or friend came by who had not been admitted to the inner circle; this was done to spare "outsiders" anxiety and to protect them in case the worst ever happened. When Anneliese Graf, Willi's sister, came to Munich to study, she stayed with Sophie and Hans for a few weeks till she found her own room. Till the very end, she knew nothing about their secret operations.

Gisela Schertling, an attractive young woman whom Sophie had met at the castle-work camp during National Labor Service days, had also come to the university this semester, to study art history. Hans had always found her appealing, but now more than ever. Perhaps her rather serene and unruffled manner helped soothe his own inner tumult; the new liaison was probably a refreshing contrast to what had become a stormy relationship with Traute—which was now over. The group was probably surprised, but accepted Gisela into their midst—but not as a member of the White Rose. Traute continued her involvement, taking risks to spread the word of the White Rose in Hamburg and Vienna.

Their double life was launched once again: lectures, clinics, roll calls, concerts; Willi took fencing lessons; he and Alex rehearsed the *Messiah* in the Bach Choir for the Christmas performance.

Christoph Probst, who had not been assigned to the front, was transferred to Innsbruck with a Luftwaffe medic unit. His wife Herta was expecting their third child, and he was reluctant to leave Munich, which was close to his home, but he had no choice. This would mean that his sober judgments and sharp criticisms would no longer be available to Hans and Alex at a time of growing danger.

The first issue at hand was how to proceed after a lapse of almost four months, although the stay in Russia had been a time of reflection and decision making for Hans, Alex, and Willi. Their outlook had changed; they wanted to break out of their Munich-student perspective and take on something larger, with more meaning and impact.

They wanted to expand their activities to other German cities. They would build cells of resistance in major German universities; from there the word would go out to the German people, informing them about the realities from which they were sealed off—informing them that the war was lost even if the lies went on, and that they must, for the sake of their own dignity and conscience, now rise up against Hitler and the Third Reich. This new program required money—much more than they ever had before—and new members, to be recruited among friends and acquaintances in every city and town where they had connections.

Most important of all, Hans and Alex felt, they had to link up with the national resistance movement. They knew now that one did exist. Listening to foreign broadcasts, they heard about the arrest by the Gestapo of Harro Schulze-Boysen and Arvid Harnack and scores of others, in Berlin, during August and September of 1942. A few hundred men and women were scooped up in a swift and terrifying move against the fluid resistance organization dubbed by the Gestapo "Die Rote Kapelle" (The Red Orchestra). The trials were held secretly; it was a subject not mentioned in the Nazi press; one never discussed it in public: if you knew about it at all, you would be under suspicion yourself.

But for the White Rose, in spite of the horror of the arrests, the torture, the trials, and the imminent executions, the fact that the Rote Kapelle existed at all was immensely heartening. One of its leaders, Harro Schulze-Boysen, was an *Oberleutnant* in the Air Ministry; his mother-in-law, a countess, was a close friend of Field Marshal Göring himself. Arvid Harnack, coming from a distinguished family of scholars, was the other major figure in the clandestine circles working in and around Berlin. A fairly high-ranking official in the Economics Ministry, he had been primarily responsible for analyzing American and Soviet economic war plans.

The unmasking of these well-known figures on the Berlin scene created a frenzied panic in Adolf Hitler: the enemies were no longer distant and formless abstractions called Communists or Social Democrats; now they were to be found right in his own lair, working in his ministries, scions of distinguished families he had almost come to trust.

Die Rote Kapelle was a widely extended network of cells and groups; they carried out their activities not only in Berlin, but in occupied Paris, Brussels, and Amsterdam, as well as in neutral Switzerland. They had begun their work in the thirties, and had even managed to survive the trauma of the Molotov-Ribbentrop Security Treaty, which temporarily turned those arch enemies, Soviet Russia and Nazi Germany, into friends. They began their secret broadcasting after the invasion of Russia in 1941. Most of the members were secret Marxists and leftists of all sorts, as well as those we would call liberals. They disseminated underground newspapers and leaflets in the Berlin area, were in contact with the German Communist party—or what was left of it—in factories in Berlin, and also had links with the foreign forced-labor communities living in barracks around the city. They helped forge papers and smuggle Jews and political fugitives out of Germany. Their major link abroad was with Soviet intelligence. They had key men placed in the higher echelons of the army, the Luftwaffe, and the navy, and were able to pass on reliable information to the Soviets on Nazi war plans.

They were betrayed by a parachutist from the Soviet Union who was caught by the Abwehr, German counterintelligence, and turned over to the Gestapo. He broke under torture and the Red Orchestra was totally shattered.

This was the first real information Hans and Alex were able to obtain about an organized resistance in Germany, and furthermore, one that had extended into the loftiest ranks of the German High Command.

The destruction of the network was a devastating blow to the German resistance movement. It had taken years to build, years of scrupulous planning, enormous caution, and training for its participants—not only in dissembling, but in coping with the tremendous risks involved, as well as in how to conduct oneself under torture and cross-examination. The men and women involved had lived a life of lies and deceit for almost a decade.

When Arvid and Mildred Harnack went on a visit to the United States in the thirties, at a time when Arvid still was considered a rising star in the Economics Ministry, their American friends pleaded with them not to return to the Third Reich. They refused to listen; many thought that Arvid's success had gone to their heads, that they had become Nazis. It was only when their terrible executions were made known that their friends abroad finally understood.

But to the handful of young Munich students, alone and without contacts, the news of these events was a wind that buoyed them up. There *was* resistance high up in the Wehrmacht, in the government itself. They were determined to somehow make contact.

Through Alex they found the link: his artist friend Lilo Ramdohr was very close to Falk Harnack, Arvid's younger brother. Hans and Alex asked her to contact him at his military unit and set up a meeting. She agreed.

At first they were concerned about traveling to Chemnitz, a city near the border of Czechoslovakia, where Harnack was stationed. They had no pass or travel permit. The controls on the trains were intensifying: the military police, the criminal police, and the Gestapo were regularly boarding trains and checking the papers of all travelers—especially trains passing near the borders of other countries. If they were picked up, they would be charged with desertion.

But they made the decision to go, and from Hans and Alex's point of view, the meeting in Chemnitz turned out to be a great success. Harnack considered himself a link among all the remaining resistance groups now that his brother was dead, and he welcomed the White Rose actions.

After some fairly severe criticisms of the White Rose leaflets they had brought along, he explained that the resistance was being built— or rebuilt—as a kind of united front, representing the military on the right and ranging all the way to the Communists on the left.

The young men agreed with this principle. They poured out a flood of questions: Was there really a military resistance? How big was it? What were they planning?

Harnack was careful not to reveal names or locations, but he did say that there was a military group planning a putsch. They intended to kill Hitler and overthrow the government.

Hans and Alex were overwhelmed. As much as they had talked and hoped, they never quite believed it would take place. Now they wanted to become part of the movement, to introduce themselves personally. They would go to Berlin.

Harnack promised to see what he could arrange, and said he would keep in touch.

With that special feeling of belonging to something larger than oneself, they returned to Munich with new confidence and authority.

Now they would build their own student and academic sub-network of the German resistance, creating university cells all over that would distribute White Rose leaflets or, if they chose, write their own.

One of the first stops on the new road they took was Stuttgart. Hans and Alex paid a visit to Eugen Grimminger, a friend of Robert

Scholl's, who had been kind enough, as a certified public accountant (or roughly its German equivalent), to take over Mr. Scholl's office while he was in prison. Grimminger was an avowed, if cautious, anti-Nazi. He was desperate to see the end of the war and the demise of the Nazis; his wife Jenny was a "full-blooded Jewess" and in constant danger of arrest and transport to a concentration camp.

They could not risk having their conversation with Grimminger overheard; they could not meet in any enclosed space—whether it be a home, a café, a restaurant. Instead, they took a long walk through the city, finally ending up at a freight-loading area on the outskirts of town.

Hans told Grimminger of their plans, spoke obliquely about a coming putsch, and apparently suggested, or at least hinted, that Grimminger could be of major importance in the new government after Hitler's fall, perhaps selected for a key political office. Hans already knew that Grimminger had contacts with industrialists in Southwest Germany who were talking about a new postwar government.

The three men paced up and down behind a deserted loading ramp, arguing intensely. Finally, on their way back to town, Hans asked Grimminger for a financial contribution. If they didn't get money, he said, the plan could not work. Grimminger hesitated, pulling back. He asked for time to think it over.

He did—and several weeks later made one of the most incautious decisions of his life. He sent a check to Hans for 500 reichsmarks, a considerable amount. But the check could be traced—and later it was—by the Gestapo.

Traute Lafrenz went home to Hamburg, bringing with her a batch of White Rose leaflets to show her old friends Heinz Kucharski and Greta Rothe. Like the Munich group, these young people and their friends met regularly to discuss the arts and the dismal state of affairs. Unlike the White Rose, however, they were aficionados of American swing and jazz.

This kind of American music had a secret, cultlike life of its own in Nazi Germany among certain groups of youths. Because it was officially frowned on and prohibited as a "racially inferior product" of the Afro-American blacks, it exerted a magnetic allure. Its free rhythms, its wild expression of feeling in sound, and its erratic and improvised beat charged up young people and drove them to find records, listen to them together, and become almost embryonic cells of conspiracy. The contrast between Benny Goodman, Glenn Miller, and Louis Armstrong and the eternal drumbeat of German military marches was so enormous that the very admission that one admired this alien form of music was a subversive statement.

At one time, Goebbels had distributed a film in Berlin showing American blacks dancing in a completely uninhibited way; the purpose of its release was to show the German public the degraded and "animal-like" behavior and movements of the black race. The film showings were always sold out; some young people went to see it ten or fifteen times. They came out smiling, they felt alive; it was an experience they would never forget. Goebbels took the film off the market, although he continued to privately screen American movies, especially Hollywood musicals, for his own pleasure.

In any event, Traute Lafrenz's friends read the leaflets with interest, said they would consider circulating them, but first would have to talk the idea over with others in the group. Some of them turned out to be willing; later, they would become known as the "Hamburg Branch of the White Rose."

Although not directly involved in White Rose affairs, Jürgen Wittenstein, the medic-student who had shared front-line experiences with Hans, Willi, and Alex in Russia, agreed to go to Berlin and contact Helmut Hartert, another mutual acquaintance, who was studying at the university there. Hartert, as it turned out, was much more cautious than Hans Scholl, and although he agreed to support the Munich group and build up a "cell" in Berlin, he wanted to write his own leaflets. He did not agree with the antimilitary tone of the White Rose. He told Wittenstein that one could not let down one's side when they were fighting for their lives, but he was willing to write leaflets urging the overthrow of the Nazis. He did get a duplicating machine and set to work.

In early December, Hans and Alex paid Kurt Huber a call at his home in the Munich suburb of Gräfelfing. The time was ripe to tell Huber the truth about the authors of the White Rose leaflets. When they did, the professor was surprised, but was still skeptical about the usefulness of leaflets when more drastic action was needed. In the small heated room where his daughter Birgit was doing her homework—the only heated room in the house—he told the young men: "If blood doesn't flow it *will not work!*" He went on to say that the Wehrmacht was the only institution capable of destroying the Nazis. Hans replied that the White Rose had contacts in Berlin with people connected to the military. Huber was astounded; he had known that there were resistance groups in the army, but he didn't know any details. Hans told him about the plans for a putsch. The professor became excited; this was good news indeed; and yes, now he certainly would support the White Rose.

The circles were widening. Another man won over by the persuasiveness of Hans Scholl was Josef Söhngen, owner of a bookshop on Maximilianplatz, right in the heart of the city. For the informed, his bookshop was the place to go if they wanted something by Franz Kafka, Thomas Mann, or many of the other banned writers. It was also a place for like-minded, *Einwandfrei*—"reliable"—customers to meet, exchange news, and share rumors and ideas.

Most of the White Rose group frequented the bookshop, but Hans became closer than the others to the proprietor, who was considered to be an eccentric bachelor. Söhngen lived alone in a flat over his shop, and there were times in the middle of the night when Hans would appear, exhausted and pale, collapse into a chair, ask for a glass of wine, and fall into a deep silence.

Söhngen had connections with an art historian, Giovanni Stepanov, who lived on Capri and had links with the Italian anti-fascist underground. Söhngen agreed to set up a meeting with Hans the next time Stepanov was in Munich on a lecture tour. An inter-European resistance movement seemed in the offing; the prospects were heady.

But it was not to be: the art historian did come to Munich, but during the Christmas holidays when Hans was home in Ulm. Stepanov was supposed to come to Munich again, in February 1943, but he ran into visa problems; the journey was postponed. When he did come again, it was too late: Hans Scholl was gone.

With frantic energy and by trial and error, the group continued to develop. Sophie was put in charge of the treasury; she doled out the money where it was needed, and tried to keep some kind of records. When she went to Ulm on weekends or holidays, she worked together with the gymnasium student Hans Hirzel and his classmates Franz Müller and Heinrich Guter; they printed leaflets and mailed them out. The work was done behind the organ in the Martin Luther Church, where Hirzel's father, who knew nothing about all this, was pastor.

Willi Graf was less persuasive with his old friends from the Gray Order—Fritz Leist, Adalbert Grindl, and Hermann Krings. They all were studying in Munich, and Willi spent a good deal of time with them; they prayed together, discussed theological questions, and worked on revising the liturgy. But Willi's friends were convinced that the ends do not justify the means, and that the use of force reduced the perpetrator to the level of the criminal. Hitler would be destroyed, they felt, by the very forces of war he had unleashed. They would not interfere in the process.

Willi's disappointments and possible self-doubts grew even stronger when he went home to Saarbrücken over the Christmas holidays with the intention of recruiting friends in the Saar and the Rhineland. At a reunion in Saarbrücken of one of the Catholic youth groups he had belonged to years before, he talked to many of his old comrades, now officers in the Wehrmacht. The general consensus among them was that the war must be won, and that something could be done about getting rid of the Nazis afterward.

Willi was disheartened by this attitude, but he did succeed in making one useful contact at the reunion. Heinz Bollinger, an assistant to a philosophy professor at the University of Freiburg, spent some time talking with Willi. They sensed their isolation from the others and the mutuality of their opinions instantly. Willi visited him a few days later. Bollinger informed him that there were anti-Nazi professors in Freiburg, and that he and his colleague Helmut Bauer were establishing a small circle there.

The young academician also introduced Willi to his brother Willi Bollinger, a medic stationed at the Saarbrücken military hospital. Willi Bollinger declared himself ready to distribute leaflets in the area, and showed Willi Graf the small depot of machine guns and pistols he had been accumulating.

Because of the Bollingers, the trip had not been a total failure. Willi Graf returned to Munich somewhat discouraged. He was determined, however, to make further recruiting attempts in the Rhineland, and intended, as soon as possible, to get a duplicating machine to Willi Bollinger in Saarbrücken.

Within a matter of two months—from November 1942 to early January 1943—the White Rose operation had been transformed from an isolated and quixotic action performed by idealistic and romantic students into an expanding network that was spreading through Southwest Germany, up to the Saarland, and was making tentative but promising leaps into the north, to Hamburg, and, most important, to Berlin.

FOURTEEN

THE GROUP reassembled in Munich in January 1943 after celebrating Christmas with their families at home.

Now was time to write another leaflet, the fifth. Contacts had been made in other cities as well as in Munich, and some money had been raised. Now "the plan" was operational. It was a new year, a year of hope for the White Rose: they believed the Allied invasion was nearly upon them, and they had a new approach that was pragmatic and had meaning.

The new leaflet, as in the past, was written—in separate drafts— by Hans and Alex. But this time they turned to Kurt Huber for his opinion and stylistic revisions. They went to his home; occasionally he came by the Scholl apartment after lectures.

The new collaboration was not easy. Huber read both drafts; he found Alex's unacceptable in content and writing style; even though Alex had not become a Communist, Huber felt, his reactions to Russia had made him less critical of the Soviet Union. Huber reluctantly accepted Hans's version—with the few corrections he made— although he made it quite clear he was not very pleased with that one either. From his point of view, the young men had changed since they came back from Russia. Perhaps he found them hardened, leaning a bit toward the left. What they called "pragmatism," he felt was a loss of the idealistic creed of individualism.

From a conservative standpoint like Professor Huber's, much that appears in the fifth and next-to-the-last leaflet of the White Rose must have been unpalatable. It is testimony to his desperation, his desire to participate, to fight back, that he agreed at all to help them. He too had now crossed the line.

For the first time, the name "The White Rose" did not appear on the leaflet. The authors now presented themselves and their work as "Leaflets of the Resistance Movement in Germany," a rather formidable title. Huber did not approve. He had admired the White Rose as a symbol of personal purity and courage; the new name implied a kind of heavy-handed organizational structure that he disliked. He was overruled by Hans and Alex.

The leaflet was headed "A Call to All Germans" and began with the warning that "the war is nearing its inevitable end. . . . Hitler cannot win the war, only prolong it."

The German people were admonished in a fairly brief paragraph to break with the Nazis, and then the leaflet discussed what kind of world the "movement" envisaged after the war was over:

> Imperialistic designs for power, regardless from which side they come, must be neutralized for all time. A one-sided Prussian militarism must never come to power again. Only in a generous, open cooperation among the peoples of Europe can the groundwork be laid for genuine reconstruction. All centralized power, like that exercised by the Prussian state in Germany and in Europe, must be eliminated. . . . The coming Germany must be federalistic. . . . The working class must be liberated from its degraded conditions of slavery by a reasonable form of socialism.

The leaflet went on to advocate basic civil rights—freedom of speech, of religion, protection of each individual from the encroachments of capricious governments—and concluded, as always, with the request to pass on the information.

There were no citations from Goethe, Schiller, or Lao-tsu, no effort to address themselves to a "cultured" audience. The leaflet was short, fairly precise; it offered a political platform for the future.

Almost every line of the political manifesto in the last few paragraphs was probably anathema to Kurt Huber. He was a passionate admirer of the Prussian state and military, in spite of his South German upbringing. The chasm between Prussia and many of the former duchies and princely states of Germany was immense. It involved not only political resentment on the part of southerners who recalled that Prussia had created and seized control of the new empire of Germany in 1871; it was also a question of style, of social habits, of values and attitudes—the eternal schism between the "cold" North and the "warm" South that seems to exist in many countries.

In the South—in Bavaria, Baden, and Swabia—Prussia stood for Spartan austerity, the pounding beat of the military boot, and the German language spoken in the imperative, a cross between a bark and a gunshot. The southerners had nursed their grievances for over seventy years; they had been taken over and unified into a nation by an unsympathetic people whose stern values and undisguised arrogance made the southerners seethe with anger.

This feeling was expressed in the White Rose leaflets: Prussia was held responsible for the rise of Adolf Hitler and for the war he decided to wage.

Kurt Huber, a deep admirer of the German idealists—Kant, Hegel, Fichte—who had developed and refined their philosophical systems within the Prussian milieu, could not accept this rather simplistic evaluation of German history that he heard time and again in the discussion groups he attended. Prussia, he believed, had contributed far more to Germany than the crack of a whip; Prussia was not responsible for the rise of Adolf Hitler, who was born in Austria—in the easygoing, softhearted "South"—and who actually launched his mass movement not in the North, not in Prussia, but in the happy-go-lucky, gracious city of Munich.

In the vehement discussions Huber had with the students, he may have objected to the expression "reasonable socialism" as well, but in no case were his suggestions to change content or tone accepted; he was simply overruled.

The leaflet was written, revised, and edited; now printing operations began. The Gestapo later estimated that between eight thousand and ten thousand copies of the *Call to All Germans* were disseminated, a twentyfold increase over the first four flyers. Alex again bought a typewriter and now a larger duplicating machine. Sophie and Traute made forays into shops all over the city in order to purchase the special paper needed, as well as envelopes and stamps. In each store, in each post office, they waited patiently in line, aware that clerks were on the alert for all suspicious behavior and out-of-the-way requests.

Even though the new press was larger than the old one, it still had to be cranked by hand. Each leaflet was turned out one by one, night after night. Stencils had to be changed, cylinders broke; again the tension was becoming unbearable. In order to stay awake and to function during the day, they took pep pills from the military clinics where the medics worked.

The bombing raids were another menace; it was not only the danger to their lives—they feared the real possibility that the atelier would be hit, and that the equipment and supplies in the cellar would lie naked in the streets, revealing all.

Hans devised a scheme: if the bombs seemed to be zeroing in on Schwabing, he would call Josef Söhngen and ask for a specific book. If the bookdealer said yes, he had that book, it meant the coast was clear. Then Hans and Alex would put the duplicator in a suitcase and carry it through the blacked-out streets, finally depositing it in Söhngen's cellar. The discovery of a printing press in a bookshop would not be as damning as in the studio of an architect.

Somehow, day by day, night by night, in spite of delays and breakdowns and unsteady nerves, the leaflets were printed and ready to go.

Gestapo headquarters in Munich was housed in the Wittelsbach Palace, one of the many residences in Bavaria built by the royal dynasty. It was a massive building in red brick, designed in the mid-nineteenth-century style of other Bavarian state buildings constructed in Munich. It is gone now, destroyed by bombs and never rebuilt, but its history will never quite disappear in the city of Munich; the experiences of men and women inside its walls reflect the ironic and tragic swings of the pendulum in the Bavarian past.

The palace had hosted, among others, royal princes and their courtesans, like Lola Montez, in the uncomplicated days of mid-nineteenth-century Europe. After the First World War, it had been the seat of the Eisner republic that was so quickly snuffed out by reactionary and right-wing forces. Now, in 1943, and since the early days of the Third Reich, it served as the focal point for Gestapo activities in Bavaria; its cellars were used for torture, its archives filled with the denunciations of zealous and envious neighbors and reports by Gestapo *Spitzel*, or "spies."

Robert Mohr was a Gestapo official who had served in a police capacity in Munich since the end of the First World War. One morning in January 1943, he was urgently summoned by the head of his department, Oberregierungsrat Schäfer. Schäfer was extremely nervous when Mohr arrived; he handed him a sheet of paper.

It was the leaflet, *A Call to All Germans*. Mohr read it and waited. Schäfer ordered him to push aside all other pending projects and concentrate on finding the authors of the leaflet. Hundreds had appeared in the city, perhaps more. The Gestapo's paid and voluntary helpers had brought them in from movie-houses, park benches, lobbies of apartment buildings, telephone booths. Schäfer added ominously that "the leaflets were creating the greatest disturbance at the highest levels of the Party and the State." Although no names were mentioned, he undoubtedly meant Heinrich Himmler, head of the SS and all security forces, including the Gestapo—and possibly even Adolf Hitler.

In a voice trembling with indignation, Schäfer told his subordinate that the Munich Gestapo had been put in charge of finding the culprits and "putting an end to the affair."

Mohr began to investigate; he quickly discovered that the leaflets were now surfacing in Stuttgart, Vienna, Ulm, Frankfurt, and Augsburg. They were sent by mail as printed matter and none were postmarked in the city where they appeared. Those received in Stuttgart were postmarked Vienna, those in Frankfurt were mailed in Salzburg.

It was a unique occurrence in the decade of Nazi rule. The Gestapo suddenly found itself confronted by what it saw as a massive bombardment of subversive literature coming from beyond the left wing, generated inside the Reich, but not from one particular location; the treasonous material seemed to spring up haphazardly all over the country. Was a small group behind it? Or, as the morale at home and on the front was deteriorating, was this the first manifestation of a nationwide resistance organization? Would the leaflets trigger a chain reaction that the Nazis could no longer contain? How strong was this resistance?

The Gestapo manhunt began in earnest.

In order to stir up the fears and anxiety that the authorities were experiencing, and to give the impression of a wide-based network, the Munich group had worked out a daring scheme. They took the leaflets in rucksacks and suitcases by train to other cities and mailed them from there to yet another city. When they boarded the train in Munich—they always traveled alone—they would leave the suitcase in one compartment on the overhead rack, and then find a seat in another compartment, as far away from the suitcase as possible.

The trains were overcrowded; often there were no seats at all, and one stood or perched on pullout benches in the long, narrow corridors. Often they didn't leave on time, since Allied bombing raids had destroyed many lines and tracks, and repair time was needed.

The expeditions of the White Rose were dark, cold, and chaotic. Travel had become a menace; not only the trains but even streetcars were controlled by the Gestapo and the military police, and sometimes pedestrians were stopped on the street. All citizens had to carry their identity papers with them at all times, and especially when traveling; the Munich students were very aware that each trip could be their last. The police were hunting not only for "subversives," deserters, and fugitives, but also for those engaged in food smuggling, a practice that had become extensive as the nation grew more and more hungry.

The trains the group took often arrived at the planned destination in the middle of the night. The students would pick up their luggage from the compartment where they had stored it and descend into darkness and often bombed-out railway stations, trying to look normal as they walked the cold, blacked-out streets, looking for mailboxes in unobtrusive places. Then, with their empty suitcases, they would return to Munich.

They had worked out plausible explanations for each journey in case they were stopped and questioned, and eventually they were even able to get counterfeit travel papers. Each one of the students made a journey like this, each one accepted the risks.

Hans went to Salzburg and posted 150 leaflets. Alex journeyed to Linz and Vienna with a suitcase filled with 1,400 leaflets; he mailed 400 from Vienna to Frankfurt, then stopped briefly in Linz and posted 200 more, and finally mailed the rest from Salzburg on his way back home, immensely relieved that the suitcase was empty.

Probably the most unpleasant aspect of these journeys was the fact that the participants undertook them alone, not in pairs. Going alone meant attracting less attention and it kept costs down, but undoubtedly these expeditions were their most terror-filled moments. But over the years they had learned to dissemble, learned how to look cool and distant, how to keep their faces inscrutable, their eyes blank, how to submit to security checks without trembling.

Sophie made her courier runs in the Augsburg-Ulm-Stuttgart area, from where she mailed about eight hundred leaflets. While at her parents' house, she had an urge to show her father one of the leaflets, which she said she had "found" in Munich. He expressed admiration over this sign of resistance, as she had hoped. But suddenly he turned to her, troubled. "Sophie, I hope you two haven't anything to do with this?"

She answered with indignation. "How can you even suspect that? Things are brewing in Munich, but we don't get involved in them."

But to Susanne Hirzel, her old friend from the days at the Fröbel Seminar, she said: "If Hitler came walking by right now and I had a pistol, I would shoot. If the men don't do it, then a woman will have to. You have to do something to avoid being guilty yourself."

While she was still in Ulm, Sophie also gave Hans Hirzel a few copies of the new leaflet, which they then reproduced in his father's church. Hirzel and Franz Müller and Heinrich Guter selected names and addresses from telephone books, typed the envelopes, and posted them.

On one occasion, Hans Scholl's new girlfriend, Gisela Schertling, helped Sophie mail a batch of envelopes in Munich. Sophie was carrying them in her rucksack; she asked her friend to keep the mailbox open so that she could throw in batches of them quickly. Gisela Schertling obliged, but never asked what it was that Sophie was doing in such a covert manner—perhaps she preferred not to know.

By far the most dangerous journey was made by Willi Graf. Without a furlough-pass or a permit to travel, he went off, in uniform, in the direction of the Rhineland. He was not only transporting leaflets in his large suitcase, but a duplicating machine as well.

He was determined to win support from among his old Catholic youth-group comrades, regardless of previous rejections. Even carrying out the precautions of separating himself from his highly charged luggage, he barely managed to slip through some tight controls.

On January 21, 1943, he was in Cologne talking to friends; he had no luck. He went on the same day to nearby Bonn, where he had once studied, and again was not warmly received, or at least his proposals were not. Traveling on, still weighed down with his heavy suitcase, he came to Saarbrücken and went to see Willi Bollinger at the military hospital where he worked as a medic.

It must have been a great relief when Bollinger took the duplicating machine and some of the leaflets to reproduce. Willi stayed with him overnight, avoiding any contact with his family. Before he left the next day, Bollinger gave him forged papers for the rest of the journey and blank travel forms, already stamped and signed, that could be used for future White Rose ventures.

Willi's next stop was Freiburg, then on to Ulm, giving a few leaflets to the two or three people he could trust and knew would support him.

It was a long trip; it meant many train connections, many chances to be checked; his suitcase had been a ticking bomb, and the enormous strain and effort had yielded some—but only some—positive results.

Willi's reactions are not known. When he returned to Munich, his diary for that day reports, he went to roll call, listened to a stupid Nazi harangue, "and in the evening a highly satisfactory cello concert."

FIFTEEN

O N JANUARY 13, 1943, for the first and last time in the Third Reich, university students rose up in protest. It was a spontaneous outbreak of rage, it occurred in Munich, it was short-lived—but it did happen.

On that day, students and faculty were summoned to the Main Auditorium of the Deutsche Museum, an enormous repository of science and technology located on an island in the Isar River, across the city from the university. The museum was chosen as the site to commemorate the 470th anniversary of the founding of the University of Munich; none of the halls at the university itself was large enough to contain so many professors and students at one time, as well as prominent officials in government, the Party, and the military.

Most of the students upon arrival were ordered up to the balcony, especially the female students, since the main hall was reserved for men in uniform: the soldier-students, the veterans who came on crutches and canes, and important officers in the SS and the armed forces. Apparently the faculty, in robes, were also permitted to sit in the orchestra; Kurt Huber was among them.

On the platform, draped with a banner to proclaim the solemn and important occasion, were local, regional, and national leaders of the National Socialist Student Association—as always, in uniform.

All exits were manned by the SS.

Since the White Rose student members had made a vow, as they said in one of their leaflets, to boycott all Nazi rallies and assemblies even if ordered to attend, they were not present. However, their friends Gisela Schertling, Anneliese Graf (Willi's sister), and

Katharina Schüddekopf, Kurt Huber's doctoral student, were in attendance, seated in the first row of the balcony.

The gauleiter of Bavaria, Paul Giesler, had replaced Gauleiter Wagner, who had had a stroke and died some months later. Giesler was to give the keynote address. Even more brutal and primitive than Wagner, he considered himself "a man of the people." He despised intellectuals and the university—a not unusual Nazi attitude.

Giesler's goal on this occasion was to whip up morale for the war effort. It was known that Adolf Hitler was furious with the people of Munich for not living up to his expectations. They were sullen and less than enthusiastic about sending their sons and fathers to the collapsing Russian front; the Führer felt they deserved all the bombing they got.

Giesler began by saying that the university was an integral part of National Socialist society, and that in a short time the students would be standing on the "command bridges" of German life. Therefore it was imperative that institutions of higher learning not remain cloistered enclaves of puerile, intellectual thought. "Twisted intellects" and "falsely clever minds," he said, were unacceptable and were not an expression of "real life." He was getting excited, and in the tradition of German political oratory, he began to bellow.

"Real life," he roared, "is transmitted to us only by Adolf Hitler, with his light, joyful and life-affirming teachings!"

No fervent crack of applause greeted that statement. He went on, praising those students who had been to the front or were to leave soon, and those who were working in factories for the war effort. Then came the attack: many were studying at the university, he said, who were "without talent" or "seriousness of purpose." They were taking away space and furnished rooms from the more deserving. Again his voice rose: the university was no rescue station for "well-bred daughters" who were shirking their war duties.

There was a growing restlessness in the hall as he spoke; by now there was shuffling of feet and catcalls. They became louder, more frequent. The auditorium was charged with tension. The women in the balcony were furious; some leaned down, calling out angry protests to the gauleiter.

Their disapproval egged Giesler on. He shouted up at the women: "The natural place for a woman is not at the university, but with her family, at the side of her husband." The girls here, he said, should be fulfilling their duties as mothers instead of studying.

The audience reaction became louder; there was movement, restlessness, shouts from all over. At this point Giesler went overboard. Women, he bellowed above the din, should present the Führer with a child every year. Then, with a grin, he added, "And for those women students not pretty enough to catch a man, I'd be happy to lend them one of my adjutants." He leered, "And I promise you *that* would be a glorious experience!"

All hell broke loose. Pounding feet in protest, shouts, tumult all over. Giesler tried to go on speaking but was drowned out.

Some twenty young women had by now stormed out of the balcony in rage; they were promptly arrested by brown-shirted students and the SS. The remaining women in the balcony were being pushed out now by the SS guards. Men from downstairs came dashing up to help them; fistfights broke out while groups of male students tried to free the arrested women.

One of the NS student-leaders was seized by the students; they shouted that they would hold him hostage till the girls were released. The fistfights continued on both floors and in the lobby outside the auditorium. By now commando squads had been summoned and were arriving on the scene. The students, with the released women, ran out of the museum, formed into small groups, and began marching in a procession along the Isar, in the direction of the university.

They linked arms as they marched and sang.

People stopped dead to stare at them; it was a sight not to be believed. There was a feeling of lightheartedness in the air, of fraternal goodwill and warmth that many had never known before in their lives.

By the time they reached Ludwigstrasse they had to disperse before the special police forces broke their ranks. The demonstration could not last.

But the moment lingered in everyone's mind: it was the talk of Munich. In the Mensa, the student cafeteria, and in the lecture halls and corridors of the university, the students talked and remembered; they used a word never used before: they spoke of "victory."

The impact of the museum "encounter" was so great that Paul Giesler felt impelled to hold another meeting with the students later in January. He begrudgingly apologized for his remarks about women, but then went on to warn the assemblage that he would close the university and pack off all the men to the front and all the women to factories if the "disorders" continued.

When they heard the news about the "uprising" at the Deutsche Museum from their friends, Willi, Sophie, Hans, and Alex were overjoyed. They saw a direct connection between their leaflets and the events; the leaflets' objective was to foment unrest: therefore their plan was working!

Their decision was to work harder. They quickly printed another 1,300 *Call to All Germans* leaflets and distributed them around Munich. They were almost beside themselves with excitement and tension. Christoph came by around this time; his wife was expecting their third child momentarily. He observed his friends and was concerned; he warned them to be careful. The realities had not changed, no matter how euphorically they viewed the future; the terror was still and always present; he felt they were in real danger.

But they didn't listen; and Willi noted jubilantly in his diary: "The stone is beginning to roll."

SIXTEEN

ALTHOUGH THE SURRENDER had actually taken place three days before, the radio announcement on February 3, 1943, hit Germany like a bolt of lightning. This time "the special bulletin" interrupting regular programming began not with triumphant fanfares but with the ominous slow beats of a drum. Then a long silence. Then again the slow roll of drums. Then the mournful second movement of Beethoven's Fifth Symphony. Finally a funereal voice began to speak: "The battle for Stalingrad is over. True, with their last breath, to their oath to the flag, the Sixth Army, under the inspirational leadership of General Field Marshal von Paulus, has been defeated. . . . They died so that Germany may live."

Despite rumors going around for weeks that the German army was surrounded at Stalingrad, and despite the silence of the Propaganda Ministry about the course of events on the southeast front, the nation went into shock. It was one of the greatest defeats in German history, and the first gigantic setback for the Wehrmacht in the Second World War. After years of listening to excited voices trumpeting new invasions and smashing victories on all fronts, this radio announcement was a staggering blow; those Germans old enough to remember the war—and who permit themselves to do so—recall precisely where they were and what they were doing when the news came on the air.

The battle for Stalingrad had begun months earlier, in September 1942. The Sixth Army, with about 300,000 men gathered from all segments of the eastern front, had attacked the city on the Volga. The press and radio at home called it the key battle to destroy Bolshevism, but after the initial announcement, no flashes came over the air about a quick victory. By mid-November, the Red Army, marshaling every man and weapon left at its disposal after eighteen months of shattering defeat, mounted an enormous counterattack and surrounded the 300,000 Germans.

As the situation grew desperate, General von Paulus asked permission to break out of the encirclement. Hitler refused. He ordered the Sixth Army to stand fast and fight till the last man. In January 1943, in a freezing Russian winter, the Soviet army launched its final push; it was all over by January 31.

As the solemn and bombastic services were held at home for the Stalingrad dead—nearly 200,000 Germans were killed in battle—no one mentioned the 90,000 prisoners taken by the Russians and led off to prison camps in Siberia. Gaunt, ill, ragged, and frozen, they were marched ever-deeper into the Russian snows, falling and dying as they walked. Goebbels, at home, canceled all theater performances, movies, and concerts to mourn the dead. The 90,000 staggering men were buried with the dead: for the Nazi leadership, there was no such word as "surrender," and those who had, were written out of history. Most of the 90,000 never came back.

Gestapo reports from Bavaria at that time noted that morale had reached the lowest point since the beginning of the war. The people were angry at Hitler, they felt manipulated and ill used; they believed that Stalingrad was the turning point of the war, and that Germany would ultimately lose. Munich and other cities in the South were experiencing a considerable influx of refugees from the industrial cities in the North that had been bombed into the ground. A feeling of exhaustion, confusion, grief, and fear hung in the air; and the people were becoming very hungry.

For Kurt Huber, Stalingrad was an enormous tragedy, as if he had experienced the suffering, the death, and the betrayal himself. He was shaken to the core; this was a moment of historic proportions for the German nation. A few days later, he made a momentous decision: he would write a leaflet himself.

He was up all night working on it, at last putting on paper all the grief and rage he had locked inside himself for ten years. Clara Huber went into his study in the early morning. She found him at the typewriter, and read over what he had written. She was deeply shocked, and begged him to destroy the essay. He told her not to involve herself, that the less she knew, the better. She saw there was no way to persuade him.

The sixth—and last—leaflet of the White Rose would not claim affiliation to "The Resistance Movement" or to the White Rose. It was simply addressed "Fellow Students"; it was meant to express the spirit of youth, of the students at the university, and of the soldiers who had died at Stalingrad.

"Our people are deeply shaken by the fall of our men at Stalingrad," it began.

> Three hundred and thirty thousand German men were senselessly and irresponsibly driven to their deaths by the brilliant strategy of that World War I corporal. Führer, we thank you! . . .
>
> We grew up in a state where all free expression of opinion has been suppressed. The Hitler Youth, the SA and the SS have tried to drug us, to revolutionize us, to regiment us in the most promising years of our lives.

Referring to the recent student uprising, Huber went on:

> Gauleiters insult the honor of women students with crude jokes, and the German women-students at the university have given a worthy response to the besmirching of their honor. German students have defended their female comrades and stood by them. . . . This is the beginning of the struggle for our free self-determination. . . .
>
> For us there is only one word: fight—against the Party! Get out of all Party organizations! Get out of the lecture halls run by SS *Unter-* and *Oberführer* and Party sycophants!
>
> Freedom and honor! For ten long years Hitler and his comrades have squeezed, debased and twisted those beautiful German words to the point of nausea. . . .
>
> . . . The name of Germany will remain forever stained with shame if German youth do not finally rise up. . . . Women students! Men students! The German people look to us! . . . Berezina and Stalingrad are aflame in the East; the dead of Stalingrad beseech us!

This essay of Huber's was eventually printed virtually untouched— except for one crucial line. The disagreement between Huber and Hans Scholl over that line was to cause the final rupture in their relationship.

Since the turn of the year, events were moving fast; by February the momentum seemed beyond control.

After hearing the Stalingrad news, during the night of February 3, 1943, Hans and Alex and Willi went out into the darkened streets and painted the words "Freedom" and "Down with Hitler" on the walls of apartment houses, state buildings, and the university. In some places they added a white swastika, crossed out with a smear of red paint.

They took turns mounting guard with a loaded pistol.

They were not caught, and the next day the reaction around the city made it worth the effort. People were gathered in front of the university, silently watching as Russian women-laborers were trying to scrub the letters off the walls, under the supervision of guards. The letters were huge, stark, clear; there was no way to avoid them, not to notice. Traute Lafrenz happened to be there as Hans Scholl came up to the university entrance that day. He walked as he always did, with long strides, head leaning slightly forward. He didn't look around, despite the clusters of people, but he had a "small triumphant" smile on his face. As he went into the building—he took no notice of the scrubbing women with their pails and brushes—his smile grew broader. An excited student came by and said to Hans: "Did you see it? Did you see it?"

Hans laughed out loud, saying, "No, see what?"

At about this time, Falk Harnack arrived in town, a significant occurrence for the White Rose. It meant that the "central body" of the resistance movement in Berlin was taking them seriously. Harnack met Alex and Hans privately, and on the next day the entire group—with the exception of Christoph—assembled at the Franz-Joseph-Strasse flat. Present were Sophie, Willi, Hans, Alex, and Kurt Huber; it was apparently on this occasion that Huber gave the draft of the sixth leaflet to Hans.

Harnack was aware that the group was charged up. They were almost feverish, their eyes glittering with exhaustion; and most of all, they seemed exalted. They believed that their work was helping create a revolutionary atmosphere in Munich.

Perhaps their efforts were not quite as crucial as they believed, but their evaluation of the mood in Munich was not far wrong. Gestapo files reporting on those February days talk about rumors going around the city that people were responding to the greeting *Heil Hitler!* with a slap in the face. The report adds: "It is also not advisable to wear the Party badge in your lapel."

As the group huddled together in Hans's unheated room, Harnack reported on the state of resistance. He said a putsch was possible at any moment, and that the Allied invasion of Europe was coming close. The German resistance movement, he said, was most interested in working with the White Rose, but they must first agree to the principle of a wide coalition of forces from left to right. He invited Hans and Alex to Berlin, on February 25, 1943; their meeting place, the Kaiser Wilhelm Memorial Church.

Harnack turned to other post-putsch plans that had to be agreed upon by the group: that all Nazi activists must be arrested and severely punished; that all members of the Party be stripped of their right to vote; and that only three political parties be permitted representation in the new parliament—Marxist, Liberal, and Christian.

The conflict became open when they talked about foreign affairs. Huber said he would not work with the Soviets, that Western individualism and democracy was the only system he could accept. Alex retorted that it was shortsighted to depend exclusively on the West. Although he personally was not a Communist, he said, he believed that the Soviet Union would develop into one of the strongest political powers in the postwar world.

Falk Harnack had to leave. The rendezvous in Berlin with Hans and Alex, or at least with Hans, was confirmed. But the atmosphere had turned sour. Kurt Huber was furious.

After Harnack's departure, the professor said that he would refuse to work with him in the future. The others disagreed, reaffirming that one of them would go to Berlin.

Huber's leaflet now came up for discussion. The group agreed to print it—with one line excised, Huber had written that students should "support our glorious Wehrmacht." Hans and Alex found that idea unacceptable. Huber wanted the line in the text; he refused to budge. Hans got excited, pointing out that the army was a pillar of the Nazi state, that there was nothing glorious about it. They must have been shouting by then: Hans and Alex telling Huber that resistance could be created among the rank-and-file troops, but not in the institution of the military.

It was then, it appears, that Huber demanded his draft back. Either the essay would be printed in its entirety—or not at all.

The others refused, saying that they considered his remarks important and that they wanted to circulate them at the university.

Apparently, he didn't insist; but Kurt Huber's brief—and per-ilous—collaboration with the White Rose was over. Angry, hurt, and deeply disappointed in the students he had come to consider his protégés, the middle-aged professor stormed out of the apartment.

He never saw Hans Scholl again.

SEVENTEEN

THEY VENTURED out twice more, on the nights of February 8 and 15, to paint the walls of the city and proclaim freedom from Nazi tyranny. They went so far as to stencil and paint the words "Down with Hitler" on the hallowed Feldherrnhalle, the huge Florentine loggia that terminates Ludwigstrasse in the downtown area of the city. This memorial to the Bavarian generals who supported Napoleon in his expedition against Russia was the site of Hitler's 1923 putsch. He had tried at that time to overthrow the Bavarian government and failed. After he took power in 1933, a memorial plaque to his martyred Storm Troopers was placed on the side of the massive loggia. It became a place of pilgrimage each year for the Nazi leadership on the anniversary of the thwarted attempt to seize power.

Now, teams of men in SS uniforms stood vigil day and night in front of the memorial plaque, with an additional SS guard post just across the street. Each citizen who passed the memorial was required to lift his arm in the "German salute"; if he did not, he was stopped and questioned by the SS.

Many Müncheners chose detours to avoid that encounter, but on one of those nights in February 1943, Hans and Alex and Willi, a few meters away from the SS honor guard, smeared the walls of the Feldherrnhalle with paint. "Freedom!" "Down with Hitler!" were the words that greeted Munich in the morning. It was unthinkable: the holiest of holies, the sacred temple of the Third Reich, had been desecrated.

About this time Christoph dropped by to see his friends; in no uncertain terms he told them that these nocturnal forays were dangerous and foolish. Christoph's tension probably matched their own: his wife had given birth to a daughter and was in the hospital with puerperal fever; but, in addition, he was deeply concerned about his friends. He argued heatedly with Hans and Alex, warning them that the Nazis had not yet been toppled from power and, if anything, were more dangerous and vicious the more terrified they became of losing their grip. Terror was rampant; individuals in various cities had been executed just for saying out loud that the war was not going well.

But Christoph did agree to one request his friends had: that he write a leaflet calling for a cease-fire and negotiations with the Allies, mainly for distribution at the front. He later sent a draft to Hans in his own handwriting. It talked about "an honorable end to the war," and even had the audacity to propose that a new international order be created after the war, perhaps under the sponsorship of Franklin D. Roosevelt, the American president.

That draft—never printed, never circulated—was to cost Christoph his life.

Although the group apparently refused to pull back and take fewer risks, they also had a feeling, growing stronger, that they were in imminent danger of being caught.

Hans's personality seemed to be undergoing a change. He walked by friends without seeing them; he seemed to be living in an inner world, unaffected by the conditions around him; his manner was distracted, no longer self-confident and eager. On one occasion, he told Gisela Schertling that he was being watched. Later Josef Söhngen, the owner of the bookshop, was to recall that Hans had given him the impression that he had secret contacts within the Gestapo itself, that perhaps he knew they were on his trail.

Since January, the Gestapo in Munich had indeed been feverishly hunting for the authors of the leaflets. When the anti-Nazi graffiti began appearing on walls, the security investigators linked that action with the student "unrest" after Gauleiter Giesler's speech, but not with the leaflets. They were focusing their attention on the university now, and circulated a bulletin offering a reward to university personnel who knew anything about the "smear campaign."

The Gestapo already had a file on Hans from his days in the underground youth movement and his arrest in 1937; they were also certainly aware of Robert Scholl's sentiments and the prison sentence he had served.

There are other troublesome and elusive scraps of information. In November 1942, Hans Hirzel, the Ulm high-school student who was a fervent admirer of Hans Scholl, had tried to enlist new supporters for the White Rose leaflet campaign. He talked to a fellow student, mentioning Hans Scholl's name, among others. The student turned out to be a Gestapo informer. When Hirzel found this out, he managed to convince the young spy that he had lost his head and was slightly mad when he told him those stories of leaflets and conspiracy. The informer seemed convinced; in any case, the Ulm Gestapo did nothing. Hans Scholl was alerted in Munich for trouble, but nothing further happened. Some time later, Hirzel again tried to persuade a student to join in the underground activities; again he was reported to the Gestapo.

On February 17, 1943, Hans Hirzel was summoned to the Ulm Gestapo headquarters and interrogated. They let him go. He was now desperate to warn Hans Scholl in Munich that there could be serious trouble. He went to the Scholl home and told Inge to contact her brother in Munich immediately, using their code for danger, *Machtstaat und Utopie* (*The Absolute State and Utopia*), the name of a book by the distinguished German historian Gerhard Ritter.

Inge promptly called her fiancé-to-be, Otl Aicher, who was on military leave and staying at Carl Muth's in Munich. She asked him to relay the message to Hans.

After contacting Hans that evening, Otl Aicher arrived, as agreed, at the apartment on Franz-Joseph-Strasse at eleven the next morning, February 18, 1943. But no one was home. He left and returned at eleven-thirty. This time the door swung open. Otl Aicher was greeted by the Gestapo.

EIGHTEEN

IN BERLIN that day, Thursday, February 18, 1943, the Sports Palace was packed with an overflowing audience of the Party faithful.

Propaganda Minister Joseph Goebbels had been planning for this moment since January: painstaking analyses of public-opinion surveys had been made; the most radical currents among the Party and population had been stirred; now, carefully chosen representatives of the German *Volk* community were gathered to greet their Führer.

But Hitler himself was sequestered in the isolation of the Wolf's Lair, his secret battle headquarters deep in an East Prussian forest. He had been brooding there ever since Stalingrad, a battle that he had promised would be a turning point toward victory. At home in the Reich, the families of those lost in Russia and everyone else were enduring bombing raids that grew with unexpected fury. The innocent and guilty alike were consumed by the tens of thousands in the green flames of clinging phosphorus.

Now Goebbels would do something significant to renew the Führer's confidence and spirits, and in the process restore himself to a paramount position in Hitler's eyes. Today was the most important demonstration of Goebbels's entire career. He would orchestrate it as if he were directing Wagner's *Twilight of the Gods*, transforming the ignominy of defeat at the hands of the Slavic "subhumans" into Germany's superhuman last stand, the apotheosis of the Thousand-Year Reich.

In the audience were fifteen thousand. Above the speaker's platform, behind Goebbels's head, hung an enormous banner with the words "Total War—Shortest War." Radio microphones were poised to transmit the words spoken on this historic occasion into every German home; newsreel cameras were already rolling, panning across the rows of faces. Grouped around the stage were casualties of the eastern front, and Red Cross nurses in white smocks, standing by. In the first rows sat ministers of government, high Party leaders, the generals of the Wehrmacht. Behind them came a sample of the German *Volk* itself, selected from all over Germany—tradesmen, office workers, artists, engineers, civil servants, ordinary soldiers, teachers—gathered to chant in unified response to the questions Goebbels would pose.

Goebbels began. His speech consisted of ten questions, designed to build excitement, bringing the audience to the highest emotional pitch. He wanted them to experience a release of energy that was orgasmic, self-abnegating.

"I ask you," Goebbels called out into the hushed silence. "Do you believe with the Führer and with the rest of us in the final total victory of the German people? Are you determined to follow the Führer through thick and thin in the struggle for victory, and to put up even with the heaviest of personal burdens?"

The audience called in a single explosion of consent. "*Ja!*"

"I ask you, are you and are the German people determined, if the Führer orders it, to work ten, twelve, or if necessary fourteen and sixteen hours a day, and to give your utmost for victory?"

The crowd called out, "*Ja!*" louder than before.

Would the German people accept the mobilization of all women? The death penalty for shirkers and profiteers?

Spontaneous demonstrations broke out, flags and banners waving, shouts of *Sieg-Heil!* and "Führer, command—we follow!"

Goebbels had the crowd at a pitch of excitement he himself had never before witnessed. Now was the time for the ultimate question.

"I ask you," he screamed, "*wollt Ihr den Totalen Krieg?*—Do you want Total War?—if necessary, more total and more radical than we can even imagine it today?"

The crowd rose to its feet and shrieked its assent in a shattering paroxysm, their hands and fingers outstretched with such fervent effort that their arms seemed almost ready to leave their shoulder sockets.

"*Do you agree,*" Goebbels called into the continuous roar, "*that everyone who goes against the war effort in any way should pay for it with his head?*"

"I asked you," he said, eyes piercing, voice choked, "and you gave me your answers. You are part of the German *Volk* and from your mouth the will of the German people has become manifest.

"Now, Nation—arise! Storm, *break loose!*"

Two days before, on February 16, Sophie had written what was to be the last letter she sent to her friend Fritz Hartnagel. When she was writing it, she already knew he was safe; he had been wounded and evacuated on one of the last planes out of Stalingrad. She wrote in her usual vein, telling him about her life, her feelings, and events at home.

"Just a short greeting before I go to my lecture," she wrote that Tuesday in Munich.

> I think I already told you that I went home for ten days to help out. This stay, even though I didn't have much time to take care of my own affairs, was so good for me, if only because my father is so happy when I come and seems so surprised when I leave, and because my mother gets involved in a thousand small chores. This love, which asks nothing in return, is something wonderful. It is one of the most beautiful things that has ever been given to me.
>
> The 150 kilometers between Ulm and Munich change me so quickly that I am astounded at myself. I'm transformed from a harmless, easygoing child into an independent and self-reliant person. This being on my own has been good for me, even if sometimes I'm not very comfortable with it because I've really been spoiled by people. But I only feel safe, secure and warm where I sense that selfless love, and that is something so relatively rare.

February 18 was a warm, springlike day in Munich. At a little after ten in the morning, Hans and Sophie left their apartment in Schwabing and strolled toward the university. Hans was carrying a large suitcase.

They arrived at the university before eleven, while lectures were still going on. The *Lichthof*, the large inner courtyard of the university with a glass-vaulted ceiling, was empty of people. Suddenly Traute Lafrenz and Willi Graf came down the marble steps toward them; they had left a lecture early in order to get to a medical clinic in another part of town where they were both taking a course. They looked at Sophie and Hans, took in the suitcase, and probably were expecting an explanation. None was forthcoming. The four agreed to meet again in the evening.

On the streetcar, Traute told Willi she had a "strange feeling." Willi only shrugged his shoulders, but she knew he was concerned too. During the lecture at the clinic, he seemed nervous and didn't doze off.

After their friends had left the *Lichthof*, Hans and Sophie opened the suitcase. They took out batches of the leaflets written by Kurt Huber and placed them in front of the doors of lecture halls, on windowsills, and on the vast stairways leading from the classrooms down to the main floor. They deposited about 700 to 1,800—estimates vary. When they finished, classes had not yet ended and they decided to leave the building.

They looked inside the suitcase and saw they still had some leaflets left. They went up the stairs to the upper floor beneath the vaulted ceiling, and there, from the balustrade, scattered the remaining leaflets down into the *Lichthof*.

At that moment two things happened: a middle-aged building custodian named Jakob Schmid was suddenly standing beneath them, shouting up, "*You're under arrest!*" and, at the same time, the lecture doors were flung open and students began pouring out. The bellowing sound of Jakob Schmid's voice must have echoed through the vast vaulted chamber. Hans and Sophie ran down the stairs, clattering along with the other students, hoping to get lost in the crowd. But Schmid was dogged and determined; a good and loyal member of the SA and the Party, this was his chance.

Jakob Schmid caught up with the young man and woman. He shouted again, "*You're under arrest!*" They stopped running and stood quietly; everything about them seemed to stop, to go limp, to be drained out.

As the horror-stricken students watched, Hans and Sophie were led without protest to Rector Wüst's office.

By now an alert had been sounded and all the exits of the university on both sides were locked. Students and faculty milled anxiously around in the great lobby, some reading leaflets, others looking nervously away; Kurt Huber was among them.

Robert Mohr's Gestapo team was summoned from the Wittelsbach Palace; at last there seemed to be a breakthrough in the leaflet mystery.

When he arrived, the young man and woman made an extremely relaxed impression. He was dubious that they were the culprits. He ordered Gestapo agents down into the lobby to collect all the leaflets; he then asked the two suspects for their identity papers. They handed them over to him, showing no signs of nervousness. The papers were in order.

He looked them over, this calm and quiet brother and sister; they didn't resemble each other very much, except both had dark hair and eyes. He realized that they were clean-cut young students, obviously from a good middle-class family. The notion that they were performing subversive acts he found inconceivable; the *Pedell* (custodian) had obviously made a mistake. He asked them why they were carrying an empty suitcase. They answered easily: they were on their way home to Ulm, had decided to leave a day earlier than usual. But why an empty suitcase? They were going to bring fresh clothes and laundry back to Munich.

Mohr was uncertain what to do; he was almost convinced of their innocence. Then, instantly, the situation changed. Mohr's men had gathered up all the leaflets from the students in the lobby and those still scattered around the corridors. They brought them up to the rector's office and were now putting the last of them into the suitcase. They fit perfectly.

Mohr gave the order to take Hans and Sophie to Gestapo headquarters; at that moment Hans pulled a piece of paper from his pocket, ripped it up into bits, and tried to stuff it down his mouth. They fell on him, and retrieved the fragments, piece by piece; it was the draft for a leaflet that Christoph Probst had written about peace a few days before.

Hans remained cool in spite of what had happened. It was a piece of paper, he said, given to him by a student he did not know; he hadn't even read it, he didn't know its contents, but felt it might in some way incriminate him.

Hans and Sophie were handcuffed and taken through the milling crowd to an unmarked car outside the entrance of the university. They looked neither right nor left; there were people in that crowd who were their friends; they would not endanger them.

Standing in the throng outside the university was Alexander Schmorell. He watched as the Gestapo took Hans and Sophie away. An escape plan had been devised by the group, and now Alex tried to put it into effect. He went immediately to Willi Graf's room; no one was there, but he left a cryptic message warning Willi. He hoped his friend could get it in time and meet Alex the next day at the Starnberger Bahnhof, a small railroad station adjacent to the Munich Central Station, from which trains went south into the alpine regions of Bavaria.

He had to kill the day somehow; he thought frantically about where in Munich he could hide safely. He called his parents. His mother answered the phone. She said quickly, "Alex! The police are here." He hung up.

In the confusion and terror, he suddenly came on the thought of his friend Lilo Ramdohr. He could trust her, and, most important, she had no direct connection with the White Rose. He would go to her and stay in her flat overnight.

Willi Graf spent the entire day at the university clinic; he had heard nothing about the arrests. He went home, with plans to meet Hans and Sophie that evening. At six-thirty, he entered his apartment on Mandlstrasse; the Gestapo was waiting. He and his sister Anneliese were taken to the Wittelsbach Palace.

Robert Mohr chose Sophie Scholl for personal interrogation and handed Hans over to another agent, Anton Mahler. Mohr was intrigued by this young, innocent-looking woman who seemed utterly unintimidated as she stood in the midst of Gestapo officials in a building of barred windows and doors. He was still not convinced of Hans's and Sophie's guilt, still debating with himself about letting them take their suitcase and go off to Ulm.

The interrogation of the brother and sister went on for seventeen hours—in separate chambers. The Gestapo learned nothing. At first the students denied any involvement, and repeated again and again that they knew no one who was engaged in such an operation. They would not budge from that position.

Then the report on the second search of the rooms at Franz-Joseph-Strasse was brought in—and the house of cards collapsed. The Gestapo had found a large batch of eight-pfennig stamps, the stamps used for mailing printed matter. And, much more devastating, they had found a letter to Hans in Christoph's handwriting: it matched the handwriting on the sheet of paper Hans had tried to destroy.

Christoph, in Innsbruck, unaware of what was happening, was in the gravest peril.

Without having the chance to consult each other, and after interrogation that continued all day Thursday and through the night into Friday, Hans and Sophie finally confessed. Both said, as had been part of the group's last option plan, that they, and only they, were responsible for the White Rose actions. They did not once deviate from this position.

When they were taken to their cells after this nonstop inquisition, they collapsed on their bunks. They were given "honorary cells," which had a barred window, a toilet, and even white sheets on the bed, but the ceiling light burned day and night, a sign that they were candidates for death. Each shared the cell with another inmate, whose main duty was to prevent any attempt at suicide.

Sophie's cellmate was a political prisoner, a woman named Else Gebel who did clerical work in Gestapo headquarters during the day and was locked up at night. Else marveled at Sophie's unruffled calm; she could not believe that this innocent girl was in any way associated with "conspiracy" and "high treason."

Before Sophie fell into her bed that Friday morning, she told Else briefly that she had not broken under cross-examination; she had made no slips, had given no names; only she and her brother were implicated—and right now that was enough of a triumph.

About the same time on Friday, the Gestapo appeared at the Bergmann School where the medic-students were stationed. Alex had not shown up for roll call. An alert was put out: a poster with his picture and description, with a banner across saying "Criminal Wanted—1000 RM Reward" was printed and circulated all over South Germany.

Alex had managed to arrive at Lilo's without difficulty; she put him up overnight as he had expected. She had been a great support to him for months lately; she had contacted Falk Harnack for him, she had stored some of his leaflets and other materials in her flat, and had even contributed some money to the White Rose venture. But she had remained apart from the group; her relationship with Alex was a private matter; when the pressure built to the point of explosion, he could flee to Lilo and his art.

Now she came to his aid again. She was able to get hold of a Yugoslav passport and had the photo replaced with one of Alex; with a trusted neighbor who was a printer, she forged travel papers. Alex's tentative plan was to flee to Switzerland. First he would temporarily disappear into a Russian POW camp near Innsbruck; later, when the atmosphere had cooled down, he would take the mountain passes through the Alps that he knew so well and reach the Swiss frontier.

On Friday, February 19, Alex and Lilo went to the Starnberger Bahnhof to meet Willi Graf. Lilo waited outside the station while Alex went in to look for Willi. After a short while Alex came out—alone. They left the area immediately; the tension was remounting. Alex told Lilo that Willi had not been there and that the station was swarming with Gestapo and police; papers and train tickets were all being checked.

As he always did on Fridays, Christoph Probst reported to the unit cashier for his weekly pay. He was on his way to see his wife, who was still in the hospital several weeks after the baby was born. Instead of getting his pay envelope, he was told to report to his superior.

When he walked into the office, the door was shut by someone behind him. Two Gestapo agents were standing in the room with his suitcase. They ordered him to take off his air-force uniform and put on civilian clothes. He was handcuffed, then pushed out the door and into a car that sped off in the direction of Munich.

It happened so fast and unexpectedly that he probably couldn't grasp the reality of it. But one menacing sign he surely recognized as a soldier: in civilian clothes he was no longer under the comparatively benign protection of the military; he had been delivered into the hands of the Gestapo.

In her cell, Sophie Scholl was told by Else Gebel that someone else in their group had been arrested. Sophie already knew that Willi Graf had been taken and was in a cell one floor above—through Else she had smuggled him a cigarette with the word "freedom" scribbled on it. Now she thought they had caught Alex. She became slightly nervous and distraught; Else promised to check out the name of the new prisoner.

When she came back later after her office work, Else told Sophie: "It's Christoph Probst."

Sophie broke down—for the first and last time. Christel: father of three babies, his wife ill, his whole world revolving around his young and growing family in the quiet village. They had all tried to keep him away from the peril; he had done almost nothing that could be called treason.

Slowly, she calmed down; she was sure he would get a relatively mild sentence; he had done nothing; and if he were imprisoned, he would be liberated as soon as the Allies invaded—a matter of maybe eight weeks. Her calm, her inner repose, seemed to return.

Friday evening Lilo went back to the Starnberger Bahnhof to reconnoiter; at home Alex was changing to a new set of clothes not described on the man-wanted poster. Lilo came back disconsolate: there was no way to get through, the police control points were still in place. Alex decided that on Saturday morning, regardless of the checkpoints, he would get on a train to Innsbruck. He had to get out of Munich.

All day Saturday the interrogations went on at the Wittelsbach Palace. Robert Mohr tried to persuade Sophie to confess her sins and declare herself for National Socialism. "I tried with all the powers of persuasion I knew," he later wrote, "to explain to her that she was not ideologically in rapport with her brother, that she had relied on him and followed him without thinking of the consequences of her actions. Sophie Scholl saw right away what I was trying to do, and decisively rejected any such assertion. This would have been in fact the only way to save her life."

She retorted that she was not led by her brother, and that she indeed knew the consequences of her acts. Mohr tried to explain the National Socialist "worldview" to her, to show her what Adolf Hitler had accomplished.

She replied: "You're wrong. I would do it all over again—because I'm not wrong. *You* have the wrong worldview."

At this point Mohr broke off the interrogation and sent her back to the cell. To her surprise, Else Gebel had prepared a small feast for her: tea, a few sausages, bread, butter, cookies, and cigarettes—all of which had been donated by prisoners and guards.

They celebrated the moment—the food, the sense of concern and solidarity that seemed to emanate from every cell and chamber.

Sophie was able to relax and even to smile; she arranged to have some of the food smuggled up to Hans.

Alex did manage to get to Innsbruck Saturday morning. When he arrived, he called a Ukrainian woman in Munich who had contacts with the Russian head of the Soviet POW camp nearby. The woman agreed to make the journey to Innsbruck and meet him. The pressure must have eased up a bit: if he could go underground in the camp, he still had a good chance.

He waited at the Innsbruck station for the Munich train. It arrived, but the woman did not appear. He stood there, alone, desperate, trying to work out a new escape route.

On Sunday morning, Sophie was summoned from her cell to receive the official indictment against her by the People's Court, Berlin. The Scholls and Christoph Probst were all accused of high treason. She returned to her cell, read the document carefully, and her hands began to shake.

She walked over to the barred window; it was an unseasonably warm day, filled with the scents and sounds of spring. People outside, dressed in their Sunday best, were strolling by, enjoying the weather. The sunlight poured into the cell. "Such a beautiful sunny day," she said softly, "and I have to go. . . ."

Again she pulled herself together, reasoned with herself, talked to herself. "How many are dying on the battlefields, how many young lives full of hope . . . what difference does my death make if our actions arouse thousands of people? The students will definitely rise up."

She turned to Else Gebel then and talked about her mother, the deepest concern she still had. How would her mother take it—two children lost at once, and another fighting in Russia. It would be unbearable for her. Her father would suffer but he would understand.

The crisis was over; her hands stopped shaking. She had accepted what would come.

From Innsbruck, Alex managed to get to Mittenwald, a familiar town from his mountain treks and skiing trips. Some time before, he had struck up a friendship with a Russian coachman who worked at Schloss Elmau, a castle turned into a health resort on the outskirts of town. He was in luck; the coachman agreed to hide him, although the man-wanted posters were now up on shop windows and in post offices in the smallest villages.

He was stopped by two local policemen who asked to see his identity papers. They looked at the Slavic name on the pass, scrutinized Alex for a moment—and let him go.

Luck had stayed with him twice. Now, if he could lie low and furtively organize the trek through the mountain passes, there was a chance he could make it.

The court-appointed defense attorney reluctantly visited Hans and Sophie in their cells. His visit was perfunctory; he was doing his duty. The trial was set for the next day, Monday, February 22, at Munich's Palace of Justice. It was to be no ordinary criminal procedure: it was under the jurisdiction of the People's Court, Berlin. That very name, and that of its presiding judge, Roland Freisler, were enough to strike terror in the hearts of even the most apathetic and uninvolved citizens. The name Freisler in a courtroom meant abuse, degradation, and death. Later, after the failure of the military plot to kill Hitler in July 1944, it was Freisler in his People's Court who mocked and abused the generals, colonels, and high government officials who had participated in the planning; most of them were subsequently executed, like the Rote Kapelle two years before, by strangulation on meat hooks. Secret films were made of Freisler's frenzied shrieking at the accused during the trials and were shown to the Führer nightly.

Whatever Sophie knew about the People's Court, she managed to react calmly, telling the lawyer that she was as responsible for the so-called crimes as her brother was, and that she expected to receive the same sentence he did. She asked if Hans had the right to execution by firing squad since he was in the army and had been at the front, thus deserving that "honor."

The lawyer was taken aback by the coolness of the question: he evaded answering. Her next query astounded him even more: she wanted to know if she would be hanged or beheaded.

Shaken by her bluntness, he withdrew as quickly as possible.

It was getting close to the end. Robert Mohr came by and suggested that the prisoners write letters to their parents.

The letters were short; they thanked their parents for the love and warmth they had given their children all their lives, and asked forgiveness for the pain and despair they were causing. They said that they could not have acted otherwise, and were sure their parents would understand, and that the future would justify their actions.

Christel wrote to his mother:

> Please do not be frightened by the fact that I did not come to you as planned last Saturday, nor be frightened by the events I must now relate. Instead of getting my usual pass last Saturday, I was arrested and brought to Munich. Through an unfortunate development I have been brought here to the Gestapo prison. Please don't think I am exaggerating when I say things could not be better with me. The treatment is good and life here in this cell seems so pleasing to me that I have no particular anxiety about being here a long time. . . .
>
> Your love is more precious than ever. Oh, that I'm causing you such anxiety! . . . The whole thing is so much bound up with our destiny that I beg you not to reproach me for being irresponsible. You all know—mother, sister, wife and children—that I live only for you. . . . I can't express how much I have felt your love, how much your love has helped my little Vincent, . . . little Herta. . . .
>
> And even if something may destroy me, I hope that these gentle and guiltless creatures may live; I cannot imagine that they should suffer. How things will turn out, I don't know. I only know that nothing is too difficult for us to endure.
>
> All good wishes to Heinz! Oh mother! You have endured so much with Herta and now I'm the unlucky one. But we do know that mothers are more important for the children than the father.
>
> I don't feel separated from you. I feel you are close by me, my own dear mother. I embrace you and remain, always, your son, Christel.

Sophie also wrote to Inge and asked her to send her last greetings to Carl Muth, and to express her deep and undying admiration for him. The last letter she wrote was to Fritz Hartnagel somewhere in Russia.

The Gestapo never sent any of these letters, but by one of those capricious quirks so common in a totalitarian state, Christoph Probst's letters to his mother and sister Angelika did survive, at least long enough to be read by the recipients in the presence of Gestapo officials after Christoph's death. The family was not allowed to take the letters with them. But Christoph's mother would never forget the words: "I thank you that you gave me life. When I think about it, it was the only way to God. Don't be sad that I sprang over part of it. Soon I'll be much closer to you than ever. I'll prepare all of you a glorious reception. . . ." He wrote Angelika: "I am dying without any hate. . . ."

The lights burned all night in their cells.

NINETEEN

ON FRIDAY, the day after the arrest, the Scholl family in Ulm got the terrible news. They were called by three friends, Traute Lafrenz, Otl Aicher, and Jürgen Wittenstein; there was no question about how disastrous the situation was. By chance, Werner, the youngest child, had gotten leave from the front and was at home with his parents. The family found out that no visitors were permitted in Gestapo headquarters over the weekend; they had to endure Saturday and Sunday at home in Ulm. They planned to leave early Monday morning for Munich.

At 7:00 AM, Monday, February 22, the three inmates were taken from their cells. Else Gebel could barely control herself as she said good-bye to Sophie, who remained calm. Later Else returned to the desolate cell to collect her things: a sheet of paper was lying on Sophie's neatly made bed: it was the official indictment. On the back, Sophie had written one word: "Freedom!"

On the bare white wall of Hans's cell they found some words scrawled in pencil: *Allen Gewalten zum Trotz sich erhalten*—"Despite all the powers closing in, hold yourself up," his father's favorite citation from Goethe.

About nine o'clock, Gestapo officials took the three prisoners to the Palace of Justice, a huge and intimidating gray edifice located several blocks from the Munich Central Station.

That a trial was held so quickly after capture and interrogation was truly an exceptional occurrence; the event was no local affair. Heinrich Himmler himself, in Berlin, had made the decisions on how the proceedings would play out. The primary goal now was to warn all students to keep away from the fires of resistance; various options on how to demonstrate this brutally and dramatically had been considered. The Munich gauleiter wanted the three students hanged publicly on the Marienplatz, the central square of Munich. Another idea was to hang them in front of their university. Himmler rejected both proposals, noting that public executions might be provocative and lead to further demonstrations. Executions would take place—but secretly and quickly.

The trial, held by the People's Court, was to follow all procedures of law, but the outcome was never in doubt.

The courtroom was packed, with invited guests only, almost all in brown or black uniforms. No family members of the accused were present; they had not been officially informed about the arrests or the trial.

The presiding judge, Roland Freisler, came out in a brilliant whirl of scarlet robes. Other judges took their seats at a long panel on either side of Freisler; these assistant judges represented the Bavarian Ministry of Justice, the SS, and the SA. Behind them on the wall hung a portrait of Adolf Hitler.

Roland Freisler has gone down in the unsavory history of the Third Reich as one of the most repellent figures in the constellations of power. His background is odd, and it is difficult to conclude whether his ideological zigzags were completely opportunistic or if they were motivated at least partially by the wild swings in conviction often associated with the true believer. As a young man, Freisler had been a prisoner of war in Russia during the First World War. There he had learned fluent Russian and became, apparently, a devout Bolshevik. He returned to Germany after the war ended, and in 1925 he suddenly emerged as a dedicated, fanatic National Socialist. He remained a great admirer of Stalinist techniques of terror, however, and studied Andrei Vishinsky's tactics as prosecuting attorney at the Moscow purge trials in the 1930s. Hitler called Freisler "our Vishinsky," but he was wrong. Freisler never brought the accused conspirators—generals, students, professors, lawyers—to their knees; they never confessed their "guilt," they did not beg to be reintegrated into the *Volk* community. In Nazi Germany, "rehabilitation" did not precede execution. By Vishinsky's standards, the Freisler techniques were a brutal failure.

On that Monday morning, the three accused students sat at the side of the chamber, each flanked by two guards. They looked wan, shrunken, exhausted, but sat upright in their chairs.

At 10:00 AM the trial opened. Hans and Sophie Scholl and Christoph Probst were officially accused of aiding and abetting the enemy and committing acts of high treason. The prosecution demanded death.

It seemed impossible to believe the string of charges, oaths, attacks, and insults that Freisler now unleashed against them. He seemed out of control; it was his style since he had become so notorious as Hitler's hanging judge. He seemed to revel in a kind of dementia that was turned off and on again without warning. The chamber was filled with silence and terror; this crazed man in dazzling red could do precisely as he wished—and they all knew it.

He shrieked, he screamed, he made wild and billowing gestures with his robed arms; the attorneys for the state and for the accused were rendered mute. The evidence was brought in: the leaflets, the duplicating machine, the paint and stencils for the wall graffiti. Three witnesses for the prosecution were ready and waiting to be called: Gestapo interrogators Mohr and Mahler, as well as the hero of the day, the custodian Jakob Schmid, who had already received a 3,000-reichsmark reward and a promotion in the university service.

But witnesses were not called: there was no need to; the three accused had already confessed. Freisler simply went on with his tirade. On several occasions a young voice broke in to contradict him: it was, astonishingly, the voice of Sophie Scholl. "Somebody had to make a start," she called out. "What we said and wrote are what many people are thinking. They just don't dare say it out loud!"

This induced more shrieks from the raised platform in front of the courtroom.

Finally the proceedings were drawing to an end. Each prisoner, in conformity now with trial procedure, was permitted to make a final statement. Sophie and Hans chose to remain silent.

Christoph Probst rose and stood at the dock. He tried to explain that what he had done was done in the interest of his country. His only desire was to end the bloodshed and to spare Germany the agony of new Stalingrads. The spectators shouted their outrage at him; from all sides insults and abuse descended upon him. Freisler interjected a remark about Christoph's proposal to turn to President Roosevelt; just that name brought on another screaming tantrum. Christoph stood quietly, looking straight ahead until the tumult died down.

Then he asked for clemency, for his life, for the sake of his sick wife and three small children.

These words were greeted by a stony silence. Suddenly Hans Scholl spoke up: he said Christoph had virtually nothing to do with the leaflet campaign, and he should be treated with leniency.

Freisler snapped at him: "If you have nothing to say for yourself, then kindly keep your mouth shut!"

It was time for the verdict to be decided upon. Suddenly there was a rushing movement at the entrance to the chamber, the sound of raised voices, shouts, confusion.

Robert and Magdalena Scholl had arrived with Werner. They had taken the early train from Ulm, only to be met at the station by a desperate Jürgen Wittenstein, who told them that the trial was already under way.

Mrs. Scholl looked at Jürgen's face and said, "Will they have to die?"

Jürgen nodded, about to weep. "If I had just one tank," he cried, "I'd get them out. Then I'd blow up the court and take them to the border!"

They all ran down the long street leading to the Palace of Justice.

Robert Scholl forced his way by the guards at the door and pushed forward down the aisle, the other members of the family following in his wake. Somehow he managed to get to his children's defense attorney. He whispered harshly in the lawyer's ear: "Go to the president of the court and tell him that the father is here and he wants to defend his children!"

The lawyer was stunned and followed Mr. Scholl's instructions. The courtroom was buzzing with curiosity and confusion. Freisler seemed perplexed; he was waiting for an explanation.

The defense attorney made his way to the platform. He whispered Scholl's request in Freisler's ear.

The judge made a dramatic and wide gesture of rejection, shrieking at the top of his lungs, and then, pointing at Robert Scholl, ordered that he be removed from court. Guards surrounded the family and hauled them out. Mrs. Scholl collapsed for a moment, but managed to revive herself.

Robert Scholl roared: "There is a higher justice!" and just as the doors were closing, he added, "They will go down in history!"

The family—Mr. and Mrs. Scholl and Werner—were left standing alone in the open-air corridor outside the courtroom.

Soon the spectators came streaming out of the chamber; Freisler and his colleagues had withdrawn to decide upon the verdicts. The Scholls sat on a bench, waiting; the others acted as if they were invisible—except for one young law student: Leo Samberger. He had received White Rose leaflets in the mail, was able to get into the courtroom, and had watched the proceedings with growing horror. He walked over to the family, introduced himself, and suggested that they put in a plea for clemency immediately, that it was the only option left.

The crowd outside was returning to hear the verdict. The Scholls waited. A few minutes later the doors were opened. The family saw it on all the faces: their children were sentenced to death.

Hans had made no statement in his own defense; but when Freisler announced the death sentence, he had called out, "You will soon stand where we stand now!" He was handcuffed, along with Sophie and Christoph, and escorted out of the courtroom. In the throng, Werner Scholl, who was in uniform, was able to push through. He shook hands with them, tears filling his eyes. Hans was able to reach out and touch him, saying quickly, "Stay strong, no compromises."

The condemned were put into a paddy wagon and taken to Stadelheim Prison, where most executions in the Munich area took place. Everything was moving fast, too fast to be comprehended.

With Leo Samberger, the Scholls ran to the state attorney's office and entered a clemency plea for their children and for Christoph. They found out where the prisoners were taken; the family made its way out to Stadelheim as quickly as possible; Munich was a city they did not know.

Somehow Robert Scholl was able to talk his way into the prison, along with his family. It was perhaps the first and last exception ever made at Stadelheim: the condemned were not allowed to receive visitors. Apparently the word had gone round the prison about how the young students had conducted themselves in Gestapo hands and at the infamous trial. The prison staff admired them; workers at the facility were not members of the SS or in the Gestapo; they considered themselves "normal civil servants" who performed their unpleasant duties no matter which regime happened to be in power.

Considering what the personnel at Stadelheim had seen and done over the years, it is a near-miracle that the White Rose were able to touch them. The guards broke the rules: they brought Hans out to see his family in a reception room. They had already made him change into the striped uniform of a convict; his face was gaunt and small. He shook hands all around over the barricade, and reassured his parents that he had no feelings of hate, that "all of that" was behind him. His father put his arms around him, saying he would go down in history and that there was justice in the world.

As Hans was about to be taken away, he sent greetings to his friends. As he uttered one name, tears rushed to his eyes. He turned away, trying to control himself.

He let the guards take him away.

Then they brought in Sophie. She was still wearing her own clothes—a jacket, blouse, and skirt. She smiled at the visitors. She seemed smaller, but her skin was fresh and clear. She accepted the sweets her mother had brought—Hans had refused them—saying yes, she was hungry, she hadn't had any lunch.

"Sophie, Sophie," Mrs. Scholl said, "you'll never come in that door again."

"Oh mother," she answered, still smiling, "what are those few years anyway?"

"Sophie . . . remember, Jesus," her mother said.

"Yes, but you too," she replied. She was taken away.

Robert Mohr found her weeping in the reception cell.

Christoph Probst had gradually become a believing Catholic. He had never been baptized, and now, in his death cell, he asked to see a priest. When the father arrived, they spoke awhile and prayed together, then they kneeled down before a small table that served as an altar. Christoph Probst received his first communion and last rites.

Hans and Sophie prayed with the Protestant chaplain, reading some of their favorite psalms in their cells. They both took communion.

Suddenly the doors of their cells were opened. They were hand-cuffed and taken out. In a hallway, near a door that led into the court-yard, they found themselves standing together, with no guard between them. Again the rules were broken: "Here, have a cigarette together," someone murmured.

They stood and smoked silently. Then Christoph said, "I didn't know that death could be so easy."

The door to the courtyard opened. Across the way was a small building with the guillotine. Sophie was the first to go. She walked erectly across the yard, escorted by the guards. She entered the building. It was five o'clock in the afternoon, three hours after the trial had ended. There was a heavy sound. It was over.

When it was Hans's turn, he walked quickly across the yard, and before he went over the threshold, he turned and shouted so that his voice could carry to all the barred windows around: "Long live freedom!"

TWENTY

T HE WEATHER continued to be balmy in Munich during most of February, filled with the scents of spring. But in the alpine regions to the south, heavy storms were blowing up.

Alex had no choice; someone in Mittenwald had recognized him and reported him to the police; he had to leave immediately. He made his way along a path in the mountains that was fast disappearing from under his feet. He did not have boots or adequate clothing, his provisions were giving out. In front of him lay a white wall of blindness. He went on for some hours, then realized it was no use. He had no strength left, no one to turn to.

He turned back; he saw no other way. He would return to Munich.

The Scholls had gone back to Ulm Monday evening, thinking their children were alive. They planned the appeal process, which they hoped could hold up the execution for months.

On Tuesday the news of the executions was made public on placards posted around the city and the university, and in special notices in the Munich press. The citizenry was informed that three students had been tried and executed the same day for high treason; they were characterized as *Einzelgänger*, outsiders and troublemakers who had defied "the spirit of the German people in a shameless manner."

Wednesday, February 24, was the anniversary of the founding of the National Socialist party. To mark that occasion—but surely also with the White Rose in mind—the Führer himself sent a proclamation to Munich, "the Capital of the Movement." Loyal Party members were exhorted to remain steadfast despite attacks, and to strengthen German resolve by ruthlessly annihilating saboteurs. "The Party has to break terror with tenfold terror," Hitler's message shrieked. "It has to extinguish the traitors—whoever they are, whatever their disguise." Apparently traitors even hid among the privileged middle-class students at the university, who in the majority were normally apolitical. To make sure they stayed that way, examples had to be made.

On February 27, Propaganda Minister Goebbels demanded that hostile university students be subjected to the free use of corporal punishment.

Gone was the heady feeling of solidarity and freedom among the students. It was as if the uprising had never happened. A special rally to demonstrate loyalty to State and Führer was held in the Auditorium Maximum, where Kurt Huber had given so many of his lectures. Hundreds of students attended to give vent to their "indignation" against the traitors who had lived in their midst. They stood up and gave a resounding ovation to the man who had saved the university from infamy and revolution, the *Pedell*, the custodian Jakob Schmid. He rose, bowed, and held his arms out wide to receive the tumultuous applause.

Not every student reacted this way. For a few days after the execution of Hans, Sophie, and Christoph, new graffiti appeared on the walls of the university: "Scholl lives! You can break the body, but never the spirit!" And on Adolf Hitler's birthday, April 20, the day after the remaining White Rose members had been tried, Hitler's portrait at the university was discovered with the added inscription "Germany's Enemy Number One." The graffito was removed immediately, but appeared again the next day, this time painted in oil.

These were the isolated and lonely responses of the few, disheartened but moved to act in whatever small way they dared. Lisa Grote, who was a student at that time, recalled later: "There had been twenty or so leaflets in our mailbox in Schwabing. I gave them out on walks through town. When the Scholls were killed, our courage was broken. I lost many other young friends, as decent and innocent as that brother and sister. But it never cut that deep again. Because of the guilt feeling—that one didn't run out screaming into the streets."

For the remaining members and friends of the White Rose— those already in prison, like Willi Graf, and those not yet taken—a terrible time of waiting had begun. One by one, they were plucked from their homes by the Gestapo and interrogated, sometimes for hours, often for days and weeks; the stain of incrimination spread from Munich to cities all over South Germany. Traute Lafrenz, Gisela Schertling, and Katharina Schüddekopf were among those in the early wave, then came the Ulm high-school student Hans Hirzel and his sister Susanne, as well as their friends Franz Müller and Heinrich Guter. In Stuttgart, Eugen Grimminger was arrested, and in Freiburg, so was Willi's university contact, Heinz Bollinger.

The waves spread even wider; the cells in the Wittelsbach Palace were filled to capacity.

On the evening of the Führer's proclamation to Munich, February 24, two days after the executions and nearly a week since the initial arrests, the RAF unleashed a furious bombing raid on the city of Munich.

A young woman named Marie-Luise was in a bunker near her apartment house, huddled together with other women. The raid seemed to be almost directly over Schwabing, in the area where she lived. She was in an advanced state of pregnancy, and like the other women in the bunker, was in an extremely agitated state.

Suddenly the bunker door opened and Alexander Schmorell walked in. He was exhausted, panting, barely able to stand. He called out, "Marie-Luise?" She had been a former girlfriend of his, and about the only one left in Munich who was not in any way connected with his activities. When he arrived at the Central Station, the attack had started, and he made his way to Marie-Luise's flat on Habsburgerplatz.

The young woman screamed: "*Shurik!*" All her neighbors stared at him with slowly dawning horror, as if he were a specter, a leper.

"Marie-Luise," he said in a weak voice, "please come out here for a moment. I have to talk to you." He stayed in the small anteroom of the bunker.

She didn't move, riveted to her seat, her face stricken with fear. She didn't answer him. Instead, she turned to her neighbors and whispered something. Alex sat down on a bench and waited. The whispering became intense. The women were telling Marie-Luise that there was only one thing to do in order to protect themselves: to call the block warden and have him arrest Alex.

He sat, waiting, perhaps catching fragments of their frantic whispers between the whistling fury of the bombs. He could not move. For seven days and nights, he had run like a hunted hare to keep his freedom. He had given his all; he had no strength left.

When the all-clear sounded, the women summoned the building superintendent, who informed Alex that he was under arrest. He did not resist. A few minutes later, a Gestapo car was in front of the house.

It is not known if the 1,000-mark reward was collected.

In Berlin the next day, Thursday, February 25, Falk Harnack waited for Hans Scholl at the Kaiser Wilhelm Memorial Church. It was to be the beginning of a new phase of national resistance, the linking up of students with the officers, government officials, and theologians of the Confessing Church, most of whom, more than a year later, would be involved in the July 20 plot to kill Adolf Hitler.

The meeting never took place. Harnack went back to his unit at Chemnitz on February 27. There he found a letter from Lilo Ramdohr. It said simply: "Our friends on the front have fallen." He knew it was a matter of days before the Gestapo would come for him.

Waiting at dawn for the knock at the door—that image has become a symbol; it expresses the texture of fear in the Third Reich for those who did not belong to the *Volksgemeinschaft:* the Jewish people and the dissidents who had crossed the line. Waiting—each day and each night, knowing that the knock would come and that there would be no mercy.

A Social Democrat named Eugen Nerdinger from Augsburg was involved in a clandestine group; he tried to articulate what it felt like in a poem published recently in a collection of the memoirs of unknown resistance-fighters. Here is a translation:

> *You sit in bed, listen to the night.*
> *How many such nights have you waited,*
> *Have you asked into the unknown:*
> *Will they come today to get me?*
> *The way, morning after morning, they came for them,*
> *Those who were your friends.*
> *The morning becomes gray, you look at your room,*
> *You see the light beyond the drapes,*
> *You know that your mother close by is awake*
> *Like you and asks like you,*

Will they come today to get me?
The house is still, no sound of life,
Only you and she are restless.
Will they come today to get me?
Still is the street, the lamps are pale.
Far away the clocks strike.
Will they come today to get me?
The neighbors sleep.
They won't stir
When they come and get you.
The stillness screams, can't be endured.
When will you finally take her and me?
A car stops, footsteps in the yard.
A knock, noise on the stairs.
They're here now.

For Kurt Huber, this time of waiting must have been agonizing. He probably had little hope that his name would not come up in the Gestapo interrogations of his students. He had been in the *Lichthof* when Hans and Sophie were seized; he must have seen that the leaflet they were distributing was his own. He followed the news of their trial, their execution; he came home and burned papers and documents, got rid of books. He knew of the wave of arrests, knew that some people, even unintentionally, were naming names. He was pale, silent, sleepless. His wife was out in the country, bartering their few precious possessions for food, and their little boy had gone along.

He lived with his daughter Birgit alone in the house, a silent ghost waiting to get through the nights and the dawn.

It was about five in the morning on Friday, February 26, that the bell rang. Birgit ran down the stairs to answer. Three men in civilian clothes were standing outside. They asked politely if her father was home. She said yes, he was sleeping. They said that didn't matter, pushed by her, and went into the house. A wave of anguish and fear went through the twelve-year-old girl; she ran by them, leaped up the stairs, tore open the door of her parents' bedroom and screamed: "Poppi, poppi, the police are here!"

Kurt Huber sat bolt upright in bed, his eyes wide-awake with terror.

They had finally come.

TWENTY-ONE

S EVERAL DAYS after the Scholl family went to Munich to bury Hans and Sophie in the cemetery near Stadelheim Prison, all of them—with the exception of Werner, who was returned to active duty—were taken into *Sippenhaft* (clan arrest). The expression, like so many others, had eased its way into the social vocabulary of the Third Reich, its shocking meaning somehow neutralized by being printed on bureaucratic forms and becoming part of the juridical and penal systems. For the authorities—and thus for the society they controlled—to arrest the parents, spouses, siblings, or children of "political criminals," with its implications that guilt is related to bloodlines, was a "normal procedure," as long as there were signed, stamped, and sealed forms in the family's file.

Again in Ulm the Gestapo was at the door, and this time all those remaining had to go. They were questioned endlessly; one agent from Munich kept talking ominously about concentration camps. Mrs. Scholl and Inge were put in solitary confinement. Inge came down with diphtheria and her mother's condition weakened each day. Finally, at the end of July 1943, the women were released.

In August, a family trial was held, and the Scholl women were at least able to see Robert Scholl again, for the first time in months. All of them were resigned to the idea of being resentenced to prison. To their surprise, the judge gave Mr. Scholl a two-year sentence, but let the women go.

Sippenhaft in Willi Graf's case meant the arrest and detention of his sister Anneliese. She was put in a cell with Christoph Probst's sister Angelika.

After the initial round-the-clock cross-examinations were over at the Wittelsbach Palace, Willi Graf was taken to another Munich prison, Neudeck. During one of the exercise rounds in the yard when political prisoners were given their airing, Willi got a chance to speak briefly to Franz Müller, the Ulm high-school student who had helped Sophie Scholl and Hans Hirzel print and circulate leaflets.

Afterward, they found themselves in the same cellblock; it soon became obvious that regardless of what had been done to him, Willi's spirit had not been broken. In a few mumbled words the two young men considered a breakout; they had even gotten so far one day, as they stood in line at the water tap, to plan how to overwhelm the guards. But then Willi was abruptly transferred to another prison.

The Schmorells were also imprisoned after their son's capture. Alex, when he was betrayed in that cellar in Schwabing, had not known that Hans Scholl was already executed. The group as a whole had agreed, a long time before, that if any one of them was captured, he would take full responsibility for all the White Rose actions. It was no longer necessary for Alex to do that, but unaware of the true situation, he did. He denied nothing; he refused to involve anyone else. The Gestapo kept at him day and night; brilliant lights were beamed into his eyes constantly as three voices questioned him in irregular, unpredictable patterns.

Falk Harnack, after his arrest, saw Alex being escorted down the corridor of the Wittelsbach Palace. Alex's eyes were burning holes, his face inflamed; as they passed each other, they "greeted each other mutely."

Kurt Huber, probably as an especially sadistic form of punishment for a sensitive, ailing professor, was put in a cell for some of the time with criminals, not political prisoners. He was stripped of his status as a university professor and civil servant, and his doctorate was declared null and void. This was not only a crushing humiliation for a man whose life was academic pursuits, but meant that Clara Huber and her children lost all rights to a pension and were left destitute. There is also some evidence—observations by other detainees in the case who saw Huber after interrogations—that he was physically beaten, perhaps worse.

Regardless of his condition, the professor began to work feverishly in his cell, between sessions with the Gestapo, on articles about folk music and, most important, on his book about Leibniz. The plunge into intellectual creativity was probably the only way he could have endured, and he thought—hoped—that his writings could somehow be of financial assistance to his family.

He did not know—and for some unknown reason, no one was allowed to tell him—that Clara Huber was also in *Sippenhaft*, along with his sister.

Mrs. Huber had returned from food "hamstering" in the country, to find out from her distraught daughter that her husband had been taken. She ran around the city looking for lawyers, advice, support; there was none. Friends and neighbors crossed the street to avoid her; shopkeepers she had known for years ignored her presence. She went to the university and stopped a professor who had been fairly close to Huber. He hissed at her as if she were a leper: "My God, get away from me! Nobody must see you with me!"

Unlike her husband, Clara Huber was ready when the Gestapo came; she knew in advance that she would be arrested. She had tried to bring food and toilet articles to the prison the day after her husband's arrest. The guards refused her admission, but she overheard their conversation: one of them said that she was going to be picked up too.

She came home, prepared mending, sewing, and darning that needed to be done, and got some warm clothes together. They came soon after that, and put her in a cell with Kurt's sister, across the row from Angelika Probst and Anneliese Graf; she, too, got to know Else Gebel. She was interrogated seven hours at a stretch, but she really knew very little, and fortunately the men in charge were "rather stupid" and their questions not difficult to evade. She was made to write letters to her husband as if she were at liberty, and that "all was well."

Birgit Huber was ordered by the Gestapo not to tell anyone that her parents were in prison, but that they had gone on a trip. The twelve-year-old child was watched and followed at all times.

Once, in a sudden and inexplicable act of mercy, she was permitted to visit her father—on two conditions: she was not to tell him that her mother was also imprisoned, and she was "not permitted to cry." She promised she would do as they ordered.

It was a brief interlude of controlled anguish for both of them. As she walked up the stairs to leave, he stood below, looking up at her. She turned back; his eyes were on her, watching her, drinking in her every movement, her every gesture. She knew she would never see him again.

But she didn't cry.

TWENTY-TWO

O N SUNDAY, April 18, 1943, New Yorkers and other Americans
sitting down to their Sunday breakfasts opened the *New York
Times* and read, "Nazi Slur Stirred Students' Revolt—Woman,
Brother and Another Soldier Beheaded for Issuing Anti-Nazi Tracts"
(see appendix 9). This was the first news of the White Rose to reach
the American public; despite the wartime blanketing of information,
the story had somehow been leaked, reaching Stockholm only a week
or so before. The *Times* article told of the riot over Gauleiter Giesler's
insulting remarks to female students, and reported that the day
following his speech, Munich house walls bore the inscription,
"Revenge for Stalingrad! We want our liberty back!" Kurt Huber's
leaflet was paraphrased, with its condemnation of the National
Socialist suppression of freedom of thought and speech, and its call
to German youth, in the name of liberty and honor, to establish a
new Europe.

The next day, in Munich, the second trial of the White Rose
was held. On April 19, one day before the Führer's next-to-last
birthday, a green paddy wagon wended its way to all the prisons of
Munich, picking up the fourteen men and women who would be tried.
In the van, it was almost like a reunion; some of the accused had not
seen each other since their arrest some two months before, and others
met for the first time. The van was sealed shut, but rays of sunlight and
glimpses of the city in spring came through the narrow slits. "Beautiful
Munich," Falk Harnack murmured, somewhat ironically. Kurt Huber
missed the irony, replying somberly, "Whom the gods love, they
punish."

The trial was not conducted in haste: two months of interrogations, analyses of files, and cross-references of dossiers were all laid out neatly for the prosecution and the judges. It was to be a show trial, a clean sweep of the White Rose. The three major defendants were Alexander Schmorell, Willi Graf, and Kurt Huber. All were charged with high treason.

The Palace of Justice was cordoned off by the police as the fourteen prisoners got out of the van.

Again Roland Freisler had come from Berlin, again he presided over the special Munich session of the Volksgerichtshof, the People's Court. The courtroom was packed, this time not only with brown and black uniforms; even the lord mayor of Munich was in attendance, as well as generals of the army and the Luftwaffe.

The trial started at nine in the morning and went on for fourteen hours; the defendants were given no refreshments, except for mugs of water brought to them by a kindly guard when everyone else was on a lunch break.

After the accused each took a seat between two guards, the five judges filed in, three of them in uniform. Roland Freisler, as always ablaze in scarlet, seated himself in the center of the panel of judges.

The names of the accused and the charges against them were read aloud. In addition to the main defendants, accused of aiding and abetting them in their subversive activities, were Eugen Grimminger from Stuttgart; Heinz Bollinger and Helmut Bauer, Willi's contacts in Freiburg; Hans and Susanne Hirzel from Ulm; Franz Müller and Heinrich Guter, also from Ulm; Traute Lafrenz, Gisela Schertling, and Katharina Schüddekopf, all students in Munich; and, finally, Falk Harnack. Most of the defendants were in their early twenties; two were middle-aged, and four were teenagers.

As the White Rose leaflets were read out loud to the court, an angry undertone began to swell in the spectators' ranks. Suddenly Kurt Huber's attorney, selected by Huber because of his useful connections in the Party and government, shot out of his seat, his arm raised in the German salute. "Heil Hitler!" he cried. He addressed Freisler; he said he could not serve as defense attorney in this case, he had to withdraw. As a German and as a guardian of German law, he could not tolerate listening to insults against his Führer.

Freisler was gratified. He gave his consent for the attorney to leave. The man bowed stiffly at Freisler, turned on his heel, and marched out of the courtroom—to a great round of applause.

The show was under way. Freisler ordered another attorney present to represent Kurt Huber. This lawyer protested that he didn't know the case, had not examined the evidence. Freisler waved away the objections.

Kurt Huber was visibly shaken by this turn of events. It was the second enormous blow he had received that day. A prominent academic, well-considered in Party circles because of his studies on race, was supposed to have served as his character witness, but he had notified the court he could not attend; he was "out of town."

The first major defendant to face the court was Alexander Schmorell. He tried to explain his emotional attachment to Russia and his Russian mother. "Drivel!" shouted Freisler, "and what did you do on the front?"

"I took care of the wounded as was my duty as a physician in training," Alex replied. He then explained why he could not shoot at Russians and why he had tried to refuse to take the oath to the Führer.

At first Freisler drummed on the table impatiently, and then, hearing Alex's explanation about why he felt "absolved" from the oath, he flew into a rage. "Traitor!" he screamed, pointing at the defendant. He went on shrieking and abusing him, and finally waved him away, dismissing him. Alex, haggard and pale, returned to his seat, sighing deeply.

Willi Graf was summoned to the dock. He stood tall, pale, his features closed, his blue eyes remote. Freisler, for some reason, chose not to attack the stoic, tight-lipped young man. Willi said almost nothing in his defense, but Freisler remarked with begrudging admiration that Willi "had almost gotten away with it," he had effectively evaded Gestapo questions. Freisler smiled at Willi, and then said teasingly, "But we are smarter than you after all!" He dismissed him.

Willi sat down, his eyes blank; it was as if his spirit had left the chamber.

Next came Kurt Huber. He had gotten over the shock about his defense attorney, and now, trembling slightly in all his limbs, he came forward and prepared the notes he had worked on for weeks as a defense speech. He stood erect and began to read it aloud. "I may state that the accusations do correspond to the spirit of my actions. I do not take a word back." He tried to explain his sense of responsibility as a German professor: "I see it not only as my right, but my natural duty, to share in the molding of the German destiny. . . . What I had in mind was the awakening of students, not through organizing, but through the power of the sheer word, not to arouse them to acts of violence, but to give them insights into what heavy damage has been done to our political life."

His goals were, he said, "a return to our own basic values, to a state based on legality, to a return of trust between man and man."

Throughout the speech, Freisler was demonstrating his boredom and disgust. He cut in time and again. At one point he shouted, "No political tirades!" At another, he interjected, "I don't know any Professor Huber or any Dr. Huber. I know the Defendant Huber. He doesn't have the right to be a German. He's a bum!"

Huber went on with his speech: "I am staking my life to make this warning, to plead for a return [to German values]. I demand the revival of freedom for the German people. We don't want to spend our brief lives in the chains of slavery, no matter if the chains are made from the gold of material abundance."

Then the professor's tone changed; his voice grew quieter. "I am leaving behind a broken wife and two unfortunate children in misery and grief." He looked up at the judges. "Won't you at least allow my poor family a small stipend so that they can live in a manner that fits the rank of a German professor?"

That was the nearest he came to asking for mercy. The words were greeted by a cold silence.

Kurt Huber paused, then lifted his voice again. "The inner worth of a university teacher, the open and courageous professing of his beliefs and his views on the state, cannot be taken away from him in trials of high treason." His voice was clear and rang through the chambers now.

I acted as an inner voice had me act. . . . I take the consequences upon myself as expressed in the beautiful words of Johann Gottlieb Fichte:

> And you must act, as if
> On you and your actions alone
> The fate of the German matter depends,
> And the responsibility were yours.

He turned and walked to his seat. Freisler was obviously bored; one of the other judges dozed off intermittently, but the proceedings continued. One after another, each defendant rose and had his interchange with Freisler.

It seemed like the middle of the night—it was after ten—when Freisler and the four assisting judges went to chambers to decide on the verdicts.

The tension rose in the courtroom; now all attention was focused again on Kurt Huber, Willi Graf, and Alexander Schmorell.

The judges filed back. The sentences for the three were read. Death. There was silence, then the other defendants heard their verdicts: Eugen Grimminger, ten years; Heinz Bollinger and Helmut Bauer, seven years; Hans Hirzel and Franz Müller, five years; Heinrich Guter, eighteen months; Susanne Hirzel, six months; Traute Lafrenz, Gisela Schertling, and Katharina Shüddekopf, one year each. Falk Harnack was released, Freisler explaining that his special and difficult circumstances as the "only remaining son" in the Harnack family were "extenuating."

Dizzy from hunger, tension, and exhaustion, the prisoners were herded back into the green van and taken to Stadelheim. They were giddy, puffing frantically at cigarettes; the trial was over. Kurt Huber took out photographs of his children and stared at them.

The van arrived in the prison yard. They were ordered out in groups: "Those sentenced to death, to the right side!" shouted a guard. "Those to prison, on the left!"

Harnack was ordered to follow the three men walking to death row. They walked through the long corridor; on each cell a board was posted with the notice: "Death sentence." Harnack noticed boxes outside each cell, intended to hold the condemned men's clothing. They were to sleep naked, manacled.

Harnack was ordered to go on. He grabbed Kurt Huber's hand and said desperately, "It was not in vain." He tried to reach Willi but the guards came between. Alex called out to him, "Give my best to Lilo, tell her I think about her often—"

The gate slammed shut. Harnack was left alone in his cell, with instructions to report to Gestapo headquarters the next day. He paced all night, interrupted once when the peephole was pushed back and a mouth appeared. "Death sentence?" the mouth asked.

"No," Harnack replied. "I report tomorrow to the Gestapo."

"Have fun" was the laconic reply as the peephole cover slammed back. He continued pacing, tortured with uncertainty about his own fate and about his friends in the other cellblock.

The next morning, he walked out of Stadelheim; for the moment, and maybe for a few hours, for some inexplicable reason, he was free.

Alexander Schmorell, Kurt Huber, and Willi Graf did not know, and would never find out, that on the very day they had faced the hanging judges—April 19, 1943—the remaining Jewish inhabitants of the Warsaw Ghetto rose up against the Nazi murderers. The news would have helped them stand even straighter under the onslaught of abuse and degradation they endured that day; it would have helped warm them in their cells all the days that were left to them. When the powerless and the oppressed, no matter how hopeless their situation, refuse to accept the will of their oppressors, we are all touched with grace.

TWENTY-THREE

THE THREE MEN waited in their solitary cells in Stadelheim; although they had been told by fellow inmates that each day they stayed alive was a form of victory, they had little faith in the petitions for clemency that had been filed on their behalf. The glimmers of hope were undoubtedly an even more terrible agony than waiting for death itself.

Alexander Schmorell was gradually transformed; as he sat alone in his cell, his restlessness, his need to move on from place to place, activity to activity, slowly disappeared. He became quiet, almost serene. He had accepted death.

He wrote his parents that "this difficult 'misfortune' was necessary to put me on the right road, and therefore was no misfortune at all. . . . What did I know until now about belief, about a true and deep belief, about the truth, the last and only truth, about God?"

His defense attorney, Siegfried Diesinger, unlike so many of the other lawyers, did not forget Alex after the trial ended. He visited him as often as he could in his cell, and his respect for the young man grew with each visit. When he first came, he was upset and nervous at the idea of seeing a young man on the brink of a terrible death, but Alex's serenity calmed him. The prisoner emanated an inner peace that affected the older man greatly. He told the attorney to inform his father "that I forgive Marie-Luise everything" (she was the young woman who had turned him in at the air-raid shelter). There was no rancor, no anger, no hatred left.

On Sunday, April 25, only one week since its previous report of the White Rose executions, the *New York Times* contained another article on the group. The execution of three German students, it said, "furnished the first sure sign that German morale was affected not only by the military sledgehammer blows of Germany's adversaries in the field but by the ruthless methods followed by the Nazi regime itself."

In Germany, the appeals for clemency dragged their way up to the highest echelons of the military. May passed into June, and finally word came back: "I reject all petitions for mercy." It was signed by Adolf Hitler.

July 13, 1943, was the date set for the execution of Kurt Huber and Alexander Schmorell. Willi's name was not on that announcement.

On that day, Alex was permitted to write to his parents:

> I'm going with the awareness that I followed my deepest convictions and the truth. This allows me to meet my hour of death with a conscience at peace. Think of the millions of young men who have lost their lives out in the field—their fate is the same as mine. . . . In a few hours I will be in a better life, with my mother, and I will not forget you; I will ask God to grant you solace and peace. Yours, Shurik.

The lawyer came to see Alex that afternoon, to stand by him in his last hours. Alex was calm and reassuring; he said he not only accepted death but welcomed it, that if someone, like the guard, could die in his place, he would refuse. "I'm convinced," he told the distraught attorney, "that my life has to end now, early as it seems, because I have fulfilled my life's mission. I wouldn't know what else I'd have to do on this earth."

Kurt Huber was working frantically, racing with time to complete the Leibniz book. After her release from prison, Clara Huber was allowed to visit him for ten minutes every fourteen days; she saw him four times before the execution. When the date was fixed, he sent a request to the People's Court for a "short delay" so that he could finish the last two chapters of the book. The request was turned down.

On July 13, he wrote a last letter to Clara and the children, thanking them for making his life rich and beautiful. "In front of me in the cell are the Alpine roses you sent. . . . I go in two hours into that true mountain freedom for which I've fought all my life. May the Almighty God bless you and keep you. Your loving father."

Execution was again scheduled for five in the afternoon, with Alex Schmorell going first.

As the two men readied themselves for the end, they were told there would be an unexpected delay. Several SS officers had suddenly appeared at Stadelheim, informing the personnel that they were to be present at the executions. They had been ordered to observe the procedure and see how long it took for each man to die; they were to make suggestions on how the process could be lengthened or shortened, if desired. When they were told that the execution was not by hanging but with the guillotine, they were extremely put out. To make sure their visit was not a complete waste of time, they demanded a detailed explanation about how the mechanism releasing the ax actually functioned. Until the site visit was over, there would be no execution.

Finally the officers left. The executioner was ready: at a signal, Alexander Schmorell, with his head high, walked across the courtyard to the small building.

A few minutes later, Kurt Huber appeared and began crossing the yard, his leg dragging slightly. The chaplain who was watching this agonizing walk to death thought he saw Kurt Huber slip suddenly in his prison slippers, catch himself, then faintly smile. He disappeared through the door.

After the terrible thudding sound, there was total silence. The priest, who had spent the afternoon with him, made the sign of the cross.

But it was not over for Willi Graf. The Gestapo found significance in his trips to the Rhineland and the Saar and in his efforts to recruit old comrades from the Catholic youth movement. They wanted names; Willi gave them none. For months they interrogated him daily. He was the only one left. They played with him, promising to change his verdict to hard labor if he cooperated; they made threats against his family.

Willi held on. Between sessions with the Gestapo, he read poetry and wrestled, as he always had, with "the ultimate question," the existence of a just God. He told himself that each day of agony was a day of hope; a day of life was a day of victory—a day closer to Allied liberation. The summer ended; it was fall again. Willi had been in solitary confinement for seven months. Suddenly the end came—with no warning.

On October 12, 1943, just before Willi followed his friends through the courtyard to the open door beyond, he was able to write a letter to his family.

On this day I'm leaving this life and entering eternity. What hurts me most of all is that I am causing such pain to those of you who go on living. But strength and comfort you'll find with God and that is what I am praying for till the last moment. I know that it will be harder for you than for me. I ask you, Father and Mother, from the bottom of my heart, to forgive me for the anguish and the disappointment I've brought you. I have often regretted what I've done to you, especially here in prison. Forgive me and always pray for me! Hold on to the good memories. . . . I could never say to you while alive how much I loved you, but now in the last hours I want to tell you, unfortunately only on this dry paper, that I love all of you deeply and that I have respected you. For everything that you gave me and everything you made possible for me with your care and love. Hold each other and stand together with love and trust. . . . God's blessing on us, in Him we are and we live. . . . I am, with love always,

Your Willi

The Graf family did not know of the execution that day. They found out when a letter they had sent to Willi was returned, stamped "deceased."

Today Willi Graf's grave lies in an old cemetery in the center of Saarbrücken, his hometown—perhaps by coincidence, right near the graves of Russian forced laborers.

Coincidence or not, Willi would have liked that.

THE AFTERMATH

A NOTHER TRIAL was held on the very day of Alexander Schmorell's and Kurt Huber's execution. The accused were all friends of the White Rose: Josef Söhngen, the bookstore owner; Harald Dohrn, Christoph Probst's father-in-law; Wilhelm Geyer, an Ulm artist who was temporarily staying in the Schwabing atelier just before the Scholls were arrested; and Manfred Eickemeyer, the architect whose studio had been such a vital part of the White Rose operation.

They all received three to six months in prison.

After his release, Harald Dohrn took part in "Action Freedom," a last-ditch resistance against the Nazis just before the Americans moved into Munich. Dohrn and his brother-in-law were seized by the SS and shot in the woods near Stadelheim Prison on the day the American tanks arrived. They are buried a few hundred yards away from Christoph, Hans, and Sophie.

In the fall of 1943, about the time of Willi Graf's execution, another chain of arrests took place, this time in Hamburg; the students arrested were "The Hamburg Branch of the White Rose." They had taken up the resistance that had been so brutally cut off in Munich, reprinting and circulating the White Rose leaflets in North Germany.

Hans Leipelt was one of that group, although he was studying in Munich. He was "half-Jewish," one of the students who had found sanctuary in Professor Wieland's Chemistry Institute in Munich. After Kurt Huber's execution, Leipelt had taken up a collection in Hamburg and Munich for Clara Huber and her children. Mrs. Huber never met him; the money was secretly handed over to her by a priest in her neighborhood. Leipelt's actions were reported to the Gestapo and he was arrested. After a year in prison, he was tried and sentenced to death. He was beheaded—like the White Rose, whom he had never met—at Stadelheim, on January 29, 1945.

In all, seven members of the Hamburg group were executed. One of its more active figures, Heinz Kucharski, was given a death sentence in April 1945, but by that time the Allies were deep inside of Germany; Kucharski was able to escape from a train on the way to the execution site in the last days of the war.

Fritz Hartnagel learned about the events in Munich when he received a letter in Poland from Mrs. Scholl saying that Sophie had been arrested; he managed to get permission to return to Germany. But when he telephoned from Berlin on his way to Ulm, he found only Werner at home, who told him that Sophie had been executed and the rest of the family was under arrest.

Knowing Sophie had transformed Hartnagel. After the war ended, he married her sister Elisabeth; he became a judge, an adviser to youthful conscientious objectors, and an active member of the antinuclear movement.

Robert Scholl was released from prison two years after the execution of his children; he was soon appointed mayor of the city of Ulm under the American occupation. His son Werner never came back from Russia, and his wife Magdalena, her heart strained beyond endurance, died not long after the war ended.

Eugen Grimminger, also released from prison by the Americans, found that his wife Jenny had been taken to Auschwitz and murdered there in December 1943.

Inge Scholl, who opened a progressive school founded on humanistic ideals after the war, dedicated herself to the preservation of the memory of the White Rose and, in particular, the role of her brother and sister. All of the surviving family members—Willi Graf's sister Anneliese, Clara Huber and her daughter Birgit (who became a psychologist), Alexander Schmorell's brother Erich and his wife, the Probst family, and the Hamburg White Rose survivors—strove to keep the spirit of the White Rose alive in publications, by granting interviews, and through the annual commemoration service held at the University of Munich every February 22, the anniversary of the first executions.

The plaza in front of the university's main building is named after Hans and Sophie Scholl, and the one across Ludwigstrasse is called Professor-Huber-Platz. In the university's courtyard there is a white rose carved in marble; above it, the names of those whose lives were taken.

But the status of individuals who resisted the National Socialist regime and were condemned as traitors was still ambiguous long after the war ended. The members of the White Rose were not specifically cleared until the 1980s, and some ex-Nazi judges were still serving in the court system well into the 1960s— including one of the judges who helped put the White Rose under the blade.

Roland Freisler himself was killed in an Allied bombing raid over Berlin while the People's Court was in session. Paul Giesler, the gauleiter of Munich, and his wife and children, committed suicide as the American troops approached the city. Jakob Schmid, the diligent custodian at the university, was arrested by the Americans and given a prison sentence. He immediately issued an appeal. He couldn't understand, he said, why he was being punished for doing his duty. He would have arrested anyone disturbing the orderly functioning of the university premises, and had even arrested Nazi students who had distributed leaflets and defaced walls before 1933. If he had not arrested the Scholls, he claimed, he would have gotten into trouble and lost his job. He was a poor man who had worked hard all his life to support his family, and therefore had to do his duty. He had no idea that the Gestapo would be called, nor was he aware of the reward money available, nor did he expect a promotion. Moreover, he could not understand why he was in a POW camp, while the rector of the university and other high officials were walking around free, some still holding office. His punishment, he felt, was unfair and unjust.

The name of the executioner at Stadelheim was Johann Reichardt. He had been at his job since 1924 and continued on under the Nazis; in the twelve years of the Third Reich, he had executed about three thousand political prisoners. Shortly after the war ended, he was reinstated. He was sent to the American war-crimes prison in Landsberg, where he hanged Nazis found guilty of crimes against humanity. He retired from his civil-service position somewhat later; he died quietly, a pensioner.

Clara Huber, shortly after her husband's execution, received a bill from the government for 3,000 marks—the cost of the execution, including "depreciation costs of the apparatus." She was destitute and she never paid. Her pension and Kurt Huber's rank and titles were restored under the American occupation.

Falk Harnack had escaped the executioner. A special deal had apparently been struck between Freisler and the Gestapo: Freisler would let him go free and the Gestapo would stalk him, in hopes he would make contacts with other resistance groups. Several months after his release, Harnack was transferred from Chemnitz to the front lines in Greece; heavy fighting was going on between the partisans and the Wehrmacht, which was now on the defensive. Suddenly Harnack was ordered arrested—under the personal instructions of Heinrich Himmler. He was warned by one of his superiors and was just barely able to escape. He joined the partisans and fought with them till the German collapse.

In spite of all the terrible executions, the indescribable tragedies, and the unrepented brutalities, the White Rose leaflets made their way throughout Germany and occupied Europe, bringing hope into the cells of condemned prisoners and into the last arena of humanity itself—the concentration camps. From Berlin they were also smuggled into Sweden and Switzerland, and from there were sent on to London.

News of the White Rose, and the spirit of their resistance, reached the American public as well, despite the blanket of silence and Gestapo intentions. On August 2, 1943—three weeks after Alexander Schmorell and Kurt Huber had gone under the executioner's blade, and while Willi Graf still lingered in prison, awaiting the same fate— an editorial appeared in the *New York Times* under the title "Young German Martyrs." It concluded with the following words: ". . . these Munich students, few or many, representative or otherwise, rose gloriously . . . protesting in the name of principles which Hitler thought he had killed forever. In years to come we, too, may honor [them]."

Once they reached the West, the leaflets of the White Rose were reprinted—now in the tens of thousands—and dropped from Allied aircraft over the cities of Germany.

The Gestapo summoned Clara Huber one day to the Wittelsbach Palace to reproach her for this; she hadn't known, till they told her, that Kurt Huber's leaflets were being scattered by Allied planes. She left Gestapo headquarters secretly and deeply proud; she only wished her husband could have known that his words, instead of bombs, were raining over the cities he loved.

The leaflets made people like Thomas Mann, in exile, weep with happiness. For those who read them or heard about them, inside or outside of Germany, they brought a sense of joy that is hard to express. They were testimony to the fact that there were Germans, locked inside the Third Reich's fortress of death, who still cared, who did not look away, who stood up, who fought back.

Ambassador Ulrich von Hassell, who himself would soon stand before Freisler to be reviled and sentenced to death for his complicity in the July 20, 1944 assassination attempt on Hitler, had this to say in his diary: "I have read the simple, splendid, deeply ethical national appeal which brought them to their death. . . . It is important for the future that such an appeal would have seen the light of day. . . . [They] died on the gallows, courageous and upright martyrs."

Friedrich Reck-Malleczewen, a member of the nobility soon to be executed at Dachau for failing, at age sixty, to answer a civil-defense conscription call, saved a special place for the White Rose in his diary.

> I never saw these . . . young people. In my rural isolation, I only got bits and pieces of the whole story of what they were doing, but the significance of what I heard was such I could hardly believe it. . . . They died radiant in their courage and readiness for sacrifice, and thereby attained the pinnacle of lives well lived. . . . We will all of us, someday, have to make a pilgrimage to their graves and stand before them in shame.

Ilse Aichinger, a poet, was a young woman at that time, living in Vienna; she was "half-Jewish." Later, after the war, she tried to describe her reaction when she first heard about the White Rose. One day she saw a familiar sight, a wall poster proclaiming the names of people who had been condemned to death.

"I read the names of the White Rose," she recalled.

> I had never heard of any of them. But as I read those names an inexpressible hope leaped up in me . . . and I was not the only one who felt this way. . . . This hope—which made it possible for us to go on living—was not just the hope for our survival. . . . It helped so many that still had to die: even they could die with hope. . . . It was like a secret light that expanded over the land: it was joy. I remember one day I went out on the street to meet a friend and he said: "Don't look so radiant, they'll arrest you!"

We didn't have much of a chance to survive, but that was not what it was about. It wasn't survival. It was life itself that was speaking to us through the death of the Scholls and their companions. . . . You can live without owning anything. But you can't live without having something ahead of you, ahead of you in the sense of something *inside* of you. You can't live without hope.

The impact of the White Rose cannot be measured in tyrants destroyed, regimes overthrown, justice restored. A scale with another dimension is needed, and then their significance is deeper; it goes even beyond the Third Reich, beyond Germany: if people like those who formed the White Rose can exist, believe as they believed, act as they acted, maybe it means that this weary, corrupted, and extremely endangered species we belong to has the right to survive, and to keep on trying.

APPENDIX 1: LEAFLETS

Leaflets of the White Rose

THE FIRST LEAFLET*

Nothing is so unworthy of a civilized nation as to allow itself to be "governed" without any opposition by an irresponsible clique that has yielded to basest instincts. It is certainly the case today that every honest German is ashamed of his government. Who among us has any conception of the enormous shame that we and our children will feel when eventually the veil drops from our eyes and the most horrible of crimes—crimes that eclipse all atrocities throughout history—are exposed to the full light of day? If the German people are already so corrupted and spiritually crushed that they do not raise a hand, unquestioningly trusting in the dubious legitimacy of historical order; if they surrender man's highest principle, that which raises him above all of God's creatures: his free will; if they abandon the will to take decisive action and turn the wheel of history and thus subject it to their own rational decision; if they are so devoid of all individuality, have already gone so far along the road toward becoming a spiritless and cowardly mass—then, yes, they deserve their downfall.

Goethe speaks of the Germans as a tragic people, like the Jews and the Greeks, but today they seem to be rather a spineless, weak-willed herd of hangers-on, who now—the marrow sucked out of their bones, robbed of their center of stability—are waiting to be hounded to their destruction. So it seems—but it is not so. Rather, by means of

---

* Four leaflets were produced by the White Rose Society under the heading, "Leaflets of the White Rose." The first two were written by Hans Scholl and Alexander Schmorell in or around June 1942, and two more swiftly followed, on which Christoph Probst offered advice and Jürgen Wittenstein provided editorial assistance. Work began on the second series of leaflets, called "Leaflets of the Resistance," in November 1942. Willi Graf and Kurt Huber helped write the fifth leaflet, which appeared in January 1943. Kurt Huber wrote the sixth, and final, leaflet, which Hans and Sophie Scholl distributed in Munich University on February 18th, where they were apprehended by the Gestapo. A hastily destroyed rough draft of a seventh leaflet written by Christoph Probst was found in Hans' pocket on his arrest.

gradual, treacherous, systematic abuse, the system has put every man into a spiritual prison. Only now, finding himself lying in fetters, has he become aware of his fate. Only a few recognized the threat of ruin, and the reward for their heroic warning was death. We will have more to say about the fate of these people.

If everyone waits for someone else to make a start, the messengers of avenging Nemesis will come steadily closer, until even the last victim has been cast senselessly into the maw of the insatiable demon. Therefore every individual has to consciously accept his responsibility as a member of Western and Christian civilization in this last hour; to arm himself as best he can to work against the scourges of humanity, against fascism and every other form of the absolute state. Adopt passive resistance—*resistance*—wherever you are, and block the functioning of this atheistic war machine before it is too late, before the last city is a heap of rubble, like Cologne, and before the last youth of our nation bleeds to death on some battlefield because of the *hubris* of a sub-human. Don't forget that every people gets the government it deserves!

From Friedrich Schiller's "The Lawgiving of Lycurgus and Solon":

Viewed in relation to its purposes, Lycurgus' code of law is a masterpiece of political science and knowledge of human nature. He desired a powerful, unassailable state, firmly based on self-created principles. Political effectiveness and permanence were the goals toward which he strove, and he attained these goals to the fullest extent possible under the circumstances. But if one compares the purpose Lycurgus had in mind with the purposes of mankind, then a deep abhorrence takes the place of the approbation we felt at first glance. Anything may be sacrificed for the good of the state except that end for which the state serves as a means. The state is never an end in itself; it is important only as a condition under which the purpose of mankind can be attained, and this purpose is none other than the development of all the abilities that man possesses. If a state prevents the development of the capacities which reside in man, if it hinders the progress of the spirit, then it is reprehensible and corrosive, no matter how excellently devised, how perfect in its own way. Its very permanence in that case amounts more to a reproach than to a basis for fame; it becomes a prolonged evil, and the longer it exists, the more corrosive it is. . . .

At the price of all moral feeling a political system was set up, and the resources of the state were mobilized to that end. In Sparta there was no conjugal love, no mother love, no filial devotion, no friendship; all men were merely citizens, and all virtue was civic virtue.

A law of the state made it the duty of Spartans to be inhumane to their slaves; in these unhappy victims of war humanity itself was insulted and mistreated. In the Spartan code of law the dangerous principle was promulgated that men are to be looked upon as means and not as ends—and the foundations of natural law and of morality were destroyed by that law. . . .

What an admirable sight it is, in contrast, to see the rough soldier Gaius Marcius in his camp before Rome, when he renounced vengeance and victory because he could not endure the sight of a mother's tears! . . .

The state [of Lycurgus] could endure only under the one condition: that the spirit of the people remained quiescent. Hence it could be maintained only if it failed to achieve the highest, the sole purpose of a state.

From Goethe's *The Awakening of Epimenides*, Act II, Scene 4.

SPIRITS:

Though he who has boldly risen from the abyss
Through an iron will and cunning
May conquer half the world,
Yet to the abyss he must return.
Already a terrible fear has seized him;
In vain he will resist!
And all who still stand with him
Must perish in his fall.

HOPE:

Now I find my good men
Are gathered in the night,
To wait in silence, not to sleep.
And the glorious word of liberty

They whisper and murmur,
Till in unaccustomed strangeness,
On the steps of our temple
Once again in delight they cry:

Freedom! Freedom!

Please make as many copies of this leaflet as possible and pass
them on!

The Second Leaflet

It is impossible to engage in an intellectual discourse on National Socialism because it cannot be defended on rational grounds. It is wrong to speak of a National Socialist philosophy, for if there were such an entity, one would have to try by means of analysis and discussion either to prove its validity or to disprove it. In actuality, however, we face a totally different situation. At its very inception this movement depended on the deception and betrayal of one's fellow man; even then it was inwardly corrupt and could only support itself by constant lies. After all, Hitler states in an early edition of "his" book (a book written in the worst German I have ever read, in spite of the fact that it has been elevated to the position of the Bible in this nation of poets and thinkers): "It is unbelievable to what extent one must betray a people in order to rule it." If at the start this cancerous growth in the nation was not particularly noticeable, it was only because there were still enough forces at work that operated for the good, so that it was kept in check. It grew larger, however, and then, in a final spurt of growth, the tumor burst, as it were, and infected the whole body. Most of its former opponents went into hiding. The German intellectuals fled to their cellars, and, like plants struggling in the dark, away from light and sun, are gradually choking to death. Now the end is at hand. Now it is our task to find one another again, to spread information from person to person, to keep a steady purpose, and to allow ourselves no rest until the last man is persuaded of the urgent need of his support in the struggle against this system. When thus a wave of unrest sweeps through the land, when "it is in the air," when many join the cause, then in a great final effort this system can be shaken off. After all, an end in terror is preferable to terror without end.

We are not in a position to make a final judgment about the significance of these historical events. But if this catastrophe can be used to further the public good, it will only be by virtue of the fact that we are cleansed by suffering; that in the midst of deepest night we yearn for the light, summon up our strength, and finally rise up to shake off the yoke which weighs on our world.

We do not intend to discuss the question of the Jews, nor do we wish to offer a defense or apology here. No, instead to demonstrate this we want to cite the fact that since the conquest of Poland *three hundred thousand* Jews have been murdered in that country in a bestial manner.

Here we see the most terrible crime committed against the dignity of man, a crime that has no counterpart in human history. For Jews, too, are human beings—no matter what position we take with respect to the Jewish question—and a crime of this dimension has been perpetrated against human beings. Some may say that the Jews deserved their fate. This assertion would be a monstrous form of insolence; but let us assume that someone said this—what position has he then taken toward the fact that the entire Polish aristocratic youth is being annihilated? (May God grant that this program has not fully achieved its aim as yet!) All male offspring of the houses of the nobility between the ages of fifteen and twenty were transported to concentration camps in Germany and sentenced to forced labor, and all the girls of this age group have been sent to Norway, into the brothels of the SS!

Why tell you these things, since you are fully aware of them—or if not of these, then of other equally grave crimes committed by this frightful sub-humanity? Because this touches on a problem that involves us deeply and forces us all to reflect. Why are the German people so apathetic in the face of all these abominable crimes, crimes so unworthy of the human race? Hardly anyone thinks about that. It is accepted as fact and put out of mind. The German people slumber on in their dull, stupid sleep and thereby encourage these fascist criminals; they give them the opportunity to carry on their depredations; and of course they do so. Is this a sign that the German people have become brutalized in their most basic human feelings, that the sight of such deeds does not strike a chord within them, that they have sunk into a terminal sleep from which there is no awakening, ever, ever again? It seems that way, and will certainly be so, if the German does not arouse himself from this lethargy at last, if he does not protest whenever he can against this gang of criminals, if he doesn't feel compassion for the hundreds of thousands of victims—not only compassion, no, much more: *guilt*. For his apathy allows these evil men to act as they do; he tolerates this "government" that has taken upon itself such an enormous burden of guilt; indeed, he himself is to blame for the fact that it came about at all! Everyone shrugs off this guilt, falling asleep with his conscience at peace. But he cannot shrug it off; everyone is *guilty, guilty, guilty*! It is not too late, however, to do away with this most reprehensible of all miscarriages of government, to avoid being burdened with even greater guilt. Now, our eyes have recently been opened, we know exactly who our adversary is, and it is high time to root out this brown horde. Up until the outbreak of the war, the larger part of the German people was blindfolded; the Nazis did not show themselves in their true aspect. But now, now that we have recognized them for what they are, it must be the sole and first duty, the holiest duty of every German, to destroy these beasts.

If the people are barely aware that the government exists, they are happy. When the government is felt to be oppressive, they are broken.

Good fortune, alas! builds itself upon misery. Good fortune, alas! is the mask of misery. What will come of this? We cannot foresee the end. Order is upset and turns to disorder, good becomes evil. The people are confused. Is it not so, day in, day out, from the beginning?

The wise man is therefore angular, though he does not injure others; he has sharp corners, though he does not harm; he is upright but not gruff. He is clear-minded, but he does not try to be brilliant.

Lao-tzu

Whoever undertakes to rule the kingdom and to shape it according to his whim—I foresee that he will fail to reach his goal. That is all.

The kingdom is a living being. It cannot be constructed, in truth! He who tries to manipulate it will spoil it; he who tries to put it under his power will lose it.

From their very nature some creatures lead from the front, others follow; some have warm breath, others cold; some are strong, some weak; some survive, others succumb.

The wise man therefore forswears excess; he avoids arrogance and does not overreach himself.

Lao-tzu

Please make as many copies of this leaflet as possible and pass them on.

The Third Leaflet

*Salus publica suprema lex**

All ideal forms of government are Utopias. A state cannot be constructed on a purely theoretical basis; instead, it must grow and develop in the same way an individual human being matures. But we must not forget that at the beginning of every civilization the state already existed in rudimentary form. The family is as old as man himself, and out of this initial bond man, endowed with reason, created for himself a state founded on justice, whose highest law was the common good. The state should reflect the divine order, and the highest of all utopias, the *civitas dei,* is the model it should ultimately resemble. We will not compare the many possible forms of the state—here democracy, constitutional monarchy, monarchy, and so on, but one issue needs to be made clear and unambiguous: every human being has the right to a just state, a state that safeguards the freedom of the individual as well as the good of the whole. For, according to God's will, man should be free and independent, while fulfilling his natural duty of living and working together with his fellow citizens, and strive to achieve earthly happiness through self-reliance and self-motivation.

But our present "state" is the dictatorship of evil. "Oh, we've known that for a long time," I hear you object, "and it isn't necessary to bring that to our attention again." But, I ask you, if you know that, why do you not rouse yourselves, why do you allow these men in power to rob you step by step, both openly and in secret, of one of your rights after another, until one day nothing, nothing at all will be left but a mechanized state system presided over by criminals and drunkards? Is your spirit already so crushed by abuse that you forget it is your right—or rather, your *moral duty*—to eradicate this system? But if a man can no longer summon the strength to demand his right, then he will definitely perish. We would deservedly be scattered over the earth like dust in the wind if we do not marshal our powers at this late hour and finally find the courage we have lacked up to now. Do not hide your cowardice behind a cloak of expediency, for with every new day that you hesitate, failing to oppose this offspring of Hell, your guilt, like a parabolic curve, grows higher and higher.

---

* Public safety is the supreme law.

Many, perhaps most, of the readers of these leaflets cannot see clearly how they can mount an effective opposition. They cannot see any avenues open to them. We want to try to show them that everyone is in a position to contribute to the overthrow of this system. Solitary withdrawal, like embittered hermits, cannot prepare the ground for the overthrow of this "government" or bring about the revolution at the earliest possible moment. No, it can only be done through the cooperation of many convinced, energetic people—people who agree on the means they must use to attain their goal. We have few choices as to these means. The only one available is *passive resistance*. The meaning and the goal of passive resistance is to bring down National Socialism, and in this struggle we can't shrink from any means, any act, whatever its nature. At *every* point we must oppose National Socialism, wherever it is open to attack. We must bring this monster of a state to an end soon. A victory for fascist Germany in this war would have inconceivable and terrible consequences. The first concern of every German is not the military victory over Bolshevism, but the defeat of National Socialism. This must be the first order of business; its greater imperative will be discussed in one of our forthcoming leaflets.

And now every resolute opponent of National Socialism must ask himself how he can fight against most effectively the present "state", how he can inflict the most damaging blows. Through passive resistance, without a doubt. We cannot provide each man with a blueprint for his acts; we can only make general suggestions, and he alone will find the best way to achieve them:

Sabotage armament industries, *sabotage* every assembly, rally, ceremony, and organization sponsored by the National Socialist Party. Obstruct the smooth functioning of the war machine (a machine designed for war that is then used solely to shore up and perpetuate the National Socialist Party and its dictatorship). *Sabotage* in every scientific and intellectual field involved in continuing this war—whether it be universities, technical colleges, laboratories, research stations, or technical agencies. *Sabotage* all cultural institutions that could enhance the "prestige" of the fascists among the people. *Sabotage* all branches of the arts that have even the slightest dependence on National Socialism or serve it in any way. *Sabotage* all publications, all newspapers, that are in the pay of the "government" and that defend its ideology and help disseminate the brown lie. Do not give a penny to public fund-raising drives (even when they are conducted under the guise of charity), for this is only a cover. In reality the proceeds help neither the Red Cross nor the needy. The government does not need this money; it is not financially interested in these fund-raising drives. After all, the presses run non-stop, printing as much paper currency as is needed. But the people must be kept constantly under tension, the pressure on the bit must never be allowed to slacken! Do not contribute to the collections of metal, textiles, and the like. Try to convince all your acquaintances, including those in the lower social classes, of the senselessness of continuing, of the hopelessness of this war; of our spiritual and economic enslavement at the hands of the National Socialists; of the destruction of all moral and religious values; and urge them to adopt *passive resistance*!

Aristotle, *Politics*: "Further, . . . [a tyrant] should also endeavor to know what each of his subjects says or does, and should employ spies everywhere . . . and further, to create disunity and division in the population: to set friend against friend, the common people against the notables, and the wealthy among themselves. Also he should impoverish his subjects; the maintenance of guards and soldiers is thus paid for by the people, who are forced to work hard and have neither the time nor the opportunity to conspire against him . . . Another practice of tyrants is to increase taxes, after the manner of Dionysius at Syracuse, who contrived that his subjects paid all their wealth into the treasury within five years. The tyrant is also inclined to engage in constant warfare in order to occupy and distract his subjects."

Please make copies and pass them on!

There is an old maxim that we tell our children: "He who won't listen will have to feel." But a wise child will not burn his fingers a second time on a hot stove. In the past weeks Hitler has chalked up successes in Africa and in Russia. As a result, optimism on the one hand and shock and pessimism on the other have grown within the German people; this is quite inconsistent with traditional German apathy. One hears among Hitler's opponents—that is, the better segments of the population—exclamations of despair, words of disappointment and discouragement, often ending with the question: "Will Hitler now, after all...?"

At the same time, the German offensive in Egypt has ground to a halt, and Rommel has to bide his time in a dangerously exposed position. But the push into the East proceeds. This apparent success has been purchased at the most horrible expense of human life, and so it can no longer be counted an advantage. Therefore we must warn against *all* optimism.

Who has counted the dead—Hitler or Goebbels? Neither of them! In Russia thousands are lost daily. It is the time of the harvest, and the reaper cuts into the ripe grain with wide strokes. Mourning enters the country cottages, and there is no one to dry the tears of the mothers. Yet Hitler feeds lies to those people whose most precious belongings he has stolen and whom he has driven to a meaningless death.

Every word that comes out of Hitler's mouth is a lie. When he says peace, he means war, and when he blasphemously uses the name of the Almighty, he means the power of evil, the fallen angel, Satan. His mouth is the foul-smelling maw of Hell, and his might is at bottom accursed. True, we must conduct the struggle against the National Socialist terrorist state with rational means, but whoever today still doubts the real existence of demonic powers has completely failed to understand the metaphysical background of this war. Behind the concrete, visible events, behind all objective, rational considerations, we find the irrational element: the struggle against the devil, against the servants of the Antichrist. Everywhere and at all times demons have been lurking in the dark, waiting for the moment when man is weak; when of his own volition he leaves his place in the order of Creation as founded for him by God in freedom; when he yields to the force of evil, separates himself from the powers of a higher order and, after voluntarily taking the first step, is driven on to the next and the next at a furiously accelerating pace. Everywhere and at all times of greatest trial men have appeared, prophets and saints who cherished their freedom, who preached the One God and who with His help enabled people to reverse of their downward course. Of course man is free, but without God he is defenseless against evil. He is like a rudderless ship, at the mercy of the storm, an infant without his mother, a cloud dissolving into thin air.

I ask you as a Christian who is wrestling to preserve his greatest treasure, if you are hesitating and playing games of intrigue and procrastination in the hope that someone else will raise his arm in your defense? Has God not given you the strength and will to fight? We *must* attack evil where it is strongest, and it is strongest in the power of Hitler.

So I returned, and considered all the oppressions that are done under the sun: and behold the tears of such as were oppressed, and they had no comforter; and on the side of their oppressors there was power; but they had no comforter.

Wherefore I praised the dead which are already dead more than the living which are yet alive.

ECCLESIASTES 4

True anarchy is the generative element of religion. Out of the annihilation of every positive element she lifts her gloriously radiant countenance as the founder of a new world. . . . If Europe were about to awaken again, if a state of states, a teaching of political science were at hand! Should hierarchy then . . . be the principle of the union of states? Blood will stream over Europe until the nations become aware of the frightful madness that drives them in circles. And then, struck by celestial music and made gentle, they approach their former altars all together, hear about the works of peace, and hold a great celebration of peace with fervent tears before the smoking altars. Only religion can reawaken Europe, establish the rights of the peoples, and install Christianity in new splendor visibly on earth in its office as guarantor of peace.

NOVALIS

We wish to make very clear that the White Rose is not in the pay of any foreign power. Though we know that the power of the National Socialists must be defeated by military means, we are trying to facilitate a renewal of the severely wounded German spirit from within. This rebirth must be preceded, however, by a clear recognition of all the guilt with which the German people have burdened themselves, and by an uncompromising battle against Hitler and his all too many minions, party members, Quislings, and the like. The chasm that separates the better section of the nation from everything identified with National Socialism must be split wide open wide with brute force. For Hitler and his followers, no punishment on this earth can be commensurate with their crimes. But out of love for coming generations we must make an example after the conclusion of the war, so that no one will have the slightest urge to attempt such actions ever again. And do not forget the petty scoundrels in this regime; note their names, so that none will go free! Having played their part in these abominable crimes, they should not be able to rally to another flag at the last minute and then act as if nothing had happened!

To reassure you, we want to add that none of the addresses of the readers of the White Rose are recorded in writing. They were picked at random from directories.

We will not be silent. We are your bad conscience. The White Rose will not leave you in peace!

Leaflets of the Resistance

A Call to All Germans!

The war is nearing its inevitable end. As in the year 1918, the German government is trying to focus attention exclusively on the growing threat of submarine warfare, while in the East the armies are constantly in retreat and invasion is imminent in the West. Mobilization in the United States has not yet reached its peak, but already it exceeds anything that the world has ever seen. It has become a mathematical certainty that Hitler is leading the German people into an abyss. *Hitler cannot win the war, only prolong it.* The guilt of Hitler and his minions exceeds all measures. Retribution draws closer and closer.

But what are the German people doing? They will not see and will not listen. Blindly they follow their seducers into ruin. *Victory at any price!* is inscribed on their banner. "I will fight to the last man," says Hitler—but in the meantime the war has already been lost.

Germans! Do you and your children want to suffer the same fate that befell the Jews? Do you want to be judged by the same standards as your critics? Are we to be forever the nation which is hated and rejected by all mankind? No. Dissociate yourselves from National Socialist gangsterism. Prove by your deeds that you think otherwise. A new war of liberation is about to begin. The better part of the nation will fight on our side. Cast off the cloak of indifference you have wrapped around you. Decide *before it is too late!* Do not believe the National Socialist propaganda that has driven the fear of Bolshevism deep into your bones. Do not believe that Germany's welfare is linked to the victory of National Socialism for good or ill. A criminal regime cannot achieve a German victory. Separate yourselves *in time* from everything connected with National Socialism. In the aftermath a terrible but just judgment will be meted out to those who stayed in hiding, who were cowardly and hesitant.

What can we learn from the outcome of this war—this war that was never a national war?

Imperialistic designs for power, regardless from which side they come, must be neutralized for all time. Prussian militarism must never come to power again. Only in a generous, open cooperation among the peoples of Europe can the groundwork be laid for genuine reconstruction. All centralized power, like that exercised by the Prussian state in Germany and Europe, must be eliminated. The coming Germany must be federalistic. At this juncture only a sound federal system can imbue a weakened Europe with new life. The working class must be liberated from its degraded conditions of slavery by a reasonable form of socialism. The illusory structure of autonomous national industry must disappear. Every nation and each man has a right to the goods of the whole world!

Freedom of speech, freedom of religion, the protection of individual citizens from the arbitrary will of criminal regimes of violence—these will be the bases of the New Europe.

Support the resistance. Distribute the leaflets!

THE SIXTH LEAFLET*

Fellow Students!

Our people are deeply shaken by the fall of our men at Stalingrad. Three hundred and thirty thousand German men were senselessly and irresponsibly driven to their deaths by the brilliant strategy of our World War I corporal. Führer, we thank you!

The German people are in ferment. Will we continue to entrust the fate of our armies to a dilettante? Do we want to sacrifice the remaining German youth to the base ambitions of a Party clique? No, never! The day of reckoning has come—the reckoning of German youth with the most abominable tyrant our people have ever been forced to endure. In the name of German youth, we demand Adolf Hitler's state restore our personal freedom, the most precious treasure that we have, out of which he has swindled us in the most wretched way.

We grew up in a state where all free expression of opinion has been suppressed. The Hitler Youth, the SA, and the SS have tried to drug us, to revolutionize us, and to regiment us in the most promising years of our lives. "Philosophical training" is the name given to the despicable method by which our budding intellectual development is smoothened in a fog of empty phrases. A system of selection leadership, at once unimaginably devilish and narrow-minded, trains up its future party bigwigs in the "Castles of the Knightly Order" to become Godless, arrogant, and conscienceless exploiters and executioners—

---

* This leaflet was written after the devastating defeat of the German Sixth Army at Stalingrad (January 31st 1943). It proved to be the last leaflet published by the White Rose. Hans and Sophie Scholl were spotted distributing it in Munich University on February 18, 1943, and were immediately arrested by the Gestapo.

Soon after their execution, Hans Leipelt, a fellow member of the White Rose, and a chemistry student at the university, together with his future fiancée Marie-Luise Jahn, started reproducing it on a portable typewriter with the new heading, "Despite everything, their spirit lives on!" They distributed them in Munich and in Hamburg, and arranged for copies to be smuggled out of Germany, as a result of which the Royal Air Force reproduced them and dropped them in their thousands all over Germany. Hans and Marie-Luise were arrested in October that year, and Hans Leipelt was later executed.

blind, stupid hangers-on of the Führer. We "Intellectual Workers" are the ones who should put obstacles in the path of this caste of overlords. Soldiers at the front are regimented like schoolboys by student leaders and trainees for the post of Gauleiter. Gauleiters insult the honor of women students with crude jokes, and the German women-students at the university in Munich have given a worthy response to the besmirching of their honor. And German students have defended their female comrades and stood by them. . . . This is the beginning of the struggle for our free self-determination, without which intellectual and spiritual values cannot be created. We thank the brave comrades, both men and women, who have set us such a brilliant example.

There is only one slogan for us: fight against the Party! Get out of all Party organizations, which are used to keep our mouths shut and hold us in political bondage! Get out of the lecture halls run by SS corporals and sergeants and Party sycophants! We want genuine learning and real freedom of expression. No threat can intimidate us, not even the closure of universities and colleges. This struggle is for each and every one of us, for our future, our freedom, and our honor under a regime that will be more conscious of its moral responsibility.

Freedom and honor! For ten long years Hitler and his comrades have squeezed, debased, and twisted those beautiful German words to the point of nausea, as only the ignorant can, casting the highest values of a nation before swine. In the ten years of destruction of all material and intellectual freedoms, of all moral fiber in the German people, they have sufficiently demonstrated what they understand by freedom and honor. The frightful bloodbath has opened the eyes of even the stupidest German—it is a slaughter that they orchestrated in the name of the "freedom and honor of the German nation" throughout Europe, and which they start anew every day. The name of Germany will remain forever stained with shame if German youth do not finally arise, fight back, and atone, smash our tormentors, and set up a new Europe of the spirit. Women students! Men students! The German people look to us! Just as in 1813 when the people expected us to shake off the Napoleonic yoke, so in 1943 they look to us to overthrow the National Socialist terror through the power of the spirit. Beresina and Stalingrad are aflame in the East; the dead of Stalingrad beseech us!

"Up, up, my people, let smoke and flame be our sign!"

Our people stand ready to rebel against the National Socialist enslavement of Europe in an impassioned uprising of freedom and honor.

A map of Germany showing the major cities where the leaflets were distributed

Draft of The Seventh Leaflet*

Stalingrad! 200,000 German brothers were sacrificed for the honor and glory of a military fraud. The conditions of surrender set down by the Russians were not disclosed to the soldiers who were sacrificed. For this mass murder, General Paulus received the Oak Leaves [medal]. High-ranking officers escaped the slaughter in Stalingrad by airplane. Hitler refused to allow those who were trapped and surrounded to retreat to the troops behind the line. Now the blood of 200,000 soldiers who were condemned to death accuses the murderer named Hitler.

Tripoli! They surrendered unconditionally to the British Eighth Army. And what did the English do? They allowed the citizens to carry on living their lives as usual. They even let the police and public officials remain in office. Only one thing did they undertake systematically: they rid the great Italian colonial city of every barbaric leader. The annihilating, irresistible superpower is approaching on all sides with absolute certainty. Hitler is less likely than Paulus to capitulate: there will be no escape for him. And will you be deceived like the 200,000 who defended Stalingrad in a hopeless cause, to be massacred, sterilized, or robbed of your children? Roosevelt, the most powerful man in the world, said in Casablanca on January 24, 1943:

---

* This draft of the seventh leaflet (presumably written after President Roosevelt's radio broadcast on February 12 announcing the Allies' agreement at the Casablanca Conference to demand Germany's "unconditionable surrender") was never finished or distributed. When Hans and Sophie Scholl were seized by the Gestapo on the morning of February 18 1943, Hans was carrying a draft of this leaflet in his pocket, which he had ripped to shreds in the hope of destroying the incriminating evidence. When questioned by the Gestapo, Hans insisted it was given to him by an unknown student in the crowd.

However, the Gestapo matched the handwritten draft to a sample of Christoph Probst's writing found in Hans' apartment, and immediately arrested him. Over the weekend, the Gestapo worked to piece it together, and the day before Christoph was executed, they showed him the reconstructed leaflet, carefully transcribed, asking him to confirm their work and fill in any gaps. The Gestapo transcript, including Christoph's additions, was discovered in East German archives after the fall of the Berlin Wall, and appears in full here for the first time.

"Our war of extermination is not against the common people, but against the political systems." We will also fight for an unconditional surrender. More contemplation may be needed before a decision can be made. This is about the lives of millions of people. Should Germany meet the same fate as Tripoli?

Today, Germany is completely encircled just as Stalingrad was. Will all Germans be sacrificed to the forces of hatred and destruction? Sacrificed to the man who persecuted the Jews, who eradicated half the Poles, and who wanted to annihilate Russia? Sacrificed to the man who took away your freedom, peace, domestic happiness, hope, and joy, and instead gave you soaring inflation? This will not, this must not happen! Hitler and his regime must fall so that Germany may live. Make up your minds: Stalingrad and defeat, or Tripoli and a future of hope? And once you have decided: act!

The hand-cranked mimeograph machine used to duplicate the leaflets

APPENDIX 2: INDICTED PERSONS RELATED TO THE WHITE ROSE

First Trial
February 22, 1943, Munich

Christoph Probst
Hans Scholl
Sophie Scholl

Second Trial
April 19, 1943, Munich

Helmut Bauer
Heinrich Bollinger
Willi Graf
Eugen Grimminger
Heinrich Guter
Falk Harnack
Hans Hirzel
Susanne Hirzel
Kurt Huber
Traute Lafrenz
Franz Josef Müller
Gisela Schertling
Alexander Schmorell
Katharina Schüddekopf

Third Trial
July 13, 1943, Munich

Harald Dohrn
Manfred Eickemeyer
Wilhelm Geyer
Josef Söhngen

Fourth Trial
April 3, 1944, Saarbrücken

Willi Bollinger

Fifth Trial
October 13, 1944, Donauwörth

Lieselotte Dreyfeldt
Wolfgang Erlenbach
Valentin Freise
Marie-Luise Jahn
Hans Liepelt
Hedwig Schulz
Franz Treppesch

APPENDIX 3: TRANSCRIPT OF THE INDICTMENT

The Indictment of Hans and Sophia Scholl, and Christoph Probst
February 21, 1943, Berlin

Reich Attorney General to the People's Court

Indictment

1. *Hans* Fritz *Scholl* of Munich, born September 22, 1918, in Ingersheim, single, no previous convictions, taken into investigative custody on February 18, 1943;
2. *Sophia* Magdalena *Scholl* of Munich, born May 9, 1921, in Forchtenberg, single, no previous convictions, taken into investigative custody on February 18, 1943; and
3. *Christoph* Hermann *Probst* of Aldrans bei Innsbruck, born on November 6, 1919, in Murnau, married, no previous convictions, taken into investigative custody on February 20, 1943;

   all at present in the jail of the headquarters, State Police (Gestapo), Munich;

   all at present not represented by counsel;

are accused:

   in 1942 and 1943 in Munich, Augsburg, Salzburg, Vienna, Stuttgart, and Linz, of committing the same acts together:

   I. of attempted high treason, namely to change the constitution of the Reich by force, and acting with intent:

   1. to organize a conspiracy for the preparation of high treason,
   2. to render the armed forces unfit for the performance of their duty of protecting the German Reich against internal and external attack,
   3. to influence the masses through the preparation and distribution of writings; and

   II. of having attempted, in the internal area of the Reich, during a time of war, to give aid to the enemy against the Reich, injuring the war potential of the Reich; and

III. of having attempted to cripple and weaken the will of the German people to take measures toward their defense and self-determination.

Crimes according to Para. 80, Sec. 2; Para 83, Secs. 2 and 3, No. 1, 2, 3; Paras. 91b, 47, 73 of the Reich Criminal Code (St GB), and Para. 5 of the Special War Criminal Decree.

In the summer of 1942 and in January and February of 1943 the accused Hans *Scholl* prepared and distributed leaflets demanding a settlement of accounts with National Socialism, disaffection from the National Socialist "gangsterism", and passive resistance and sabotage. In addition, in Munich he adorned walls with the defamatory slogan "Down With Hitler" and with canceled swastikas. The accused Sophia *Scholl* participated in the preparation and distribution of the seditious materials. The accused *Probst* composed the first draft of a leaflet.

I

Summary of Results of Investigations

1. Up to 1930 the father of the accused Hans and Sophia Scholl was mayor of Forchtenberg. Later he was Economic Adviser in Ulm on the Danube. The accused Scholls have two sisters and a brother, who is now serving in the armed forces. Against the accused Hans Scholl, as well as against his brother Werner and his sister Inge, charges had previously been brought on the part of the Reich Police Headquarters, Stuttgart, concerning conspiratorial acts, which led to the temporary arrest of the above-named. Hans Scholl attended the local secondary school and in 1937 he enlisted in the army. In 1939 he began his studies in medicine, which he continued during his period of active service in the army in April, 1941. He was last assigned to the Student Company in Munich with the rank of sergeant. He covered the cost of tuition out of his army pay and out of an allowance from his father. In 1933 Scholl joined the *Hitler Jungvolk* and was later transferred to the *Hitler Jugend.*

2. The accused Sophia Scholl worked first as a kindergarten teacher and since the summer of 1942 has been studying science and philosophy at the University of Munich. Until 1941 she belonged to the *Bund deutscher Mädel,* serving finally as Group Leader.

3. The accused *Probst* attended the *Gymnasium* in Nuremberg and, after finishing his Labor Service, volunteered for the army. Later he became a medical student and most recently belonged to the Student Company in Innsbruck with the rank of sergeant in the medical service.

II

During the summer of 1942 the so-called Leaflets of the White Rose were distributed through the mail. These seditious pamphlets contain attacks on National Socialism and on its cultural-political policies in particular; furthermore, they contain statements concerning the alleged atrocities of National Socialism, namely the alleged murder of the Jews and the alleged forced deportation of the Poles. In addition, the leaflets contain the demand "to obstruct the continued functioning of the atheistic war machine by passive resistance, before it is too late and before the last of the German cities, like Cologne, become heaps of ruins and German youth has bled to death for the "*hubris* of a subhuman." According to Leaflet No. 2, a wave of unrest must spread through the land. If "it is in the air," if many participate, then in a great final effort this system can be shaken off. An end with terror, the leaflet stated, is preferable to terror without end. In Leaflet No. 3 the idea is developed that it is the intent and goal of passive resistance to bring down National Socialism. In this struggle one should not hesitate to take any course, to do any deed necessary. National Socialism must be attacked at all points, wherever it may be vulnerable. Rather than military victory, the first concern of every German should instead be the defeat of National Socialism. Every committed opponent of National Socialism must therefore ask himself how he can most effectively struggle against the present "state" and deal it the most telling blows. To this end sabotage in armament plants and war industry, the obstruction of the smooth functioning of the war machine, and sabotage of all National Socialist functions, as well as in all areas of scientific and intellectual life, is imperative.

A total of four separate leaflets of this sort were distributed in Munich at that time.

In January and February of 1943 two separate seditious leaflets were distributed by means of random scattering and through the mail. One of these bears the heading "Leaflets of the Resistance Movement in Germany" and the other "Fellow Fighters in the

Resistance!" or "German Students!" The first leaflet states that the war is approaching its sure and certain end. However, the German government is trying to direct all attention to the growing submarine threat, while in the East the armies are falling back ceaselessly in retreat, in the West the invasion is expected, and the armament of America is said to exceed anything that history has heretofore recorded. Hitler (it states) cannot win the war; he can only prolong it. The German people, who have blindly followed their seducers into ruin, should now dissociate themselves from National Socialist sub-humanity and through their deeds demonstrate that they do not agree. National Socialist propaganda, which has terrorized the people by fostering a fear of Bolshevism, should not be given credence, and people should not believe that Germany's future is tied to the victory of National Socialism for better or for worse.

The second leaflet, referring to the battle of the Sixth Army at Stalingrad, states that there is a ferment among the German people, and the question is raised whether the fate of our armies should be entrusted to a dilettante. The breaking of National Socialist terror, the leaflet expects, will be the work of students—to whom the German people are looking for guidance and who will achieve their goal through the power of the intellect.

III

1. The accused Hans *Scholl* long considered the political situation. He arrived at the conclusion that in 1918, and after the seizure of power by the National Socialists in 1933, it was not the German masses but rather the intellectuals who had failed politically. This is the only explanation, in his opinion, why mass movements with simplistic slogans had succeeded in drowning out all rational thought. Accordingly, he felt it his duty to remind the middle-class intellectuals of their political obligations, one of which was to take up the struggle against National Socialism. He therefore decided to prepare and distribute leaflets intended to carry his ideas to the broad masses of the people. He bought a duplicating machine, and with the help of a friend, Alexander *Schmorell*, with whom he had often discussed his political views, he acquired a typewriter. He then drafted the first leaflet of the "White Rose" and claims to have singlehandedly prepared about a hundred copies and to have mailed them to addresses chosen from the Munich telephone directory. In so doing, he selected

people particularly in academic circles, but also restaurant owners who, he hoped, would spread the contents of the leaflets by word of mouth. Subsequently he prepared three additional leaflets of the "White Rose," which were likewise written by him. The contents of these leaflets are reproduced above, in Part II of this indictment. Again these were distributed through the mail.

He was prevented from issuing more leaflets by his assignment to active duty on the eastern front in July 1942. He claims that in part he himself paid for the materials used in preparing the leaflets; some portion of the costs were given to him, he claims, by his friend Schmorell.

The name "The White Rose," according to the statements of the accused Hans Scholl, was chosen arbitrarily and took its inception from his reading of a Spanish novel with this title. The accused claims that at first he did not plan an organization; only later, namely early in 1943, did he draw up the plan for an organization which was to propagate his ideas. He claims that he has not yet attempted to bring together a group of like-minded persons.

Early in 1943 the accused Hans Scholl, who in the meantime had been given leave from army service in order to study at the University of Munich, came to the conclusion, as he relates, that there was only one means of saving Europe, namely by shortening the war. To publicize this idea, he drafted two more leaflets, in editions totaling about 7,000, and with the titles mentioned above in Part II of this indictment. Of these he scattered about 5,000 copies in the inner city of Munich, in addition to mailing numerous other copies. At the end of January he traveled to Salzburg, and from the railway post office he posted some 100 to 150 letters containing the leaflets he had prepared. In addition, about 1,500 of the seditious papers were distributed through the post in Linz and Vienna by Schmorell, who traveled to these cities at Scholl's request. Scholl contributed to the cost of train tickets. Finally Scholl had his sister Sophia take about 1,000 letters containing seditious leaflets to Augsburg and Stuttgart, where she put them in the mail. After the news of the reverses in the East, Hans Scholl again prepared leaflets in which he reproduced the text of his student leaflet under a new title. Of these he sent several hundred by post. He took the addresses from a University of Munich directory. On February 18, 1943, he and his sister scattered more seditious papers. On this occasion he was observed by the witness *Schmied* and placed under arrest.

Early in 1943 the accused Hans Scholl requested that his friend, the accused Probst (with whom he had for a long time exchanged ideas about the political situation), write down his ideas on current political developments. Probst then sent him a draft, which without doubt was to be duplicated and distributed, though there was no time for such action. This draft was found in Scholl's pocket at the time of his arrest.

At the end of January 1943 the accused Hans Scholl, at the suggestion of Schmorell, decided to make propaganda by painting defamatory slogans on walls. Schmorell prepared a stencil for him with the text "Down With Hitler" and with a swastika which was canceled through, and he provided paint and brush. In early February 1943 Hans Scholl, together with Schmorell, painted such slogans in black tar on several houses in Munich, on the columns in front of the University, on the buildings of the National Theater and the Ministry of Economics, the Schauspielhaus Theater, and elsewhere.

2. The accused Sophia *Scholl* as early as the summer of 1942 took part in political discussions, in which she and her brother, Hans Scholl, came to the conclusion that Germany had lost the war. Thus she shared with her brother the view that agitation against the war should be carried out through leaflets. She claims to be unable to remember whether the idea of the preparation of leaflets had its inception with her or with her brother. She claims that she had no part in the preparation and distribution of the leaflets with the title "The White Rose" and that she did not become aware of them until a friend showed her a copy. On the other hand, she admits to having taken part in preparing and distributing the leaflets in 1943. Together with her brother she drafted the text of the seditious "Leaflets of the Resistance in Germany." In addition, she had a part in the purchasing of paper, envelopes, and stencils, and together with her brother she actually prepared the duplicated copies of this leaflet. She also helped her brother address the envelopes for mailing. Furthermore, at the request of her brother she traveled by express train to Augsburg and Stuttgart and put the prepared letters into various mailboxes, and she took part in the distribution of the leaflets in Munich by depositing them in telephone booths and parked automobiles.

The accused Sophia Scholl was also implicated in the preparation and distribution of the student leaflets. She accompanied her brother to the university, was observed there in the act of scattering the leaflets, and was arrested when he was taken into custody.

The accused Sophia Scholl was not involved in the act of deface-
ment of buildings, though when she learned about it, she offered to
assist on future occasions. She even expressed the view to her brother
that it might be a good form of concealment to have a woman taking
part in this activity.

The accused Sophia Scholl knew that her brother spent considerable sums of money in the preparation of the seditious papers. In fact,
she took charge of her brother's finances, since he was little concerned
about money matters; she kept financial records and issued to him the
sums he needed for these purposes.

3. The accused Probst, who was often in the company of brother
and sister Scholl and who shared their ideas, wrote at the request of
the accused Hans Scholl the draft, mentioned above, of his estimate
of the current political scene. He claims, to be sure, that he did not
know that Scholl intended to use the draft for a leaflet, but he did
admit that he was aware that it might be used for illegal propaganda.

IV

The accused were on the whole willing to admit to their acts.

Testimony and Exhibits

  I. The statements of the accused in the Supplementary Volumes
I–III;
 II. The Judge of the Police Praesidium of Munich: H 9 R;
III. The witnesses:

    1. Custodian Jakob Schmied, Munich, Türkenstrasse 33/I,
    2. and
    3. Officials of the Police yet to be named;

IV. Exhibits:

    1. The confiscated typewriters, duplicating machine, duplicat-
ing master, paint, and brushes;
    2. the leaflets and photographs in the appended volume of
exhibits.

With the concurrence of the Chief of Staff of the Supreme Command of the Armed Services and the Reich Minister of Justice, the
case is transferred to the People's Court for action and decision.

APPENDIX 4: TRANSCRIPT OF THE SENTENCES

The Transcript of the Sentence of Hans and Sophia Scholl and Christoph Probst

February 22, 1943

Transcript
I H 47/43

In the Name of the German People

In the action against
1. *Hans* Fritz *Scholl,* Munich, born at Ingersheim, September 22, 1918,
2. *Sophia* Magdalena *Scholl,* Munich, born at Forchtenberg, May 9, 1921, and
3. *Christoph* Hermann *Probst,* of Aldrans bei Innsbruck, born at Murnau, November 6, 1919, now in investigative custody regarding treasonous assistance to the enemy, preparing to commit high treason, and weakening of the nation's armed security,

the People's Court, first Senate, pursuant to the trial held on February 22, 1943, in which the officers were:

> President of the People's Court Dr. Freisler, presiding,
> Director of the Regional (Bavarian) Judiciary Stier,
> SS *Group Leader* Breithaupt,
> SA *Group Leader* Bunge,
> State Secretary and SA *Group Leader* Köglmaier, and, representing the Attorney General to the Supreme Court of the Reich, Reich Attorney Weyersberg,

find:

That the accused have by means of leaflets in a time of war called for the sabotage of the war effort and armaments and for the overthrow of the National Socialist way of life of our people, have propagated defeatist ideas, and have most vulgarly defamed the Führer, thereby giving aid to the enemy of the Reich and weakening the armed security of the nation.

On this account they are to be punished by

Death

Their honor and rights as citizens are forfeited for all time.

Grounds

The accused Hans Scholl has been a student of medicine since the spring of 1939 and, thanks to the solicitude of the National Socialist government, has begun his eighth semester in those studies. He has served meanwhile on temporary duty in a field hospital in the campaign in France and again from July to November 1942 on the eastern front as a medical aide.

As a student he is bound by duty to give exemplary service to the common cause. In his capacity as soldier—on assignment to medical study—he has a special duty of loyalty to the Führer. This and the assistance which he was expressly granted by the Reich did not deter him in the first half of the summer of 1942 from writing, duplicating, and distributing leaflets of the "White Rose." These defeatist leaflets predict the defeat of Germany and call for passive resistance in the form of sabotage in war industries and for sabotage in general, to the end that the German people would be deprived of the National Socialist way of life and thus also of their government.

All this because he imagined that only in this way could the German people survive the end of the war!

Returning from Russia in November 1942, Scholl requested his friend, the accused Probst, to provide him with an article which would open the eyes of the German people! In actuality Probst furnished Scholl with a draft of a leaflet as requested, at the end of January 1943.

In conversations with his sister, Sophia, the two resolved to carry on propaganda in the form of a leaflet campaign against the war and in favor of collaboration with the plutocratic enemies of National Socialism. Brother and sister, who had quarters in the same rooming house, collaborated in the writing of a leaflet, "To All Germans." In it they predicted Germany's defeat in the war, they urged a war of liberation against "National Socialist gangsterism," and demanded the establishment of a liberal democracy. In addition, they drafted a leaflet, "German Students!" (in later versions, "Fellow Fighters!"), wherein they called for a struggle against the Party. They wrote that the day of reckoning was at hand, and they were bold enough to compare their call to battle against the Führer and the National Socialist way of life with the War of Liberation against Napoleon (1813). In reference to their project, they used the military song, "Up, up, my people, let smoke and flame be our sign!"

The accused Scholls, in part with the help of the accused Schmorell, duplicated the leaflets and by common agreement distributed them as follows:

1. Schmorell traveled to Salzburg, Linz, and Vienna and put 200, 200, and 1,200 leaflets addressed to places in those cities in the mail; in Vienna an additional 400 were directed to Frankfurt am Main.

2. Sophia Scholl posted 200 in Augsburg and on another occasion 600 in Stuttgart.

3. Hans Scholl, with the aid of Schmorell, scattered thousands of leaflets in the streets of Munich at night.

4. On February 18 the Scholls deposited 1500–1800 copies in bundles in the University of Munich, and Sophia Scholl let fall a large number from the third floor down the light well of the building.

Hans Scholl and Schmorell also, on the nights of August 8, 1942, and February 14, 1943, defaced walls in many places in Munich, and in particular the University, with the words "Down With Hitler," "Hitler the Mass Murderer," and "Freedom." After the first incident Sophia Scholl learned of this action, was in agreement with it, and requested—though without success—to be allowed to help in the future!

Expenses were covered by the accused themselves—in all, about 1,000 marks.

Probst likewise began his medical studies in the spring of 1939 and is now in his eighth semester, a soldier on student duty. He is married and has three children aged two and a half, one and one fourth years, and four weeks. He is a "nonpolitical man"—hence no man at all! Neither the solicitude of the National Socialist Reich for his professional training nor the fact that it was only the National Socialist demographic policy which made it possible for him to have a family prevented him from writing at the behest of Scholl—in cowardly defeatism—a "manuscript" which takes the heroic struggle in Stalingrad as the occasion for defaming the Führer as a military swindler and which then, progressing to a hortatory tone, calls for opposition to National Socialism and for action which would lead, as he pretends, to an honorable capitulation. He supports the promises in this leaflet by citing—Roosevelt! And his knowledge about these matters he derived from listening to British broadcasts!

All the accused have admitted the facts stated above. Probst offers as excuse his "extreme depression" of the time he drafted the leaflet, a depression which he claims arises from Stalingrad and the childbed illness of his wife. But such explanations do not excuse a reaction *of this scope.*

Whoever has, like the three accused, committed the acts of high treason, weakening the home front and thereby in time of war the security of the nation, and by the same token has aided the enemy (Par. 5 of Special War Decree and Par. 91b of the Criminal Code), raises the dagger for a stab in the back of the Front! That applies also to Probst, though he claims that his manuscript was not intended for use as a leaflet—since its tone and style proves the opposite. Whoever acts in this way—and particularly at this time, when we must close our ranks—is attempting to cause the first rift in the unity of the battle front. And German students, whose traditional honor has always called for self-sacrifice for *Volk* and fatherland, were the ones who acted thus!

If a deed of this sort were to be punished otherwise than by death, we would be forging the first links of a chain whose end—in an earlier time—was 1918. Therefore, for the protection of the *Volk* and the Reich at war, the People's Court has found but one just punishment: death. The People's Court knows that it is at one with our soldiers in this decision.

Through their treason to our *Volk*, the accused have forever forfeited their citizenship.

As criminals who have been found guilty, the accused will pay the court costs.

Stier.

Dr. Freisler
(signed)

Certified True Copy
Landesarchiv Berlin
Berlin-Charlottenburg
December 22, 1960
(Seal)   (signature illegible)

APPENDIX 5: ARTICLE IN THE *MÜNCHENER NEUESTE NACHRICHTEN*

Article in the *Münchener Neueste Nachrichten* reporting the sentencing and execution of Hans and Sophie Scholl and Christoph Probst.
February 22, 1943

Death Sentences

For Preparing to Commit Treason

On February 22, 1943, the People's Court, convened in the Court of Assizes Chamber of the Palace of Justice, sentenced to death (together with loss of the rights and privileges of citizenship) the following persons: Hans Scholl, aged 24, and Sophia Scholl, aged 21, both of Munich, and Christoph Probst, aged 23, of Aldrans bei Innsbruck, for their preparations to commit treason and their aid to the enemy. The sentence was carried out on the same day.

Typical outsiders, the condemned persons shamelessly committed offenses against the armed security of the nation and the will to fight of the German *Volk* by defacing houses with slogans attacking the state and by distributing treasonous leaflets. At this time of heroic struggle on the part of the German people, these despicable criminals deserve a speedy and dishonorable death.

APPENDIX 6: ARTICLE IN THE *VÖLKISCHER BEOBACHTER*

Article in the *Völkischer Beobachter,* Munich edition, reporting the sentencing of Alexander Schmorell, Kurt Huber, Wilhelm Graf, and others.
April 21, 1943

Just Punishment of Traitors to the Nation at War

The People's Court of the German Reich, sitting in Munich, dealt with a number of accused persons who were involved in the high treason of the Scholl siblings sentenced on February 22, 1943.

During the years 1942–43, at a time of arduous struggle for our people, Alexander Schmorell, Kurt Huber, and Wilhelm Graf of Munich collaborated with the Scholls in calling for sabotage of our war plants and in spreading defeatist ideas. They aided the enemy of the Reich and attempted to weaken our armed security. Through their violent attacks against the community of the German people, these accused have voluntarily excluded themselves from that community, and were punished by *death.* They have forfeited their rights as citizens forever.

Eugen Grimminger of Stuttgart furnished funds in support of this action, though, to be sure, he was not fully aware of its details. The Court was unable to establish that he consciously gave aid to the enemy of the Reich. Furthermore, he gave considerable assistance to his employees who were serving in the armed forces, though on the other hand he was aware that the money might be used for purposes injurious to the state. He has been sentenced to ten years in jail. Heinrich Bollinger and Helmut Bauer of Freiburg had knowledge of the treasonous acts of the above-named accused but failed to report them, despite the fact that they are mature adults, and in contravention of the obligation of every German to report treasonous plans of this sort. In addition, they listened to enemy broadcasts. They have been sentenced to seven years in jail, and have forfeited their honor as citizens for the same length of time.

Hans Hirzel and Franz Müller of Ulm, immature youths, aided in the distribution of the treasonous leaflets. In consideration of their age they were sentenced to five years' imprisonment.

The accused Heinrich Guter of Ulm, likewise a young person who knew of the treasonous acts but failed to report them, was sentenced to eighteen months' imprisonment. Three girls who were guilty of the same act were sentenced to one year's imprisonment.

One other accused person, who assisted in the distribution of the leaflets but who did not know their contents, was given a sentence of six months in jail because she failed to carry out her obligation to inform herself about the contents of the leaflets.

APPENDIX 7: RADIO SERIES *GERMAN LISTENERS,* THOMAS MANN

Excerpt from the Deutsche Hörer ("German Listeners") Radio Series by Thomas Mann:

June 27, 1943

I tell you: Respect the people of Europe! Let me add, though at the moment it may sound strange to many of you who are listening, pay respect to the German people and show compassion for them! The idea that it is impossible to distinguish between the German *Volk* and Nazism—that to be German and National Socialist are one and the same thing—is heard at times in the Allied countries, and put forward with some passion. But this idea is untenable and will not prevail. Too many facts testify to the contrary. Germany has set up its defenses and continues to resist, exactly as the other nations do. . . .

The world is deeply moved by the recent events at the University of Munich, about which we have received information through the Swiss and Swedish newspapers, at first just rumors and then with specific facts that fascinate us more and more. We know now about Hans Scholl, survivor of the Battle of Stalingrad, and his sister. We know of [Chistoph] Probst, Professor Huber, and all the others; about the Easter demonstration of students against the obscene speech of a Nazi bigwig in the *auditorium*; we know of their martyrdom on the block; about the leaflet which they had distributed and which contains words that go far to make up for many of the sins against the spirit of German freedom committed in these unhappy years at the German universities. Indeed, this susceptibility of German youth—the youth in particular—to the National Socialist revolution of lies was painful. Now their eyes are opened, and they put their young heads on the block for their insight and for the honor of Germany. They go to their death after telling the president of the court to his face, "Soon you will be standing here, where I now stand," and after bearing witness in the face of death that a new faith in freedom and honor is dawning.

Good, splendid young people! You shall not have died in vain; you shall not be forgotten. The Nazis have raised monuments to indecent rogues and common killers in Germany—but the German revolution, the real revolution, will tear them down and in their place will memorialize these people, who, at the time when Germany and Europe were still enveloped in the dark of night, knew and publicly declared: "A new faith in freedom and honor is dawning."

APPENDIX 8: LEAFLET ISSUED BY THE NATIONAL COMMITTEE FOR A FREE GERMANY

To the German Fighting Forces on the Eastern Front:

Lower the flags
Over the fresh graves
Of German freedom fighters!

A short time ago we heard the terrible news that three young Germans, Hans and his sister Sophie Scholl and Christoph Probst, were executed at the end of February.

The three belonged to the group of noble and courageous spokesmen for German youth who refused to witness the terrible sufferings of their Fatherland in passive and silent acceptance any longer.

They were students at the University of Munich. Hans Scholl had returned just a few months before on study leave from the eastern front. He had been a courageous soldier and had received the Purple Heart, the Iron Cross Second Class, and the Eastern Front Medal.

Under Hans Scholl's leadership the Munich students were the first to raise the flag of freedom. They distributed leaflets and organized impressive demonstrations

against Gestapo terror and the betrayal of the masses;

against total mobilization, which reduces the German people to total misery;

against the debauched and squanderous high-life carousers of the SS, the SA, and the Hitlerian big-wigs;

against warmongers and prolongers of the war who, in their insatiable greed for profit or in stubborn fanaticism, let millions of Germans bleed to death;

against the whole arbitrary Hitler regime, which is out to achieve world rule and the enslavement of peoples, which has brought upon Germany the infinite sufferings of total war, mass air raids, ruin, and misery;

against Hitler, the betrayer of peoples, the mad self-styled general, who through his quixotic policy of conquest, his fomenting of racial hate and bloody terrorizing of the occupied areas, has incited the hatred of the nations against Germany; who has ruined and decimated the German family, the German farmer and the middle classes; who has caused Germany to be overrun with foreign nationals; who has crushed and undermined the foundations of our existence and halted the processes of our historical growth.

These were the slogans of the young demonstrator in Munich in February 1943.

The demonstrations were broken up by the SS. Several students were arrested, brutally mistreated, and hauled before the Military Court.

They were called a "Threat and Danger to the German *Volk*" and "Communists."

"I am no communist; I am a German," stated Hans Scholl before the Court.

And as a German, as a soldier at the front, as a man with concern for the fate of his homeland and his people, this brave young freedom fighter defied his judges.

"You can execute me, but the day will come when you will be judged. The people, our German homeland, will judge you!"

The ax of the Hitler executioner was raised three times; three times it descended; and three young heads rolled from the block.

Three heroes died, but their spirit, their love and their hate, their struggle for peace and German freedom lives on in the hearts of hundreds of thousands and millions of young Germans. . . .

The renown of the brave is eternal.

Ulm—the home of the Scholls—and Munich—where they fought and died—will one day dedicate monuments in gratitude and respect to these heroes.

"Germany puts its hopes in its youth!" said Scholl in his last speech.

"As once in the Wars of Liberation in 1813–1814, now again German youth must rescue the fatherland from dishonorable tyranny, shame, misery, and war exploitation," added his sister.

Young Germans in uniform: Heed the call of alarm of the heroes of freedom from distant Munich. There speaks to you the voice of your unhappy homeland.

The most evil enemies and destroyers of Germany stand behind you. Yes, they give you your orders and incite you to self-destructive, utterly dangerous warfare.

Know the truth. Know the real enemy!

You alone can save our people, our homeland, from ruin and misery.

Officers and Soldiers: Do not be misled by lying, inflammatory slogans. Follow your own reason, your conscience, and your love for country.

For a free and peaceful Germany!

For the preservation and security of the German people, the German family!

Fight against the Hitler war and the Himmler terror!

Fight against Göring-Krupp war profiteering and Goebbels-Ley lies!

Fight against the enmity between nations and total war!

Bring the war to an end. Bring Hitler down!

German Youth, awake!

APPENDIX 9: *NEW YORK TIMES* ARTICLES

Articles on the White Rose from *The New York Times*, 1943

NAZI SLUR STIRRED STUDENTS' REVOLT

Official Was Jeered When He Told Girls It Was Duty to Bear Children Without Marriage

THREE WERE GUILLOTINED

Woman, Brother and Another Soldier Beheaded for Issuing Anti-Nazi Tracts

By GEORGE AXELSSON
Wireless to THE NEW YORK TIMES.

STOCKHOLM, Sweden, April 17—The pictorial weekly Veckojournalen reports that a woman was among the three Munich University students who were executed last February for spreading anti-Nazi tracts. The others, it says, were soldiers, one a Stalingrad Sixth Army survivor who had been decorated with two Iron Crosses—first class and second class.

The weekly asserts the victims were a medical student, Sergeant Hans Scholl, Veteran of Stalingrad and son of an official of Ulm; his sister, Maria Scholl, a philosophy student, and another medical student, Private Adrian Probst.

They were guillotined after Gauleiter Gieseler of Munich had demanded that they be publicly hanged on the campus.

Details Are Reported

The background of the incident was reported as follows:

Gauleiter Gieseler in a speech at a university festival Feb. 11 denounced women students for using studies as a pretext to escape war service and declared in an insulting fashion that if they did not want to work in munitions factories they ought at least to bear children, without marriage.

The women students retorted with jeers. Men students formed lines protecting the girls when policemen charged. A riot ensued in front of the University.

The following day Munich house walls bore the inscription: "Revenge for Stalingrad! We want our liberty back!"

The student body issued two tracts, one an appeal to men and girl students, protesting against Nazism and its suppression of individual thinking and the free expression of opinion and also against the attempt to force uniformity on students.

The tract praised the men for protecting the girl students and called for a fight to recapture the right of the individual to decide his own destiny "without which no spiritual values can be created."

The tract concluded with a call to battle against the Nazi party by resigning from Nazi organizations and by refusal to attend lectures by pro-Nazis. The war was condemned and German youths were urged to establish a new Europe.

"A new faith in liberty and honor dawns," it said.

The university was occupied by the police and Scholl and Probst were arrested for distributing the tracts. They were tried the next day on charges of "favoring the enemy."

When Sergeant Scholl was accused of communist activities he replied, "I am not a Communist; I am a German." To Judge Freisler he said, "You will soon stand where I stand now."

The executions were carried out immediately after the sentence. For several ensuing nights the City walls bore inscriptions: Scholl lives! You can break the body but never the spirit."

SUNDAY, APRIL 18, 1943

YOUNG GERMAN MARTYRS

When Germany arrives at the crossroads where Italy stands today— as she surely will—some of her people may be able to find words for what they think of Nazism in a manifesto issued by students in Munich last spring. What is believed to be the authentic text of this document has just been published in this country by the International Student Assembly, on the authority of Paul Hagen, research director of American Friends of German Freedom. After a bitter at attack on Hitler's generalship and Nazi methods of education the manifesto declares:

> Honor and liberty! For ten years Hitler and his comrades cruelly twisted, distorted and ridiculed those two fine German words, as only

unscrupulous men can who throw the highest values of a nation to the swine. What honor and liberty mean to them they have demonstrated clearly enough in the ten years in which they have destroyed all the material and spiritual freedom and all the moral substance of the German people. The horrible bloodshed in which they, in the name of the liberty and honor of the German nation, have plunged all Europe, and which they daily perpetuate, has opened the eyes of even the dumbest German. The name of Germany will be shamed forever if German youth does not finally rise to take revenge, to destroy its tormentors and to create a new Europe, a Europe of the spirit.

Students! The German people are looking to us. They expect much of us. Just as in 1813 Napoleon's terror was broken, so in 1943 the National Socialist terror shall be broken by the strength of the spirit. The Stalingrad dead implore us! * * * Our people are rising against the enslavement of Europe by National Socialism, in a new break-through for liberty and honor.

Six Munich students, one of them a girl of 20, are said to have been executed following the issuance of this manifesto. If it is genuine, and there is no reason to doubt that it is, we can see in it the beginning of the end of the nightmare period in Germany itself. It was natural that the older generation, growing to manhood in a civilized country, should be at least lukewarm toward the hideous nonsense of Nazism, but there was doubt as to what could be expected of young people who had never known anything else. An animal brought up in a sty may be expected to behave like a pig. But these Munich students, few or many, representative or otherwise, rose gloriously out of the mud, protesting in the name of principles which Hitler thought he had killed forever. In years to come we, too, may honor Sergeant Hans Scholl, Sophia Scholl, Christophe Probst, Alexander Schmorell, Karl Huber and William Graf, slain in Munich for a cause that is also ours.

MONDAY, AUGUST 2, 1943

SOURCES

BOOKS AND JOURNALS

Asgodom, Sabine, ed. *"Halts Maul—sonst kommst nach Dachau!": Frauen und Männer aus der Arbeiterbewegung berichten über Widerstand und Verfolgung unter dem Nationalsozialismus* ("Shut your mouth—or you'll end up in Dachau!": Women and men from the labor movement report on resistance and persecution under National Socialism). Cologne, 1983.

Axelrod, Toby. *In the Camps: Teens Who Survived the Nazi Concentration Camps.* New York, 1999.

Bonhoeffer, Dietrich. *Letters and Papers from Prison.* London, 2001.

Bracher, Karl Dietrich. *The German Dictatorship.* New York, 1970.

Brysac, Shareen Blair. *Resisting Hitler: Mildred Harnack and the Red Orchestra.* Oxford and New York, 2002.

Burden, Hamilton T. *The Nuremberg Party Rallies: 1923–1939.* New York, 1967.

Burleigh, Michael. *The Third Reich: A New History.* New York, 2000.

Burleigh, Michael. *The Racial State: Germany 1933–1945.* New York, 1991.

Campt, Tina. *Other Germans: Black Germans and the Politics of Race, Gender, and Memory in the Third Reich.* Ann Arbor, 2003.

Die deutsche Universität im Dritten Reich: 8 Beiträge (The German university in the Third Reich: A series of 8 contributions). Munich, 1966.

Donohoe, James. *Hitler's Conservative Opponents in Bavaria, 1930–1945.* Leiden, 1961.

Drobisch, Klaus, ed. *Wir schweigen nicht!: Eine Dokumentation über den antifaschistischen Kampf Münchener Studenten, 1942–43* (We will not be silent!: A documentation of the antifascist struggle of the Munich students, 1942–43). East Berlin, 1968.

Dumbach, Annette E. "'Without Love There is No Fatherland': German Youth and the German Resistance: A Neglected Legacy in the Struggle Against Right-Wing Extremism." Paper presented in the Sunday

Scholars Series of the Washington Hebrew Congregation, Washington DC, March 1995.

Focke, Harald, and Uwe Reimer. *Alltag unterm Hakenkreuz: Wie die Nazis das Leben der Deutschen veränderten* (Everyday life under the swastika: How the Nazis changed the lives of the Germans). Hamburg, 1979.

Frankenberg, Günter, and Franz J. Müller. "Juristische Vergangenheitsbewältigung: Der Volksgerichtshof vorm BGH" (Juridical overcoming of the past: The People's Court before the Supreme Court of the Federal Republic). *Kritische Justiz* 16, no. 2 (1983): 145–163.

Fürst-Ramdohr, Lilo. Freundschaften in der Weissen Rose. Munich, 1995.

Gamm, Hans-Jochen. *Der Braune Kult: Das Dritte Reich und seine Ersatzreligion* (The brown cult: The Third Reich and its substitute religion). Hamburg, 1962.

Giesecke, Hermann. *Vom Wandervogel bis zur Hitlerjugend* (From *Wandervogel* to the Hitler Youth). Munich, 1981.

Glaser, Hermann. *Das Dritte Reich: Anspruch und Wirklichkeit* (The Third Reich: Expectations and Reality). Freiburg, 1961.

Green, Martin. *The von Richthofen Sisters.* New York, 1974.

Grunberger, Richard. *The 12-Year Reich: A Social History of Nazi Germany, 1933–1945.* New York, 1971.

Haecker, Theodor. *Journal in the Night.* New York, 1950.

Hanser, Richard. *A Noble Treason.* New York, 1979.

Hassell, Ulrich von. *The Von Hassell Diaries, 1938–1944: The Story of the Forces against Hitler inside Germany.* Garden City, N.Y., 1947.

Heyer, G. W. *Die Fahne ist mehr als der Tod* (The flag is greater than death). Munich, 1980.

Hoffmann, Peter. *German Resistance to Hitler.* Harvard, 2005.

Hohoff, Curt. *Woina-Woina: Russisches Tagebuch, 1941–1944* (War-war: A Russian diary, 1941–1944). Düsseldorf, 1951.

Holler, Eckard. Hans Scholl zwischen Hitlerjugend und dj.1.11—Die Ulmer Trabanten. Puls 22, Verlag der Jugendbewegung, Stuttgart, 1999.

Huber, Clara, ed. *Kurt Huber, zum Gedächtnis: Bildnis eines Menschen, Denker und Forscher, dargestellt von seinen Freunden* (Kurt Huber, in remembrance: Portrait of a man, thinker and researcher, presented by his friends). Regensburg, 1946.

Hirzel, Susanne. Vom Ja zum Nein: Eine schäbische Jugend, 1933–1945. Tübingen, 1998.

Insdorf, Annette. *Indelible Shadows: Film and the Holocaust.* Cambridge and New York, 2002.

Jens, Inge. ed. *At the Heart of the White Rose: Letters and Diaries of Hans and Sophie Scholl.* New York, 1987.

Kardoff, Ursula von. *Berlin: Diary of a Nightmare, 1942–1945.* 1960.

Kirchberger, Günther. *Die Weisse Rose* (The White Rose). Munich, 1980.

Klee, Ernst. *"Euthanasie" im NS-Staat: Die "Vernichtung lebensunwerten Lebens"* ("Euthanasia" in the National Socialist state: the "extermination of life unworthy of living"). Frankfurt, 1983.

Klönne, Arno. Jugendbewegung Jugend im Dritten Reich: Die Hitler-Jugend und ihre Gegner. Cologne, 1984

Knoop-Graf, Anneliese, ed. *Willie Graf: Briefe und Aufzeichnungen.* Frankfurt am Main, 1988.

Koch, H. W. *Hitler Youth: The Duped Generation.* New York, 1972.

——. *The Hitler Youth: Origin and Development.* New York, 1975.

Kohn, Hans. *The Mind of Germany.* New York, 1960.

——. *The Rise of Nationalism.* New York, 1962.

Köllmayr, Friedrich. *Unser München: Antifaschistischer Stadtführer* (Our Munich: An antifascist guide to the city). Frankfurt, 1983.

Kulturamt der Reichsjugendführung [The Reich Youth Leadership's Bureau of Culture]. *Freude, Zucht, Glaube: Handbuch für die kulturelle Arbeit im Lager* (Joy, racial breeding, belief: Handbook for cultural work in camp). Potsdam, 1937.

Leibholz-Bonhoeffer, Sabine. *Vergangen, erlebt, überwunden* (Things past, lived through, overcome). Gütersloh, 1976.

Leiser, Erwin. *Nazi Cinema.* New York, 1975.

Leisner, Barbara. *Sophie Scholl: "Ich würde es genauso wiedermachen."* Munich: 2000.

Lusane, Clarence. *Hitler's Black Victims: The Historical Experiences of Afro-Germans.* London, 2002.

Malvezzi, Piero, and Giovanni Pirelli. *Letzte Briefe zum Tode Verurteilter aus dem europäischen Widerstand* (Last letters of those condemned to death in the European resistance). Munich, 1962.

Maschmann, Melitta. *Account Rendered: A Dossier on my Former Self.* London, New York, Toronto, 1965.

Matties, Kurt. *Ich hörte die Lerchen singen: Tagebuch aus dem Osten, 1941–1945* (I heard the larks singing: Diary from the East, 1941–1945). Munich, 1956.

Moll, Christiane. "Acts of Resistance: The White Rose in the Light of New Archival Evidence," in Resistance Against the Third Reich, 1933–1990, pp.172—200. Michael Geyer and John W. Boyer, eds. Chicago, 1992

Mosse, George. *Nazi Culture.* New York, 1966.

Mosse, George. Nationalism and Sexuality. Madison, 1985.

Müller, Franz, ed. "The White Rose: The Resistance by Students Against Hitler, Munich, 1942/43." The White Rose Foundation, Munich, 1991.

Newborn, Jud. "The Ghostly Cries of the White Rose Echo in Germany," Newsday, May 3, 1985.

Newborn, Jud. "Will We Carry the White Rose Into the Next Millennium?" *Daily Press*, Virginia, 1999.

Newborn, Jud. "Work Makes Free: The Hidden Cultural Meanings of the Holocaust." Dissertation, University of Chicago, 1994.

Pabst, Helmut. *Der Ruf der aussersten Grenze: Tagebuch eines Frontsoldaten* (The call of the outer limits: Diary of a front-line soldier). Munich, 1953.

Petry, Christian. *Studenten aufs Schafott: Die Weisse Rose und ihr Scheitern* (Students on the scaffold: The White Rose and its failure). Munich, 1968.

Peukart, Detlev. *Inside Nazi Germany: Conformity, Opposition and Racism in Everyday Life*. New Haven, 1989.

Preis, Kurt. *München unterm Hakenkreuz* (Munich under the swastika). Munich, 1980.

Reck-Malleczewen, Friedrich Percyval. *Diary of a Man in Despair*. New York, 1945.

Rothfels, Hans. *Die deutsche Opposition gegen Hitler* (The German opposition against Hitler). Frankfurt, 1958.

Scholl, Inge. *The White Rose: Munich 1942–1943*. New York, 1983.

Schüddekopf, Charles, ed. *Der Alltägliche Faschismus: Frauen im Dritten Reich* (Everyday fascism: Women in the Third Reich). Berlin, 1982.

Seydewitz, Max. *Civil Life in Wartime Germany: The Story of the Home Front*. New York, 1945.

Shirer, William L. *The Rise and Fall of the Third Reich*. New York, 1960.

Steinert, Marlis G. *Hitler's War and the Germans: Public Mood and Attitude during the Second World War*. Athens, Ohio, 1977.

Terkel, Studs. *The Good War: An Oral History of World War II*. New York, 1985.

Toller, Ernst. *Eine Jugend in Deutschland* (A young life in Germany). Hamburg, 1983 (orig. ed., 1933).

Traven, B. *The White Rose [Die Weisse Rose]*. Westport, 1976 [Berlin, 1929].

University of Munich Library. *Die Weisse Rose: Studentische Widerstand im Dritten Reich, 1943. Gedenkausstellung Universitätsbibliothek München, 1983* (The White Rose: Student resistance in the Third Reich, 1943. Memorial exhibit at the University of Munich Library, 1983). Munich, 1983.

Verhoeven, Michael, and Mario Krebs. *Der Film "Die Weisse Rose": Das Drehbuch* (The film *The White Rose:* The script). Karlsruhe, n.d.

——.*Die Weisse Rose: Der Widerstand Münchener Studenten gegen Hitler. Information zum Film* (The White Rose: The resistance of Munich students against Hitler. Information about the film). Frankfurt, 1982.

Vielhaber, Klaus, Hubert Hanisch, and Anneliese Knoop-Graf. *Gewalt und Gewissen: Willi Graf und die Weisse Rose. Eine Dokumentation* (Force and conscience: Willi Graf and the White Rose. A documentation). Freiburg, 1964.

Vinke, Hermann. *The Short Life of Sophie Scholl*. New York, 1984.

Weisenborn, Günther. *Der lautlose Aufstand: Bericht über die Widerstands-bewegung des deutschen Volkes, 1933–1945* (The silent uprising: Report on the resistance movement of the German people, 1933–1945). Hamburg, 1962.

Wünsche, Frederic. Marie-Luise Schultz-Jahn. Haspa-SchulService, Hamburg, 1999–2002

ARCHIVAL SOURCES

Gestapo Interrogation Transcripts:
Bundesarchiv Potsdam
Hauptstaatsarchiv Düsseldorf
Staatsarchiv München
Staatsarchiv Ludwigsburg

MAJOR NEWSPAPER AND MAGAZINE ARTICLES

Münchener Abendzeitung, 25 Feb. 1968.
New York Times, 18 Apr., 25 Apr., 2 Aug., 21 Aug., 1943.
Stern, Feb. 1968.
Süddeutsche Zeitung, 1 Nov. 1946.

PERSONAL INTERVIEWS

Clara Huber   Dr. and Mrs. Erich Schmorell
Birgit Weiss-Huber   Katharina Schüddekopf
Franz Müller   Michael Verhoeven
Dr. Leo Samberger

STATEMENTS, REPORTS, RECOLLECTIONS, AND LETTERS FROM THE COLLECTION OF THE WHITE ROSE, INSTITUT FÜR ZEITGESCHICHTE, MUNICH

Josef Fürtmeier   Traute Lafrenz
Hubert Fürtwangler   Robert Mohr
Else Gebel   Angelika Probst
Wilhelm Geyer   Gestapo Officer Rechtsteiner
Günther Groll   Gisela Schertling
Lisa Grote   Jakob Schmid
Heinrich Guter   Inge Scholl
Falk Harnack   Herta Siebler Probst
Helmut Hartert   Josef Söhngen
Karl Hepperle   Jürgen Wittenstein

INDEX

235